"Be warned. This looks like a book on how Calvin thought about living the Christian life. But open it and you will discover that Mike Horton is driving you on a grand Calvin tour of the whole of theology. And that, of course, is Professor Horton's (and John Calvin's) point: it takes the whole biblical gospel to make a whole Christian life. By employing the classical formulation of the two natures of Christ ('distinct but not separate'), Dr. Horton provides readers with a key to help unlock Calvin's teaching. But more than that, he shows why the Genevan Reformer's vision of the Christian life remains unsurpassed. Thoroughly satisfying, thoroughly enjoyable, and thoroughly recommended."

Sinclair B. Ferguson, Professor of Systematic Theology, Redeemer Seminary, Dallas, Texas

"Learned and lucid, masterfully organized and vigorously expressed, this full, solid, and exact study of Geneva's reforming pastor is an outstanding piece of work. In all four sections Calvin comes to vigorous life. Calvin's reputation for godly wisdom, and Horton's for vivid writing, will certainly be enhanced."

J. I. Packer, Board of Governors' Professor of Theology, Regent College

"*Calvin on the Christian Life* provides an amazingly personal and comprehensive portrait of the Reformer's passions and positions, constantly connecting them to issues of belief and practice in our day. Far more than a synthesis of Calvin's thought and practice, this book provides readers with an intimate glimpse into his private piety."

Nancy Guthrie, Bible teacher; author, Seeing Jesus in the Old Testament Bible study series

"Scholar and pastor Michael Horton has provided us with a well-researched introduction to John Calvin's doctrine of *piety*—Calvin's word for the reverence and love that the gospel produces in all our relationships. One of the most intriguing aspects of Horton's book is the way he traces the theme of 'distinction without separation' through the Christian life, whether with respect to the two natures of Christ, grace and the sacraments, or church and state. This book will enlighten beginners and refresh and challenge veterans in the field."

Joel R. Beeke, President, Puritan Reformed Theological Seminary

"Using the most recent Reformation research, as well as letting the sources speak for themselves, Michael Horton has given us a wonderful overview of how John Calvin saw the life of the Christian. The book demonstrates the open attitude Calvin had toward living in this world and does away with the caricatures that still surround this Reformer. Horton's book is both academic and practical—a rare but very welcome combination."

Herman Selderhuis, Director, Refo500; President, The International Calvin Congress

CALVIN

on the Christian Life

THEOLOGIANS ON THE CHRISTIAN LIFE

EDITED BY STEPHEN J. NICHOLS AND JUSTIN TAYLOR

CALVIN

on the Christian Life

GLORIFYING AND ENJOYING
GOD FOREVER

MICHAEL HORTON

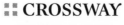

CROSSWAY

WHEATON, ILLINOIS

Calvin on the Christian Life: Glorifying and Enjoying God Forever

Copyright © 2014 by Michael Horton

Published by Crossway
        1300 Crescent Street
        Wheaton, Illinois 60187

Cover design: Josh Dennis
Cover image: Richard Solomon Artists, Mark Summers

First printing 2014

Printed in the United States of America

Scripture quotations are from the ESV® Bible (*The Holy Bible, English Standard Version®*), copyright © 2001 by Crossway. 2011 Text Edition. Used by permission. All rights reserved.

Trade paperback ISBN: 978-1-4335-3956-5
PDF ISBN: 978-1-4335-3957-2
Mobipocket ISBN: 978-1-4335-3958-9
ePub ISBN: 978-1-4335-3959-6

Library of Congress Cataloging-in-Publication Data

Horton, Michael Scott.
   Calvin on the Christian life : glorifying and enjoying God forever / Michael Horton.
      pages cm. — (Theologians on the Christian life)
   Includes bibliographical references and index.
   ISBN 978-1-4335-3956-5 (tp)
   1. Calvin, Jean, 1509–1564. 2. Spirituality—Christianity.
3. Christian life. 4. Spiritual life—Christianity. I. Title.
BX9418.H645   2014
248.4'842—dc23   2013030010

Crossway is a publishing ministry of Good News Publishers.

VP		24	23	22	21	20	19	18	17	16	15	14
15	14	13	12	11	10	9	8	7	6	5	4	3	2	1

To W. Robert Godfrey,
Calvin scholar, mentor, and friend

We see that our whole salvation and all its parts are comprehended in Christ. We should therefore take care not to derive the least portion of it anywhere else. If we seek salvation, we are taught by the very name of Jesus that it is "of him." If we seek any other gifts of the Spirit, they will be found in his anointing. If we seek strength, it lies in his dominion; if purity, in his conception; if gentleness, it appears in his birth. For by his birth he was made like us in all respects that he might learn to feel our pain. If we seek redemption, it lies in his passion; if acquittal, in his condemnation; if remission of the curse, in his cross; if satisfaction, in his sacrifice; if purification, in his blood; if reconciliation, in his descent into hell; if mortification of the flesh, in his tomb; if newness of life, in his resurrection; if immortality, in the same; if inheritance of the Heavenly Kingdom, in his entrance into heaven; if protection, if security, if abundant supply of all blessings, in his Kingdom; if untroubled expectation of judgment, in the power given to him to judge. In short, since rich store of every kind of good abounds in him, let us drink our fill from this fountain, and from no other.

JOHN CALVIN, *INSTITUTES OF THE CHRISTIAN RELIGION* 2.16.19.

CONTENTS

SERIES PREFACE

Some might call us spoiled. We live in an era of significant and substantial resources for Christians on living the Christian life. We have ready access to books, DVD series, online material, seminars—all in the interest of encouraging us in our daily walk with Christ. The laity, the people in the pew, have access to more information than scholars dreamed of having in previous centuries.

Yet for all our abundance of resources, we also lack something. We tend to lack the perspectives from the past, perspectives from a different time and place than our own. To put the matter differently, we have so many riches in our current horizon that we tend not to look to the horizons of the past.

That is unfortunate, especially when it comes to learning about and practicing discipleship. It's like owning a mansion and choosing to live in only one room. This series invites you to explore the other rooms.

As we go exploring, we will visit places and times different from our own. We will see different models, approaches, and emphases. This series does not intend for these models to be copied uncritically, and it certainly does not intend to put these figures from the past high upon a pedestal like some race of super-Christians. This series intends, however, to help us in the present listen to the past. We believe there is wisdom in the past twenty centuries of the church, wisdom for living the Christian life.

Stephen J. Nichols and Justin Taylor

ACKNOWLEDGMENTS

Those to whom I am indebted for this book are too numerous to name. I was introduced to Calvin's writings in my teenage years mostly by thoughtful laypeople in churches that claimed no direct lineage to the Genevan Reformer. From there, R. C. Sproul, J. I. Packer, and James Boice helped to continue my odyssey.

In seminary, and even before, I fell under the spell of an extraordinary church historian by the name of W. Robert Godfrey. And now, as a colleague, I continue to find myself in awe of his mastery of Calvin's corpus and historical context down to the most minute points. I am grateful also to later teachers, such as Cambridge historian Peter Newman Brooks and my doctoral supervisor at Wycliffe Hall, Oxford, Alister McGrath.

I owe a debt of gratitude to my colleagues at Westminster Seminary California and to my students—especially in my course on the *Institutes*; to my comrades at the White Horse Inn; to my church family at Christ United Reformed Church; and to my Crossway editor, Thom Notaro. His expertise and attention to detail ensured a much better book than this might otherwise have been.

As always, a special thanks is due to my wife and children for their encouragement and patience with a writer who sometimes gets lost in the clouds. And, above all, I am grateful to our Lord for sending faithful servants into his harvest like John Calvin and the countless unheralded ministers who gather and feed Christ's flock.

CHAPTER I

CALVIN ON THE CHRISTIAN LIFE: AN INTRODUCTION

"The spirituality of John Calvin is seldom examined."[1] There are notable exceptions to this verdict by Howard Hageman. Yet it seems generally true that even those who consult Calvin on theological or exegetical questions may be inclined to look elsewhere for spiritual direction. I suspect that a principal reason for this oversight has to do with what we mean by "spirituality."

A Different Time

Once upon a time, daily rhythms were ordered by the tolling of the church bell and the annual cycle punctuated by the church calendar. People passed into the church to mark life's milestones through rows of headstones. From baptisms to funerals, God's presence was felt at least tacitly across the whole of life. Faith was a shared public frame of reference, not a private hobby of those who, in the words of modern theologian Friedrich Schleiermacher, "have a talent for religion" or "a taste for the Infinite." God's hand was discerned in floods, fires, and plagues as well as in fruitful harvests. Of course, there were plenty of people for whom this was all unreflective

---

[1] Howard Hageman, "Reformed Spirituality," in *Protestant Spiritual Traditions*, ed. Frank C. Senn (New York: Paulist, 1986), 60.

gibberish more than genuine belief. However, no one assumed a world in which religion or spirituality was a corner of private life.

The Reformation and the Heart of the Matter

Whatever ways in which the Reformation anticipated the modern age, it belonged to the world shaped by Christendom. Especially for the Reformers and their successors, faith and reason, doctrine and life, sacred and secular were on speaking terms. It is striking to us in our contemporary context to discover the same theologian writing a sermon or a lecture, a poem on nature or a hymn to nature's Creator and Redeemer, a Hebrew or Greek grammar, and some calculations on planetary movements—in the same week. Truth, goodness, and beauty drew all disciplines together in a unified body of knowledge. No less when exploring the heavens than when poring over Scripture, one was engaging in pious meditation upon God's works.

It is difficult to justify the claim that the Reformation brought unalloyed blessing. Yet it is even more implausible to suggest, as some recent writers have, that it launched the drift toward secularism.[2] First, by various measurements it can be easily shown that late medieval Christendom was already coming apart at the seams. It was held together precariously but firmly by the vast network of magisterial power. Centuries of papal tyranny and abuses created widespread cynicism and provoked myriad reform movements. For a while "conciliarists"—urging papal submission to councils—gained the upper hand, but "papalists" finally won out.

An especially anxious moment came in the fourteenth century, when three popes claimed Peter's chair. Begun in 1309, the Western Schism (often called "the Babylonian Captivity") was only concluded with the Council of Constance in 1417, a century before Luther posted his Ninety-Five Theses. In 1987, before becoming Pope Benedict XVI, Cardinal Joseph Ratzinger explained:

> For nearly half a century, the Church was split into two or three obediences that excommunicated one another, so that every Catholic lived under excommunication by one pope or another, and, in the last analy-

---

[2] A recent example is University of Notre Dame historian Brad Gregory, *The Unintended Reformation: How a Religious Revolution Secularized Society* (Cambridge: Harvard University Press, 2012). For a quite different interpretation, see Scott H. Hendrix, *Recultivating the Vineyard: The Reformation Agendas of Christianization* (Louisville: Westminster John Knox, 2004).

sis, no one could say with certainty which of the contenders had right on his side. The Church no longer offered certainty of salvation; she had become questionable in her whole objective form—the true Church, the true pledge of salvation, had to be sought outside the institution.[3]

At least from the perspective of the Reformers, this was only the tip of the iceberg. Satires of the Roman curia and the monks were common. Yet Reformers like Luther and Calvin went to the heart of the matter: the doctrine, and not just any doctrine, but the substance of the gospel message itself.

However, as the word *reformation* suggests, they did not set out to create a new church, nor did the movement become mired in mere critique. The aim was essentially constructive: namely, to re-evangelize Christendom.

First, the Reformation sparked a renewal of Christian piety by *deepening* it. In his preface to his Small Catechism, Luther expressed alarm at widespread biblical illiteracy. Yet more than a century earlier, University of Paris chancellor and theologian Jean Gerson wrote a treatise complaining that even many priests were ignorant of the basic message, figures, and plotline of Scripture. Going back to the sources to rediscover a lost treasure, those who embraced the Reformation were so deeply knowledgeable about it and invested in it that they were willing to die for it if necessary. Those who embraced the Reformation were convinced that they had truly understood the gospel of God's free grace in Christ for the first time.

The Reformation also ignited genuine piety by *widening* the circle. The monks and nuns engaged in full-time prayer and contemplation were called "the religious." Basically, they were surrogates, fulfilling spiritual disciplines on behalf of the secular layperson. Monks were often targets of the period's equivalent of stand-up comics. Yet the Reformers were troublesome not because they joined in mocking abuses, laziness, ignorance, and vice, but because they challenged the legitimacy of the monastic vocation itself.

While all roads led to the cathedral or local parish, the church's leaders felt obliged to issue edicts requiring attendance at Mass at least once a year. Even then, the average worshiper could not understand the liturgy enough to participate in it, and the Communion cup was withheld entirely

---

[3] Joseph Cardinal Ratzinger, *Principles of Catholic Theology* (San Francisco: Ignatius, 1987), 196.

from the laity. Sermons were rare, except when traveling (mendicant) preachers came to town. Essentially, the Mass was a spectacle—a sumptuously staged event that the people observed from afar, separated by a screen. It was becoming increasingly clear that at least on the street, the veneer of Christianity was peeling away to reveal a canvas of various native (pre-Christian) folk paganisms. As Cambridge historian Patrick Collinson concludes, the Reformation was an "episode of re-christianization or even primary Christianization" that interrupted "a process of secularization with much deeper roots."[4]

With the gospel as the fountain, believers now had full and equal access to God's mercy through his means of grace. They heard the Word expounded in their own languages. The screen was removed, and the congregation participated in the public liturgy, receiving Communion—not only the bread, but also the cup, and frequently rather than once a year. Soon, even poorer saints obtained Bibles and brought their own Psalters to church, from which they sang in their daily chores on the farm and in the shop, as well as in their homes around the dinner table. It became so common for martyrs to spend their final time on earth singing God's praises as they passed the watching crowds that the authorities resorted to cutting out martyrs' tongues before they were escorted to the pyres.

Imitating the example of the ancient church, the Reformers produced catechisms. Teenage evangelicals—girls as well as boys—were more familiar with the content and rationale for their faith and practice than were many priests. In fact, the Catholic Counter-Reformation produced its own catechism and other means of instruction (including the Jesuit order) in an effort to stem the tide of conversion to evangelical faith and practice.

Breaking down the wall separating the monks in "full-time Christian service" from the average believer not only deepened and widened piety in public worship; it also entailed a liberating view of callings in the world. Even milking a cow to the glory of God and for the neighbor's good was a spiritual activity.

John Calvin and Life *Coram Deo*

If the modern world was becoming more secular, this was the very opposite of Calvin's piety. He was not a progressive anticipating the Enlighten-

---

[4] Patrick Collinson, *The Religion of Protestants: The Church in English Society 1559–1625* (Oxford: Clarendon, 1982), 199.

ment's autonomous individualism, but an evangelical humanist crying, "Back to the sources!" The faith he encouraged was deeper and wider than the popular piety of his day. Like any pious Augustinian, Calvin viewed every aspect of life *coram Deo*, before the face of God. Calvin would not have even comprehended the idea that is usually assumed in the word *spirituality* as we use it today: namely, as a private island of subjective and imaginative irrationality surrounded by a sea of objective and public reason.

"Piety" (*pietas*), not spirituality, is the Reformer's all-encompassing term for Christian faith and practice. Even this term has lost its value in modernity. We've learned to draw a line between doctrine and life, with "piety" (like "spirituality") falling on the "life" side of the ledger. The ancient church saw it differently: *eusebia* encompassed doctrine and life. It could be translated "piety" or "orthodoxy" without any confusion. Calvin assumed this overarching horizon. Doctrine, worship, and life are all of one piece. The doctrine is always practically oriented, and practice is always to be grounded in true doctrine. In fact, "justification by faith . . . is the sum of all piety."[5] The root of piety is faith in the gospel. Love is the yardstick for all duties, and God's moral law in both Testaments stipulates the character of this love on the ground, comprehending "piety toward God" and "charity toward men."[6] Calvin even defined his *Institutes* as "a sum of Christian piety."

If historical distance makes us work harder to understand Calvin's view of piety, it also forces us to appreciate the extent to which the Reformer himself would have been embarrassed to be singled out for a distinctive view of the Christian life. Indeed, the label Calvinist was coined in 1552 by Lutheran polemicist Joachim Westphal, and Calvin did not treat it as a term of endearment. As I point out in the next chapter, Calvin stood on the shoulders of giants from the past and fellow Reformers who helped shape many of his own views that are erroneously attributed to his unique genius.

In short, Calvin has been given too much blame by critics and too much credit by fans. His real genius is to be found in his remarkable ability to synthesize the best thought of the whole Christian tradition and sift it with rigorous exegetical skill and evangelical instincts. His rhetorical rule

---

[5] Calvin, *Institutes of the Christian Religion*, ed. John T. McNeill, trans. Ford Lewis Battles (Philadelphia: Westminster, 1960), 3.15.7.
[6] Ibid., 3.3.1; 3.3.16.

was "brevity and simplicity," and this, combined with a heart enflamed by truth, draws us back to his wells for refreshment in many times and places—especially when we seem to have lost our way.

The Making of an Unlikely Reformer

In 1536, a red-headed preacher, Guillaume Farel, begged the young French author of a popular little book to stay in Geneva to help him complete the work of reformation in the church there. The author was Jean Calvin, and his book was the first edition of the *Institutes of the Christian Religion*, at that point a brief summary of the evangelical faith. Calvin reverently declined the honor, explaining that he only wanted to be left alone to pursue his scholarship. Unexpectedly, the fiery preacher who had led Geneva to embrace the Reformation threatened his timid fellow-Frenchman with God's judgment on his studies if he should refuse God's calling to assist with reformation where it was needed. Persuaded by Farel and a few others, Calvin agreed, but initially only to the post of Bible lecturer, to which was added soon thereafter regular preaching and pastoral duties.

Geneva was basically a client state of the Reformed city of Bern. After a year of pushing for greater independence of the church from Geneva's magistrates (as well as Bern's), Farel and Calvin—along with two other ministers—were sent packing. Calvin found a new home and ministry in Strasbourg, where the leading pastor, Martin Bucer, became a spiritual father. It was Bucer (along with Peter Martyr Vermigli) who would have a large impact on the course of the English Reformation, even helping Cranmer revise the Book of Common Prayer. Here in Strasbourg the Reformation was already established—precisely as the young Reformer would have hoped for Geneva. Calvin was pastor to five hundred French exiles and started a youth hostel with his new wife, Idelette. He participated in imperial conferences, completely revised the *Institutes* from six chapters to sixteen, and wrote his important Romans commentary. Finally, he felt that he had found a home.

Yet only three years after Calvin and his colleagues had been summarily dismissed from Geneva, an ambassador was dispatched to Calvin's door with the official plea: "On behalf of our Small, Large, and General Councils . . . we beg you very affectionately to decide to come to us and return to your former place and ministry."[7] Happily ensconced in Strasbourg,

---

[7] Quoted in Scott M. Manetsch, *Calvin's Company of Pastors: Pastoral Care and the Emerging Reformed Church, 1536–1609* (New York: Oxford University Press, 2012), 25.

Calvin "stated plainly that he would not return," according to the biography written by his successor, Theodore Beza. To one close friend he confided, "Rather would I submit to death a hundred times than to that cross on which I had to perish daily a thousand times over."[8]

The Genevans recruited Bucer to their cause. Tearing a page out of Farel's playbook, Bucer "appealed to the example of Jonah" to encourage Calvin to return to his former post.[9] Calvin mourned the prospect of returning to Geneva—"not because I have hated it," he told Pierre Viret, "but because I see so many difficulties presented in that quarter which I do feel myself far from being equal to surmount."[10] He could at least stall the Genevans by writing from Germany that he still had important business to do for Strasbourg at these imperial meetings.[11] Yet, as he expressed to Farel, "When we come back, our friends here will not refuse their consent to my return to Geneva. Moreover, Bucer has pledged himself that he will accompany me."[12]

Nothing seems to have been less agreeable to his frame. "But when I remember that I am not my own, I offer up my heart, presented as a sacrifice to the Lord."[13] This motto is enshrined in Calvin's crest: a hand holding up a heart.

A short time later, a lovely carriage arrived with the Genevan ambassador to transport Calvin and his new family back to Geneva, where he was greeted at the gates with a hero's welcome. Entering the pulpit of St. Pierre's once again the following Sunday, Calvin did not refer to his exile, rail against vicious enemies who still agitated against his return, or offer flattering speeches about the welcome that may have compensated for such an unseemly dismissal. He simply picked up preaching at the very verse at which he had left off when he had been asked to leave.

A Revealing Episode for Calvin's Life and Ministry

This episode illumines Calvin's wider life and ministry. First, it points up his shyness—and, at least in his own view, "cowardice"—in becoming

---

[8] T. H. L. Parker, *John Calvin* (Tring, UK: Lion, 1975), 96.

[9] Theodore Beza, "Life of Calvin," in *Selected Works of John Calvin: Tracts and Letters*, ed. Henry Beveridge and Jules Bonnet, 7 vols. (Grand Rapids: Baker, 1983), 1:xxxvii.

[10] Calvin, "To Viret" (Ulm, March 1, 1541), in *Selected Works of John Calvin*, 4:230. "I am so perplexed, or rather confused, as to the call from Geneva that I can scarce venture to think what I ought to do."

[11] This he did on two occasions, drafting nearly the same letter to the Genevan leadership. See Calvin, "To the Seigneury of Geneva" (Strasbourg, October 23, 1540), in *Selected Works of John Calvin*, 4:208, and again (Strasbourg, February 19, 1541), 4:225.

[12] Calvin, "To Farel" (Strasbourg, August 1541), in *Selected Works of John Calvin*, 4:280.

[13] Ibid., 281.

embroiled in public controversies. "I must confess that by nature I have not much courage and that I am timid, faint-hearted and weak."[14] Nothing could have proved more of a challenge to those natural tendencies and aspirations than ministry in Geneva: a backwater city of perpetual conflict, with passionate factions—political as well as religious. From his flight from France to constant public controversies that taxed his patience, each calling seemed to be imposed on him. Yet if God had called him to the post through the voice of the church, he could—indeed must—accept it. Bucer's Jonah analogy may have been apt after all.

Second, it points up the complexity of Calvin's ministry in Geneva. While those who are sympathetic to his convictions can only celebrate his uncompromising dedication to God's Word, those who are not can only regard him as an inflexible despot. The truth is more complicated than either of these views.

One of the reasons for Calvin's surreptitious ejection by the city council along with Farel and two other pastors was a riot that broke out when they refused to celebrate the Supper with unleavened wafers after a synod of Swiss Reformed churches upheld Bern's requirement of the practice. For his own part, Calvin did not even know about his senior colleagues' decision until it was done, and in retrospect he thought it was a petty issue. Yet it was more a test case for a larger contest: namely, whether the political authority had the last word in the church's affairs and whether, in particular, Bern's church and city council could determine every aspect of the Genevan church's life.

On some occasions, Calvin displayed youthful brashness, confusing stubbornness with fidelity and impatience with courage. Nevertheless, as he matured in these conflicts, Calvin became a remarkably flexible and ecumenical leader, willing to compromise even on points that he considered quite important, if it held out hopes of greater unity in the church. At a time of bitter inter-confessional polemics, he grew rather quickly in his ability to promote common ground and consensus while refusing to yield to the slightest confusion on what he considered the weightiest matters. In moments when others were given to vehemence, he could be the sweet voice of reason and compromise. Calvin was a complicated man in a complicated situation.

---

[14] Calvin, preface to the *Commentary on the Psalms*, quoted by Herman J. Selderhuis, *Calvin's Theology of the Psalms* (Grand Rapids: Baker Academic, 2007), 27–28.

Third, in spite of the complex and sometimes contradictory attitudes he sometimes exhibited, the episode highlights the conviction that was his consistent, unyielding, and unvarying North Star: *the absolute priority of God's glory and therefore of God's Word.* So upon his return to the pulpit, he simply picked up at the verse where he left off. Like Luther's defense at the Diet of Worms, Calvin's whole ministry can be considered one long "here I stand" speech before emperors and popes abroad and magistrates and ministers at home. Even many who quarreled with his interpretations had to conclude that his conscience indeed was captive to the Word of God.

Calvin as Pastor

Calvin was a pastor. We may remember him for other things, but as he grew into this office for which at first he felt unsuited, "minister of Word and sacrament" became the core of his identity.

On the one hand, the Reformer was remarkably patient and comforting to the "bruised reed" and "flickering candle." Indeed, he saw himself in these terms and spoke more openly of his faults than of his virtues. He refers frequently in his writings to moments when he misunderstood Scripture on a certain point and was corrected or learned wisdom from one of his parishioners.[15]

Precisely because they took God's Word seriously, struggling pilgrims found their own faith and repentance weak and halting. Christ is the friend of sinners, Calvin constantly taught, and the minister's main calling is to assure tender consciences that God is favorable toward them in Jesus Christ. He never ridiculed or demeaned. "With regard to manners," Beza recalled,

> although nature had formed him for gravity, yet, in the common intercourse of life, there was no man who was more pleasant. In bearing with infirmities he was remarkably prudent; never either putting weak brethren to the blush or terrifying them by unseasonable rebukes, yet never flattering their faults.[16]

So Calvin never had trouble with those who, like himself, *fell short* of God's Word—in doctrine or in life.

---

[15] Calvin gives us an interesting example in his commentary on Ps. 115:16. I discovered this reference in ibid., 13.

[16] Beza, "Life of Calvin," xcviii.

On the other hand, Calvin showed little patience toward those—especially leaders in the church—who displayed either explicitly or implicitly that they did not take God's Word *seriously*. The obvious examples for him were the priests and monks. However, Calvin was even more irritated when, whether out of laziness, ignorance, or pride, those who had embraced the clear evangelical message failed to fulfill their office. Failure to take Scripture seriously was also evidenced by laypeople who mocked Christ and his ordinances despite having the benefit of faithful ministers.

Especially in these instances where God's Word was ignored or trivialized, Calvin did display that censorious temperament that Beza found even in the reports of his friends of youth. He was harder on himself in that regard than he was on others, but he was also hard on others. As Calvin was suffering various illnesses in his last few days, Beza says that whenever he and others would beg Calvin to rest from dictating and writing, Calvin would reply, "What, would you have the Lord to find me idle?" When Calvin was assured that God's Word required a certain position or action to be taken, the only appropriate response was obedience: sooner rather than later. For example, he rebuked privately Bucer and Lutheran theologian Philipp Melanchthon for conceding too much to Rome on justification at an imperial conference. The great Reformed theologian in Bern, Wolfgang Musculus, called Calvin "an always-drawn bow."[17]

Yet he was an ecumenical activist in a situation that seemed to favor the most factious spirits. Even in the wake of the anathemas of Trent, Calvin agreed to participate in the Colloquy of Poissy with Roman Catholic leaders. Though Calvin was prevented from making the trip by health (and the city leaders' concern for his safety), Beza attended as the Genevan representative. Calvin worked tirelessly at healing the Lutheran-Reformed breach. Melanchthon dubbed him "The Theologian."[18]

Calvin called Luther "my ever-honored father," and via Bucer the German Reformer sent greetings to Calvin, whose books he read "with special delight."[19] Luther and Pomeranus asked Melanchthon to pass on their commendation: "Calvin has acquired great favor in their eyes."[20] In fact, it is reported that after reading his treatise on the Supper, Luther told a friend that "I might well have entrusted this controversy to him from the beginning. If

---

[17] Philip Benedict, *Christ's Churches Purely Reformed: A Social History of Calvinism* (New Haven, CT: Yale University Press, 2002), 94.
[18] Beza, "Life of Calvin," xxxvi.
[19] Quoted in Parker, *John Calvin*, 162.
[20] Quoted in ibid.

my opponents had done the same, we should soon have been reconciled."[21] T. H. L. Parker relates, "When some mischief makers showed Luther a passage where Calvin criticized him all he said was: 'I hope that Calvin will one day think better of us; but in any event it is good that he should even now have some proof of our good will toward him.'" In response, Calvin said, "If we are not affected by such moderation, we are surely of stone," and in his Romans commentary he apologized for his immoderate critique.[22]

In 1557 he proposed to Melanchthon "a free and universal council to put an end to the divisions of Christendom." When Archbishop Thomas Cranmer proposed a general synod to unite all evangelical churches, Calvin replied that for his part he "would not grudge to cross ten seas if it were necessary" for the project.[23] In spite of misgivings, and a rocky relationship with Heinrich Bullinger, Calvin initiated a joint statement on the Supper that, while not wholly satisfactory to the Reformer, moved Zurich away from Zwinglian memorialism.

By temperament and conviction, Calvin was a conservative Reformer. "Rashness" he frequently identified as a besetting sin of many whose zeal exceeded their pastoral instincts. He had learned quickly that even in primary matters, the church could be reformed only by consistent and patient instruction. There could be no "top-down" approach; the people, especially the leaders, had to be brought along to embrace the conclusions by persuasion from Scripture.

Unmovable as he was where key principles were at stake, Calvin was as sharp in his rebukes toward those who exceeded the bounds of "due moderation," especially when they provoked controversies over secondary matters. He rebuked John Knox and other exiles in the Frankfurt church for provoking controversy with the Lutherans over ceremonies. He warned French exiles in London not to demand everything to be patterned on his model, making "an idol of me" and "a New Jerusalem of Geneva."[24]

Through the many controversies he endured, Calvin matured as a person and as a pastor, frequently holding his tongue when assailed. More than most of his contemporaries in the battle, he picked his fights with growing discernment and continued to name as friends those who showed themselves to be suspicious and even sometimes open adversaries.

---

[21] Quoted in ibid.
[22] Calvin, quoted in ibid., 163.
[23] Calvin, quoted in ibid., 165.
[24] Calvin, quoted in Irena Backus and Philip Benedict, introduction to *Calvin and His Influence, 1509–2009*, ed. Irena Backus and Philip Benedict (New York: Oxford University Press, 2011), 10.

While there is abundant evidence of Calvin's impatience with and disregard for human flattery, there is just as much to demonstrate that he was generally open-minded and willing to listen to criticism. When a pastor in the Church of Neûchatel criticized one of Calvin's books on a few points, the Reformer replied, "So far from being offended because of your opinions, I am greatly delighted with this straightforward plainness. Nor does my perversity reach to such a degree as to allow myself a freedom of opinion which I would wish to take away from others."[25]

Overcoming Caricatures

If caricatures are the price of historical fame, then Calvin may be one of the most famous leaders in history. For few figures have unfounded rumors by enemies been allowed to stand more persistently as historical fact. The "tyrant of Geneva," a "Protestant Pope," Calvin is reviled as a killjoy whose pastime was ruminating with relish on the fate of the damned and ensuring that the present life of his subjects was as close to that fate as possible. Ignoring the conclusions of specialists, Philip Jenkins repeats the slur in a recent book.[26] Not surprisingly, there is not a substantiating footnote.

If later legends of a repressed Geneva evolved after Calvin's death, his contemporary enemies created quite different caricatures. According to Roman Catholic polemicists, Geneva was a cauldron of debauchery and a refuge for hedonists of every kind.[27] It is true that there were taverns as well as plays, which Calvin attended without scruple. He even rebuked a fellow minister for criticizing a play from the pulpit, criticism that, Calvin thought, showed contempt for the actors. "Our play narrowly escaped being converted into a tragedy," he told Farel.[28] Thomas Norton, who made the

---

[25] Calvin, "To Christopher Libertet" (Basle, September 4, 1534), in *Selected Works of John Calvin*, 4:43.

[26] See, for example, Philip Jenkins, *God's Continent: Christianity, Islam, and Europe's Religious Crisis* (New York: Oxford University Press, 2007), 260. Jenkins expresses astonishment at novelist Salmon Rushdie's hope for a Muslim equivalent of the Protestant Reformation, since Calvin was "a revolutionary who established a repressive theocratic regime in Geneva, with moral and religious orthodoxies enforced by the full force of state power."

[27] Francis Higman, "The Origins of the Image of Geneva," in John B. Roney and Martin I. Klauber, *The Identity of Geneva: The Christian Commonwealth, 1564–1864* (Westport, CT: Greenwood, 1998). See also Gillian Lewis, "Calvinism in Geneva in the Time of Calvin and of Beza," in *International Calvinism, 1541–1715*, ed. Menna Prestwich (Oxford: Clarendon, 1985). After crossing swords with the Reformer repeatedly, Jerome Bolsec became the first Calvin muckraker. Sexually profligate (with men and women), Calvin was simultaneously a libertine and a despot, according to Bolsec's 1577 biography. Critical scholarship has exposed these misunderstandings, and yet rumors die hard.

[28] Calvin, "To Farel" (Geneva, July 4, 1546), in *Selected Works of John Calvin*, 5:61. The senate asked Calvin his opinion, but he said he would only add his voice to the ministers as with one voice. One of the ministers (named Michael) inveighed in a sermon against the actors, and many people came to Calvin with

first English translation of the *Institutes*, coauthored with Thomas Sackville *Gorboduc*, the first English tragedy ever staged. Calvin's associate, Theodore Beza, wrote the first stage drama in the French language.[29] As Spitz summarizes, "Calvin himself had an unusually good wine cellar. God does not forbid us to laugh, he said, and was himself very adept at punning."[30]

However, not a single charge was brought against Calvin for personal misconduct in a disorderly city that, under his ministry, became widely noted for its justice, civility, and (eventually) kindness to strangers. Calvin was especially devoted to the cause of the poor exiles who flooded the city and were often mistreated by the proud Genevans. Ignoring the pleas of the magistrates, Calvin tended to the spiritual needs of plague victims in the hospital. Marilynne Robinson reminds us that Calvin's entire life was burdened with a deep sense of obligation to the suffering and that from its very first edition the *Institutes* was written to defend victims of persecution.[31]

The survival of such contradictory legends—Calvin the moralistic dictator and Calvin the debauched godfather of vice—is perhaps an indicator of the historical significance of Geneva, and Calvin in particular, for friend and foe alike.

Even the popular legends of Calvin burning witches and ruling Geneva with an iron fist have become laughable as historians investigate the primary records. A brief summary will suffice to make this point.

Before the city embraced the Reformation, the bishop was also the head of state, on behalf of the Duke of Savoy, with whom he had constant quarrels over power. The duke's tyranny galvanized the city fathers to seek political independence just as they also embraced the Reformation.

If anyone came close to a dictator in Geneva during Calvin's lifetime, it was his implacable foe Ami Perrin, a tempestuous buffoon whom Calvin dubbed privately "our comic Caesar." Calvin, however, refused to use his office for any political agenda. On the contrary, as Scott M. Manetsch notes, the city council even "prosecuted heretics and serious moral offenders,"

---

strong complaints. It nearly led to a riot. "I endeavoured in the second discourse to appease their exasperation, observing moderation, for I judged that he had acted imprudently in having at an unseasonable time chosen such a theme for declamation. But his extravagance was the more displeasing, since I could by no means approve of what he had said." "They threateningly assert that they would have killed Michael were it not that they revered me. . . . Viret is present as a spectator, who has again returned, according to arrangement, with a view to restore our furious friend to sanity" (5:62).

[29] Marilynne Robinson, preface to *John Calvin, Steward of God's Covenant: Selected Writings*, ed. John F. Thornton and Susan B. Varenne (New York: Vintage, 2006), xxiv.

[30] Lewis Spitz, *The Protestant Reformation: 1517–1559* (St. Louis: Concordia, 2003), 159.

[31] Robinson, introduction to *John Calvin*, xiii–xiv.

appointed church officers, and dictated the schedule for the church calendar. "For their part, Geneva's ministers were employees of the state who could be dismissed at any time . . . and who were not permitted to sit on any of the citizen councils."[32]

Geneva rewarded Calvin with citizenship only late in his ministry. Far from assuming political powers, even at the height of the respect he enjoyed he was never able to push through city hall all of his desired reforms of the church. If the pope considered himself the ultimate ruler of Christendom, the Lutheran and Reformed churches regarded the prince (or city council) as their "nursing father." Along with Farel and Viret, Calvin sought greater independence of the church from the state. Even after his *Ecclesiastical Ordinances* was approved, the senators wanted to retain the right to excommunicate. To Calvin, this violated the distinction between the spiritual and the temporal jurisdictions, especially since it involved civil punishments that Calvin thought entirely out of place in the church's discipline.

It is true that in the 1540s the senators asked Calvin to draft the republic's constitution. This was not because he was a Protestant ayatollah, since he was at the same time still being rebuffed in attempts to secure the liberty of the church's consistory over its own affairs. Rather, the appeal reflected the simple fact that no one else came close to his command of Greco-Roman civil history and law. After all, his first work, a commentary on Seneca's *On Clemency*, was a textbook used in the law schools of French universities. Yet if ever there might be a moment when the Reformer might set his allegedly theocratic system in stone, this was it. What was the result? "Calvin seems only to have pruned the law," according to historian William Monter, "to make punishment less severe, while attempting to ensure that all men were equal before the law and that the laws were actually enforced." Equity and clemency were urged over against tyrannical rigor. His friend Germain Colladon updated Calvin's draft in 1568 and "it remained the foundation of Genevan public law until the end of the republic."[33] It is hardly the work of an aspiring despot. Rather, it is typically regarded as a document in early constitutional republicanism.

When Ami Perrin plotted to abolish the consistory (church leadership) and take absolute control of the state (with some French collusion), the senate tried him for sedition. New elections were held, and now Farel, Calvin,

---

[32] Manetsch, *Calvin's Company of Pastors*, 27.
[33] William Monter, *Calvin's Geneva* (New York: John Wiley and Sons, 1967), 152.

and the other ministers received support to pursue their reforms. So, surely from this moment forward we would see the despotic Reformer emerge to reign with a free hand. Instead, the senators determined that such power would never be entrusted to a single person again.[34]

Far from pastors monitoring every aspect of behavior, with spies and secret police, the church registers "provide the impression that the pastors were really absorbed in their supervision of the missionary campaign," notes Robert M. Kingdon.[35] Recently, Scott Manetsch's comprehensive study of the church records demonstrates a concern primarily "with educating the ignorant, defending the weak, and mediating interpersonal conflicts."[36] Women and children were often little more than property in medieval Europe, and the records display the patience and seriousness with which pastors and elders pursued resolution of conflict. In fact, a merchant confronted for beating his wife with a stool "complained that 'the Consistory is the paradise of women' and that city magistrates 'pursue men and protect women.'"[37] "It petitioned the Small Council to provide gainful employment for young women" and "defended the cause of helpless orphans, poor laborers, mistreated prisoners, despised refugees, and social misfits."[38] Although the myth is still perpetuated, there was not a single case of execution for blasphemy in Geneva during Calvin's ministry, even though blasphemy was a capital offense in medieval law.[39]

Calvin and the other pastors repeatedly affirmed that the consistory could not administer legal or temporal punishments, but could correct only with "the spiritual sword of God's Word," and that "corrections are nothing but medicine to bring sinners back to our Lord." The *Ecclesiastical Ordinances* and the records of actual cases demonstrate the remarkable extent to which this stated intention was followed.[40] Indeed, whereas Rome claimed authority to anathematize, Calvin argued that the consistory exercises the keys of Christ with warnings to the erring member and "calls him back to salvation."[41] Calvin warned against discipline degenerating

---

[34] Ibid., 88.

[35] Robert M. Kingdon, *Geneva and the Coming of the Wars of Religion in France, 1555–1563* (Paris: Librairie Droz, 2007), 31.

[36] Manetsch, *Calvin's Company of Pastors*, 183–84.

[37] Ibid., 200.

[38] Ibid., 215.

[39] Monter, *Calvin's Geneva*, 153.

[40] Manetsch, *Calvin's Company of Pastors*, 184. "During the 1540s Calvin's Consistory suspended a relatively small number of Genevans from the sacrament of the Table—on average of one or two dozen per year" (185). This is remarkably small considering that the whole population belonged to the church.

[41] Ibid., 189.

into "spiritual butchery."[42] This undue rigor was something he detected in both Roman Catholic and Anabaptist discipline.

Many of the matters that came before the consistory had to do with making sure that parishioners knew the Christian faith well enough to receive Communion. For example, they could not receive Communion if they secretly embraced Roman Catholic or Anabaptist beliefs and practices, but the form of discipline was instruction. Others were admonished for drunken outbursts (even urinating) during services.[43] As one might expect, the magistrates frowned on practices like dancing naked at weddings, but the civil laws of Geneva were identical to those in Europe, even Italy.[44]

Alarmed at the condition of marriage in his day, Scott H. Hendrix notes, Luther urged princes and magistrates to tighten laws: "In 1539 he wrote that people who wished to be Christian would keep houses of prostitution out of their towns while those who tolerated such houses were no better than pagans."[45] Lutheran church orders barred from Communion "open adulterers, whores, rowdies, regular drunkards, blasphemers, and others who lead a shameful life." If they still resist, after being "earnestly admonished by one or two preachers to change their life," "they are to be regarded as unchristian and people who are damned, just as Christ teaches us by the judgment he renders in Matthew 18:15–20." "They are not to be admitted to the sacrament, to their greater condemnation, until they publicly change their life, because they have publicly sinned. They can attend the sermon, however."[46]

The same policy was followed in Geneva—suspension from the Table, but not from the ministry of the Word—in the hope that offenders would be led to repentance. In fact, Manetsch reports that "only around 13 percent of all suspensions in Geneva were for sexual sins such as fornication, adultery, and solicitation" during both Calvin's and Beza's lifetimes.[47] Meanwhile, in Roman Catholic and Anabaptist discipline, excommunication meant typically being barred not only from the church entirely but from the social community as well.

---

[42] Ibid.

[43] Ibid., 193. A particularly egregious abuse of discipline did occur when a young husband and school-teacher was suspended briefly from Communion for lying about his sexual impotence. Yet what is interesting is that this happened a year after Calvin's death, and his parents "complained bitterly that 'if Monsieur Calvin had still been alive, [the consistory] would not have behaved in this fashion.'"

[44] Monter, *Calvin's Geneva*, 216.

[45] Hendrix, *Recultivating the Vineyard*, 62.

[46] Ibid., 112, quoting the Hamburg church order adopted in 1529.

[47] Manetsch, *Calvin's Company of Pastors*, 202.

By design, excommunication was to be rare, "only around 3–4 percent of all interdictions" between 1542 and 1609.[48] Furthermore, these matters had to remain private; gossip, too, could provoke a letter from the consistory. The way it actually worked out, Elsie Anne McKee observes, only non-repentance could lead to excommunication. In fact, "a repentant murderer might be received, an unrepentant quarreler would not."[49]

It should be noted that no minister or elder—even Calvin—could exercise discipline individually. Rather, all actions were those of the consistory—ministers and elders—as one body, in common consent. Monter reminds us, "Calvin was a pastor—as well as the permanent Moderator of the Genevan Company of Pastors—and he had no other kind of authority in Geneva."[50] Manetsch relates that on one occasion the Company, acting on evidence, removed a minister who had groped his female servant. Vehement in his response, the minister accused the Company of injustice—and especially Calvin of abusing his authority in the matter as moderator of the Company. At an emergency session, "Calvin requested that the Company judge whether he had exceeded his authority as moderator and minister" in the process. "The ministers dismissed Calvin and Ferron from the meeting and discussed the case in private before finally exonerating Calvin and upholding the charges against Ferron." The offending minister was suspended from the ministry by the city council, and he left Geneva.[51] It is hardly a despot who asks his fellow pastors to judge whether he had exceeded his authority. Furthermore, there was no partiality: ministers also were removed from office for various indiscretions.[52]

Calvin even insisted that pastors rotate throughout the parish churches so that the people would be attached to the ministry rather than the minister. In fact, Monter says, "it is worth noting, as special evidence of Calvin's lifelong struggle against what the twentieth century calls the cult of personality, that neither he nor his successor was dispensed from routine pastoral work in order to fulfill these pan-European responsibilities."[53] "Despite the common picture of a Genevan theocracy," Stanford historian (and Lutheran) Lewis Spitz concludes, "Calvin was deeply concerned to

---

[48] Ibid., 193.

[49] Elsie Anne McKee, "Context, Contours, Contents: Towards a Description of Calvin's Understanding of Worship," in *Calvin Studies Society Papers, 1995, 1997: Calvin and Spirituality; Calvin and His Contemporaries*, ed. David Foxgrover (Grand Rapids: CRC Product Services, 1998), 84n48.

[50] Monter, *Calvin's Geneva*, 107.

[51] Manetsch, *Calvin's Company of Pastors*, 63.

[52] Ibid., 194.

[53] Monter, *Calvin's Geneva*, 142.

separate the church with its spiritual functions from state control."[54] This was true even in the tragic affair that hangs like a dark cloud over Calvin's memory: the burning of Michael Servetus.

The Case of Michael Servetus

Calvin knew of Servetus from the past, before fleeing Paris. In fact, he had risked his life by agreeing to meet with the outspoken Anabaptist and anti-Trinitarian in private, but Servetus never showed. Fleeing imprisonment in France, where he was awaiting execution at the hands of the Inquisition, Servetus arrived in Geneva imagining that he could with impunity interrupt Calvin's sermon by attacking the Trinity—"that triad of impossible monstrosities"—and was quickly arrested.[55]

Declaring himself "First Syndic" (sole ruler), it was the redoubtable Ami Perrin who, after a trial, condemned Servetus to the flames on October 27, 1553. "Perhaps the most eloquent commentary on Genevan justice came from its most famous victim, Michael Servetus, who at one point in his trial was asked whether he preferred to be tried in Geneva or be sent back to France. Servetus fell on his knees and implored *Messieurs* to be tried in Geneva."[56]

Perrin and the city council sought advice from various Protestant cities, and all returned the same judgment: an anti-Trinitarian with an international reputation like Servetus's must be burned at the stake, according to the common law of Christendom. The Inquisition sentenced the escaped prisoner to death *in absentia*—"in a slow fire."[57] Would Protestants even tolerate those who strike at the heart of the catholic faith, thus justifying the immediate dispatch of every army in Christendom against the republic?

Calvin pleaded repeatedly with Servetus to recant, but to no effect. The "slow burning" demanded by the Inquisition was ignored, but the magistrates insisted on burning. Monter explains, "Calvin tried to have the sentence lightened to simply execution, but without success."[58] Even "gentle Melanchthon" wrote to Calvin, "To you also the Church owes gratitude at the present moment, and will owe it to the latest posterity. . . . I affirm

---

[54] Spitz, *The Protestant Reformation*, 159.
[55] Parker, *John Calvin*, 139.
[56] Monter, *Calvin's Geneva*, 155.
[57] Parker, *John Calvin*, 145.
[58] Monter, *Calvin's Geneva*, 84.

also that your magistrates did right in punishing, after a regular trial, this blasphemous man."[59]

Concerning Servetus, Monter reminds us, "His was the only case, but at the same time an extremely significant case, of a man put to death for his religious opinions in Calvin's Geneva. Other victims followed him in nearby Protestant states."[60] Indeed, fully Trinitarian evangelicals were being sent to the flames, gallows, and sword every day across Europe, especially in Calvin's homeland. In these cases, the Reformer vehemently protested any attempt to take up the sword in defending the gospel or, in its defense, their own lives.

However, Calvin compounded his complicity in the affair by writing a defense of capital punishment for notorious anti-Trinitarians like Servetus. Apparently Calvin—like the other Reformers—saw no contradiction between Servetus's execution and his own teaching on the spiritual reign of Christ by his Word alone. It is unworthy of the truth that he proclaimed to exonerate Calvin in this affair simply as a man of his time, especially when others were appealing to the Reformer's own writings to defend religious toleration. At the same time, even in this tragic episode he played not the role of a despot, but the role that was assigned to him—and which he willingly accepted—as a pastor in Christendom.

"He was not trying to Calvinize France or to make Genevan Calvinism international," observes Hendrix. Like Luther's, his missionary concern was to recultivate Christ's vineyard in so-called Christendom and to extend the gospel beyond Europe.[61] And yet, under his ministry, Geneva did provide an international model. Refugees—many of them students—poured in not only from all of Europe but also from Russia, Crete, Malta, and Tunisia. And the first Protestant missionaries were sent from Geneva to the New World: Brazil. As Philip Benedict points out, Geneva's population more than doubled during Calvin's ministry. Despots repress their populations, but the complaint of Genevans was that their new republic was being overrun by foreign refugees.[62] Given his own experience, it is not surprising that Calvin's favored metaphors for the Christian life are exile, pilgrimage, feast, refugee, and finding asylum only in Christ.

As we explore Calvin's view of the Christian life, we discover a teacher

---

[59] Philip Schaff, "Protestant Intolerance," in *History of the Christian Church*, vol. 8, accessed November 10, 2011, http://www.ccel.org/ccel/schaff/hcc8.iv.xvi.iv.html.
[60] Monter, *Calvin's Geneva*, 84.
[61] Hendrix, *Recultivating the Vineyard*, 94.
[62] Benedict, *Christ's Churches Purely Reformed*, 108.

who arrived at his convictions not out of ivory-tower speculation or monastic contemplation, but out of constant crises, tests, disappointing setbacks, and personal suffering. Perhaps this introduction finds its most eloquent conclusion in the words of a Pulitzer Prize–winning novelist: "His life might be seen as a great tragedy were it not for the strength of his work, which has had an incalculable impact on the thought and culture of the West and the whole Christian world."[63]

---

[63] Robinson, preface to *John Calvin* , xv.

CHAPTER 2

CALVIN ON THE CHRISTIAN LIFE: IN CONTEXT

Some misunderstandings of Calvin's theology and piety are due to friends, not just foes. The first step in disentangling Calvin from the many uses that we have made of him, then, is to examine Calvin's piety in his own context.[1]

The Catholic Calvin

First, there is the "Catholic Calvin." Here "Catholic" encompasses the consensus of all Christians everywhere. It is broader than the term *Roman Catholic*. Although we know what people mean when they say, "I was raised Catholic, but I'm a Christian now," Calvin would have been baffled by this way of putting it. He always considered himself more Catholic than his Roman critics. Indeed, he was hardly the first to have thought so, since the Christian East has long pointed out the oxymoron in "Roman Catholic." After all, "Catholic" means universal, and "Roman" refers to a part rather than the whole. The bishop of Rome was originally one among other key leaders. Even the sixth-century Roman bishop Gregory the Great said that "universal pontiff" was "a form of proud address" and that any bishop who

---

[1] See David Steinmetz, *Calvin in Context*, 2nd ed. (New York: Oxford University Press, 2010), for a rich summary of Calvin's views on various subjects with a keen eye toward situating him in his own world rather than ours.

assumed that title was "a precursor to Antichrist."[2] The current pope was schismatic, in Calvin's view, and the Reformers were simply calling the church back to its sources.

Although Calvin's father, Gerard, had destined him for the priesthood, it was a course that young Jean enthusiastically embraced. At the age of twelve he was the local bishop's secretary and even received the monk's tonsure (distinctive haircut). His gifts and zeal won the patronage of the distinguished Montmor family, allowing him to attend the most prestigious colleges of the University of Paris (Sorbonne). At the Collège de la Marche he acquired his celebrated command of Latin under the distinguished teacher Mathurin Cordier, who would eventually come to evangelical convictions and to teach at Geneva's Academy. Calvin then studied theology and philosophy at the Collège de Montaigu, after Erasmus and just before Ignatius of Loyola, founder of the Jesuits. Here the "new learning" (classical humanism) was breathing new energy into the conservative university. Although his memories of the strict regimen were as unpleasant as Erasmus's, Calvin became a student of classical Greek and Roman literature while at the college and also began his Hebrew and Greek study of Scripture.

When his close friend Nicolas Cop, son of the king's surgeon, became the president of the University of Paris, Calvin helped to draft the inaugural speech. Peppered with calls for evangelical reform, the address provoked the ire of university and royal authorities, and the pair narrowly escaped. Their libraries were burned, they fled to Basel together, and Nicolas's brother Michel—a noted Hebraist—made Calvin proficient in Hebrew.

Alongside his close study of Scripture in the original languages, Calvin devoured the writings of the ancient church fathers, especially Irenaeus, Chrysostom, and the Cappadocians in the East and Ambrose, Hilary, and Augustine in the West. He even called upon the testimony of "the better theologians" of the medieval church, such as Thomas Aquinas, Bernard, and Bonaventure. They left an indelible stamp on his exegesis and theological formulations, as well as his liturgical and devotional writings. In fact, he frequently swayed audiences in favor of the Reformation with his arguments from these sources, cited nearly verbatim from memory.

Writing to the French King Henri II, whose policy of persecution was even more violent than his father's, Calvin said, "We have here laid down with simplicity a brief confession of the faith we hold, which we trust you

---

[2] *Letters of Pope Gregory the Great*, book 5, epistle 18.

will find in accordance with that of the Catholic church."[3] Richard Muller reminds us that although the Reformation provoked controversy over justification, the sacraments, and the church, "the doctrines of God, the Trinity, creation, providence, predestination, and the last things were taken over by the magisterial Reformation virtually without alteration."[4] Later Reformed pastors and theologians would identify themselves not as Calvinists but as "Reformed Catholics."[5]

Radical Protestants—particularly the Anabaptists—did not appeal to antiquity. As contemporary Anabaptist scholar Leonard Verduin notes, "They were not interested in any continuity with the Church of the past; for them that Church was a 'fallen' creature."[6] Calvin, on the other hand, was eager to maintain every possible connection with the ancient church and the best heritage of Christian faith and practice down to his own day. Far from anticipating the Enlightenment ideals of progress and individual autonomy, Calvin upbraided the pope for having an itch for novelty—creating doctrines and forms of worship without scriptural warrant and the example of the ancient church. Luther and Calvin were Catholic Reformers, not radical modernizers.

The Evangelical Calvin

An earthy, gregarious, and sometimes boisterous son of German peasant stock, Luther peppered his sermons and conversations with homely—sometimes even crude—illustrations that resonated with the average Wittenberger. In his translation of the Bible, he searched diligently for the most familiar word or phrase in everyday German that would communicate the original text. With a larger-than-life personality, which he felt quite at home in divulging, Luther seems especially suited to the role that providence gave him. It is perhaps not surprising that Luther's informal table-talk conversations were recorded for posterity.

Hailing from an upper-middle-class French home and taken under the wing of a distinguished family for a privileged education, Calvin was more refined. Temperamentally, he was reserved and private—even shy,

---

[3] Calvin, "To the King of France" (Geneva, October 1557), in *Selected Works of John Calvin: Tracts and Letters*, ed. Henry Beveridge and Jules Bonnet, 7 vols. (Grand Rapids: Baker, 1983), 6:373.
[4] Richard Muller, *The Unaccommodated Calvin: Studies in the Foundation of a Theological Tradition* (New York: Oxford University Press, 2001), 39.
[5] Richard Muller, *Calvin and the Reformed Tradition: On the Work of Christ and the Order of Salvation* (Grand Rapids: Baker Academic, 2011), 54.
[6] Leonard Verduin, *The Reformers and Their Stepchildren* (Grand Rapids: Eerdmans, 1964), 156.

avoiding autobiography. Contemporaries report the congeniality of a man whose home was often filled with guests. In Strasbourg, he and his wife, Idelette, were at the center of activity in a bustling youth hostel that they founded. However, he was the type of person who would have been uneasy with note takers hovering about over dinner recording the conversation. In short, though serious about the matters at hand, Luther seems at home on the stage of history, while Calvin seems genuinely to have preferred a peaceful obscurity.

Also, many changes had occurred in the two decades that separated the Reformers in age (they never met personally). Luther, the Augustinian monk, was fond of the German mystics and became the pioneering Reformer; Calvin was shaped in student days by the French humanists and early Reformers, who displayed little interest in mysticism. Their contexts were different, too. The Lutheran Reformation was an event in the history of the Holy Roman Empire (basically Germany), with Luther as the central figure who had come under the protection of now evangelical princes. However, Reformed churches emerged primarily in independent cities, whose magistrates embraced the Reformation usually after a public Roman Catholic–Reformed debate. Although Bucer came close, there was no one comparable religious authority to Luther or political equivalent of the united princes. Consequently, consensus was reached more by mutual consent of the cities and their church leaders. Calvin was but a rising star in a constellation of already established leaders. Furthermore, while Luther was at home in Wittenberg, with a free hand even sometimes to meddle in political affairs, Calvin was a foreigner and exile in a city whose leaders often stifled his attempts simply to reform the church.

There were similarities as well. Luther was destined by his father for law and then the priesthood; the reverse in Calvin's case. Both knew firsthand the most rigorous expressions of late-medieval theology and practice. In fact, far from youthful rebels, both confessed the depth to which they had devoted themselves to Rome. They were censorious of themselves and others who failed to invest themselves fully and sincerely in the form of medieval piety in which they had been reared.

After embracing the gospel Calvin also shared Luther's concern to pursue reform cautiously. "For it is not possible that the public government of the church can be all at once changed," he told the king of Poland (Sigismund Augustus), a Reformed monarch known as a pioneer of religious liberty.[7] Although he was more concerned than Luther to purge remnants of false worship, he counseled toleration and patient instruction where there were differences of opinion. Like Luther, he never abandoned the church, but sought to reform it by going back to its own source in Scripture. And, like Luther, he was excommunicated by the papacy, he was hunted by the Inquisition, and his writings were placed on the index of forbidden books.

Calvin also shared with Reformers like Luther and Bucer a deep conviction that sound doctrine is the soul of piety, not an intellectual game. He described the dogma of implicit faith (assenting to whatever the church teaches) as ignorance disguised as humility. Surely faith requires knowledge. Nevertheless, faith is supremely trust in a person—namely, Christ as he is clothed in his gospel. This Word of God captures our whole person, not just our mind or will or affections. In fact, "true faith consists more in living experience than in high-flown speculations that flit about in the brain."[8] "I have censured the curiosity of those who would agitate questions which are truly nothing else than mere tortures to the intellect," he said.[9] Theology is not abstract theory, but the most practical knowledge of all.

In fact, knowledge and experience are inseparable. Calvin repeatedly raises the objection that Roman critics of justification have not really experienced a crisis of conscience before a holy God. They are not only ignorant of Scripture but also experientially naïve. "It is not strange, however, that addle-pated monks who, having never experienced any struggle of conscience . . . should thus prate the perfection of the Law," despite their hypocrisy. "With the same confidence do they talk of a heaven for hire, while they themselves meanwhile continue engrossed with the present hire, after which they are always gaping." They fail to realize, he says, "that there is no work untainted with impurity, until it be washed away by the blood of Christ."[10] He adds, "Were regeneration perfected in this life the observance of the law would be possible. . . . But there is no wonder that they speak so boldly of things they know not. War is pleasant to those who have never tried it."[11]

Calvin had tried it. Like Luther, he was more devoted to medieval piety

---

[7] Calvin, "To the King of Poland" (Geneva, December 5, 1554), in *Selected Works of John Calvin*, 6:108.
[8] Calvin, *Institutes of the Christian Religion*, ed. John T. McNeill, trans. Ford Lewis Battles (Philadelphia: Westminster, 1960), 1.5.9.
[9] Calvin, "Psychopannychia," in *Selected Works of John Calvin*, 3:418.
[10] Ibid., 145.
[11] Ibid., 156.

than most of his peers. He wanted to get it right. He wanted to *be* right before God. If such faithful young men of the church became leaders of the Reformation, it was because they had taken Rome's piety further and deeper than most, and it left them destitute. In response to the Council of Trent's canon condemning those who teach that we should not expect our good works to be rewarded with eternal life, Calvin writes, "Such boldness is not strange in men who have never felt any serious fear of Divine judgment."[12]

The same concern is expressed even more directly in his passionate letter to Cardinal Jacopo Sadoleto:

> Hence, I observe, Sadoleto, that you have too indolent [lazy] a theology, as is almost always the case with those who have never had experience in serious struggles of conscience. For, otherwise, you would never place a Christian man on ground so slippery, nay, so precipitous, that he can scarcely stand a moment if even the slightest push is given him.[13]

Calvin imagines that he is standing with Sadoleto before Christ on judgment day: "I, O Lord, as I had been educated from a boy, always professed the Christian faith," but did not really know what it was.

> I believed, as I had been taught, that I was redeemed by the death of thy Son from liability to eternal death, but the redemption I thought was one whose virtue could never reach me. I anticipated a future resurrection, but hated to think of it, as being an event most dreadful. . . . They, indeed, preached of thy clemency toward men, but confined it to those who should show themselves deserving of it.[14]

In spite of "some intervals of quiet, I was still far off from true peace of conscience; for, whenever I descended into myself, or raised my mind to thee, extreme terror seized me—terror which no expiations nor satisfactions could cure" and which could only be ignored. Then I heard "a very different doctrine," which actually

> brought me back to its fountainhead. . . . Offended by the novelty, I lent an unwilling ear, and at first, I confess, strenuously and passionately

---

[12] Ibid., 158.
[13] Calvin, "Reply by John Calvin to Cardinal Sadoleto's Letter," in *Selected Works of John Calvin*, 1:52.
[14] Ibid., 61.

resisted; for . . . it was the greatest difficulty I was induced to confess
that I had all my life long been in ignorance and error. One thing in particular made me averse to those new teachers; namely, reverence for the
Church.[15]

Yet, Calvin says, once he opened his ears, he understood the truth from
those who treasured it. "They spoke nobly of the Church and showed the
greatest desire to cultivate it."[16]

The Certainty of the Gospel

Calvin felt the sting of the Devil's taunt to Luther, "Are you alone wise
among men?" We are certain of the gospel because it is so clearly revealed
in Scripture—in contrast with the teachers of Rome.

> I do not dream, however, of a clarity of faith which never errs in discrimi-
> nating between truth and falsehood, is never deceived, nor do I figure
> to myself an arrogance which looks down as from a height on the whole
> human race, waits for no man's judgment, and makes no distinction be-
> tween learned and unlearned.

Indeed, it is better to suspend judgment than to rashly criticize and raise
dissent. "I only contend that . . . the truth of the word of God is so clear and
certain that it cannot be overthrown by either men or angels."[17]

The Reformed have no controversy at all with the true Catholic church,
Calvin contends.[18] "You know, Sadoleto," he daringly presses, "that our
agreement with antiquity is far closer than yours" and that we are only
trying to "renew that ancient form of the church" that has been "distorted
by illiterate men" and "was afterwards flagitiously mangled and almost
destroyed by the Roman Pontiff and his faction."[19] Every aspect of the
church's ministry—its doctrine, the sacraments, ceremonies, and discipline—had been profaned by Rome. "Will you obtrude upon me, for the
Church, a body which furiously persecutes everything sanctioned by our

---

[15] Ibid., 62.
[16] Ibid., 63.
[17] Ibid., 54.
[18] Ibid., 37.
[19] Ibid.

religion, both as delivered by the oracles of God and embodied in the writings of the Holy Fathers, and approved by ancient Councils?"[20]

Even Calvin's humanist sympathies were tested by the evangelical emphasis. In many ways, the Dutch humanist Desiderius Erasmus (1466–1536) was a founding father of both the Reformation and the Counter-Reformation. However, behind Erasmus stands the broader influence of the Brethren of the Common Life, also known as the *devotio moderna* (modern devotion). This is especially worth mentioning because I think contemporary evangelical spirituality bears more in common with this movement than with the Reformation.

Founded in the fourteenth century by Gerard Groote, the Brethren represent a mystical-pietist reform effort. Among their distinguished alumni were cardinals and a pope, as well as Erasmus, Luther, Bullinger, Anabaptist leaders like Balthasar Hubmaier and Hans Denck, and the founder of the Jesuits, Ignatius of Loyola. Everything turned on "the imitation of Christ," which was the title of the devotional best seller written by Brethren member Thomas à Kempis. However, what set the Reformers apart was that they challenged the *doctrine* of the medieval church. For the most part, the Brethren were not interested in church doctrine and ritual, and they were generally inclined toward more optimistic views of free will and justification as inner transformation.

As he approached the fork in the road, Calvin declared, "I am a pupil of Luther's." Addressing Emperor Charles V, he said, "God roused Luther and the others, who carried the torch ahead, in order to recover the way of salvation; and by whose service our churches were founded and established."[21]

Also like Luther, Calvin thought of justification not as merely one doctrine among many, but as the heart of the dispute with Rome. Of this doctrine he said, "This is the main hinge on which religion turns. . . . For unless you first of all grasp what your relationship to God is, and the nature of his judgment concerning you, you have neither a foundation on which to establish your salvation nor one on which to build piety toward God."[22] All of the other abuses—pilgrimages, merits, satisfactions, penances, purgatory, tyranny, superstitions, and idolatry—flow from this fatal fountain of denying justification, Calvin argues pointedly. As for the pope

---

[20] Ibid., 38–39.
[21] Calvin, "The Necessity of Reforming the Church," in *Selected Works of John Calvin*, 1:125.
[22] Calvin, *Institutes* 3.11.1.

and his retinue, "Did they not decide that their only security was in arms and cruelty?"[23]

Distinctive Characteristics in Calvin's Piety

Finally, Calvin also contributed a distinctively Reformed inflection of the catholic and evangelical faith and even contributed to an emerging consensus at a time of some internal incoherence. On the one hand, he disdained novelty and desired nothing more than unity of all the churches in the gospel. On the other hand, having cast off the pope, he was perturbed by the sycophantic tendency of many evangelicals—Reformed and Lutheran—to wrap themselves around a Protestant leader. "If I were never to dissent from Luther," he wrote to the chancellor of Saxony, "to undertake the task of interpretation would be absurd."[24] He also grew impatient with the partisans of Zwingli. By his own report, Calvin was unimpressed with Zwingli's writing and in fact ignored it as long as possible.[25] "They flare into a rage if anyone dares to prefer Luther to Zwingli," Calvin complained. "This is not harming Zwingli in any way, for if they are compared with each other, you yourself know how much Luther is to be preferred."[26]

We will encounter Calvin's distinctive contributions along the way, some of which may be mentioned here.

First, Calvin insisted more than other Reformers that Scripture alone must determine faith and practice. Neither the pope nor the prince, but Christ by his Word, determines every aspect of the church's doctrine, worship, life, and discipline. Beyond Scripture, the church has no authority to bind consciences.

Second, the formula "distinction without separation" pervades Calvin's thinking. The ecumenical Creed of Chalcedon (AD 451) affirmed that the eternal Son assumed our flesh in such a way that the two natures are united in one person. Nevertheless, each nature retains the attributes proper to it—without separation *or* confusion. Drawing on the early fathers, Calvin's christology—and the "distinction without separation" formula in particular—shapes his view not only of the relation between the saving reality and creaturely sign in the Supper, but also of the relation between God and the world, Christ's saving office and the ministry of the church, and Christ

---

[23] Calvin, "Reply by John Calvin to Cardinal Sadoleto's Letter," 60.
[24] Calvin, "To Francis Unhard" (Geneva, February 27, 1555), in *Selected Works of John Calvin*, 6:154.
[25] T. H. L. Parker, *John Calvin* (Tring, UK: Lion, 1975), 162.
[26] Calvin, quoted in ibid., 154.

and culture. Also, in Calvin's treatment of the Supper his richly Trinitarian theology becomes especially evident, with a greater emphasis on the Spirit's work. He underscores the importance of Christ's bodily ascension, which opens up space for the Spirit's work of uniting us here and now to the Christ who has ascended and will return in the flesh.

Third, Calvin was a pioneering covenant theologian, emphasizing God's promise in Christ as the basis and a communion of saints as the result. The unity of the covenant of grace across Old and New Testaments is woven throughout his teaching on the Christian life. It is not just a supporting argument for the baptism of covenant children, but a hermeneutical lens through which he interprets the whole of Scripture and applies Scripture to the daily life of families and individuals. This covenantal emphasis is also at the heart of Calvin's corporate and ecclesial understanding of piety. Private disciplines are important, but the public ministry of the church is like a fountain from which God's good gifts flow out to families and individuals and then, through them, out into the world. In short, private piety arises out of public piety, not vice versa. This emphasis on corporate worship included congregational singing, and the continuity of the covenant of grace in both Testaments gave the Psalms the prominence that they had in better days. In short, for Calvin at least, piety is not just something that is taught; it is also "caught": as we pray, so we believe (*lex orandi, lex credendi*). True doctrine is inculcated not only by direct instruction but also by the patterns of public worship and fellowship in the communion of saints, in family life, and in everyday callings. Reading, praying, and singing the Psalms were among the most significant distinctives of Reformed piety.

All of these distinctive emphases will become clearer in the following chapters. We begin our exploration of Calvin's spirituality now with Calvin's own prayer at the beginning of his lectures: "May the Lord grant that we may engage in contemplating the mysteries of his heavenly wisdom with really increasing devotion, to his glory and to our edification. Amen."

PART I

LIVING BEFORE GOD

CHAPTER 3

KNOWING GOD AND OURSELVES

At least in the popular imagination, especially in our self-obsessed culture, Calvin's theology is so God-centered that there is no room for human beings. Consequently, it is seen as cold and rationalistic. We can only bow before an utterly sovereign God of blinding majesty.

We do not need to go any further than the opening line of his *Institutes* to conclude otherwise: "Nearly all wisdom we possess, that is to say, true and sound wisdom, consists in two parts: the knowledge of God and of ourselves." And these two are "inseparable."[1]

Created in God's image and likeness for covenantal fellowship, we were made not for ourselves, but for God and for each other. No doubt Calvin recalled Augustine's opening in his *Confessions*, even expressed in the intimacy of prayer: "You have made us for yourself and our hearts find no peace until they rest in you."[2] God doesn't need us, but freely chose to create us as his covenant partners. So the moment we think of God, we cannot help but think also of ourselves—and vice versa. Knowing God is inseparable from experiencing God.

For, how can the thought of God penetrate your mind without your realizing immediately that, since you are his handiwork, you have been made

---

[1] Rightly rejecting the prevalent notion of a "central thesis" in Calvin's work (viz., predestination), Mary Potter Engel speaks of Calvin's thought generally as "a dynamic perspectival structure," *John Calvin's Perspectival Anthropology* (Atlanta: Scholars Press, 1988), xi.

[2] St. Augustine, *Confessions*, trans. R. S. Pine-Coffin (New York: Penguin Classics, 1961), 21.

over and bound to his command by right of creation, that you owe your life to him?—that whatever you undertake, whatever you do, ought to be ascribed to him? . . . For, to begin with, the pious mind does not dream up for itself any god it pleases, but contemplates the one and only true God. And it does not attach to him whatever it pleases, but is content to hold him to be as he manifests himself.[3]

Standard medieval textbooks began with the question, "What is God?" In other words, what is his essence, God as he is in himself? It was basically a philosophical question that could be answered in this way before even examining God's self-revelation in Scripture. The same was true in considering ourselves. "What is humanity"—the essence that distinguishes us from all other creatures, and even my inmost self from my body? Typically, as in Greek speculation, medieval theology discoursed on the sublimity of the soul as a sort of "spark of divinity," immortal and indestructible, although humans were considered more like the beasts in their bodily nature.

In Scripture, though, the context of the question is always concrete covenantal history. Calvin states up front, "What is God? Men who pose this question are merely toying with idle speculations. It is more important for us to know of what sort he is and what is consistent with his nature. . . . *What help is it, in short, to know a God with whom we have nothing to do?*"[4] "They are mad who seek to discover what God is," he says. "The essence of God is rather to be adored than inquired into."[5] "Indeed, his essence is incomprehensible; hence, his divineness far escapes all human perception. But upon his individual works he has engraved unmistakable marks of his glory, so clear and so prominent that even unlettered and ignorant folk cannot plead the excuse of ignorance."[6]

In fact, besides numerous scriptural passages, Calvin picked up this emphasis from the ancient fathers, especially those in the East, who insisted that we can know God according to his works, but never in his essence.[7]

---

[3] Calvin, *Institutes of the Christian Religion*, ed. John T. McNeill, trans. Ford Lewis Battles (Philadelphia: Westminster, 1960), 1.2.2.

[4] Ibid., emphasis added. See note 6 in the Battles translation of this passage, where he suggests that Calvin also had Zwingli in mind in this criticism. In a letter to Zwingli's successor, Heinrich Bullinger (January 1552), Calvin faults Zwingli's work on God's providence for being rife with "knotted paradoxes" (*Corpus Reformatorum: Johannis Calvini opera quae supersunt omnia*, 14.253).

[5] Calvin, *Institutes* 1.2.2.

[6] Ibid., 1.5.1.

[7] Gregory of Nyssa, "On 'Not Three Gods' to Ablabius," in *A Select Library of Nicene and Post-Nicene Fathers of the Christian Church*, series 2, vol. 5, trans. S. D. F. Salmond (Grand Rapids: Eerdmans, 1973), 333; John of Damascus, "An Exact Exposition of the Orthodox Faith," in *A Select Library of Nicene and Post-Nicene*

Though we dare not speculate about what God *is in himself*, we can know what God *is like*—in other words, his attributes—from Scripture. "Thereupon his powers are mentioned, by which he is shown to us not as he is in himself, but as he is toward us: so that this recognition of him consists more in living experience than in vain and high-flown speculation."[8] What God reveals is true knowledge, but God gives it to serve our desperate need to be reconciled to him rather than to satisfy our curiosity.

> Now, the knowledge of God, as I understand it, is that by which we not only conceive that there is a God but also grasp what befits us and is proper to his glory, in fine, *what is to our advantage to know of him*. Indeed, we shall not say that, properly speaking, God is known where there is no religion or piety.[9]

The goal for Calvin, then, is not to find a "what" but a "who"; not an essence, but an active agent in history. That requires a story, not a speculation. We know the Giver through his gifts, and we know ourselves as the beneficiaries of those gifts.

So Calvin's view is far from the popular caricature of a distant deity of sovereign majesty who renders humanity nothing but a shadow. André Biéler puts it succinctly: "The Protestant Reformation has not only been a rediscovery of God. It has also been a decisive answer to the question: 'Who is man?'"[10] As T. F. Torrance observes of Calvin's approach:

> This Biblical knowledge of man is gained: (a) Through the law, which enables man to see himself as he really is in comparison with his original truth which is the law of his being. . . . (b) Through the Gospel, which not only reveals to man what he actually is [in Christ], but brings him regeneration so that he may become what he is meant to be.[11]

Thus, anthropology "has no independent status" for Calvin.[12] And the place

---

Fathers of the Christian Church, series 2, vol. 9, trans. S. D. F. Salmond (Grand Rapids: Eerdmans, 1973), 1. See B. B. Warfield, *Calvin and Augustine*, ed. Samuel Craig (Philadelphia: Presbyterian and Reformed, 1956), 153. As Warfield noted, "He is refusing all a priori methods of determining the nature of God and requiring of us to form our knowledge of him a posteriori from the revelation He gives us of Himself in His activities." See further Warfield's excellent summary of this reticence in Calvin and the tradition generally to explore the "whatness" (139–40).

[8] Calvin, *Institutes* 1.10.2.

[9] Ibid., 1.2.1.

[10] André Biéler, *The Social Humanism of Calvin*, trans. Paul T. Fuhrmann (Richmond, VA: John Knox, 1961), 9.

[11] T. F. Torrance, *Calvin's Doctrine of Man* (Westport, CT: Greenwood, 1957), 13.

[12] Ibid., 14.

where we come to know God and ourselves most definitely is a person: Jesus Christ, both God and human.

When we come to these questions in this way—searching for the truth that "is to our advantage to know" rather than for speculations that "merely flit about in the brain"—we are no longer in the driver's seat. We are prepared to be surprised—even overwhelmed—by the truth. It will get close to us, in fact cut into us. Yet this is precisely what Calvin means by "piety." Even in pagan wonder at someone or something beyond nature there are remnants of this piety that he has in mind. "Even if there were no hell," says Calvin, a pious person "would still shudder at offending [God] alone." "And we ought to note this fact even more diligently: all men have a vague general veneration of God, but very few really reverence him."[13]

Knowing God is like knowing other people; it requires intellectual content, to be sure, but it is above all a relationship of love and trust based on reliable communication. God speaks to us not primarily to inform us, but to encounter us in judgment and grace.

Piety is the loving respect of a child for a parent, of a subject for his or her monarch; it is a relational knowing that involves the whole person—reason, will, feeling, and body—standing under God, waiting to hear whatever he is pleased to reveal about himself *and* about us. We are never detached observers or spectators in this enterprise. The progression of Calvin's argument in the *Institutes* echoes Paul's speech in Athens (Acts 17) and his argument in the first three chapters of Romans. Elsie Anne McKee does a wonderful job of summarizing Calvin's argument as a logical progression from the broadest circumference of piety to the most specific—namely, "Christ as he is clothed in the gospel."[14]

Everyone Knows God

Many today assume that the gospel offers a personal relationship with God. Yet Calvin assumes that this is already the case. Created in a covenantal relationship to God, everyone knows God by nature. "There is within the human mind, and indeed by natural instinct, an awareness of divinity [*sensus divinitatis*]." "This we take to be beyond controversy," Calvin says.[15]

---

[13] Calvin, *Institutes* 1.2.2.
[14] Elsie Anne McKee, "Context, Contours, Contents: Towards a Description of Calvin's Understanding of Worship," in *Calvin Studies Society Papers, 1995, 1997: Calvin and Spirituality; Calvin and His Contemporaries*, ed. David Foxgrover (Grand Rapids: CRC Product Services, 1998), 69.
[15] Calvin, *Institutes* 1.3.1.

In fact, much of this entire first section of the *Institutes* is a running commentary on Cicero's *On the Gods*. There are people who suppress this general revelation even to the point of denying God's existence. "Yet there is, as the eminent pagan [Cicero] says, no nation so barbarous, no people so savage, that they have not a deep-seated conviction that there is a God"— which is "a tacit confession of a sense of deity inscribed in the hearts of all. Indeed, even idolatry is ample proof of this conception."[16]

So even after the fall, this sense of divinity "can never be effaced"; it is "naturally inborn in all."[17] Even in ancient Greece, atheism was rare. "Although Diagoras and his like may jest at whatever has been believed in every age concerning religion, and Dionysius may mock the heavenly judgment, this is sardonic laughter, for the worm of conscience, sharper than any cauterizing iron, gnaws away within." This is a "law of their creation."[18] "There are innumerable evidences" to which "astronomy, medicine, and all natural sciences" attest.

> Indeed, men who have . . . even tasted the liberal arts penetrate with their aid far more deeply into the secrets of the divine wisdom. Yet ignorance of them prevents no one from seeing more than enough of God's workmanship in his creation to lead him to break forth in admiration of the Artificer.[19]

Each creature should lead us in a bread-crumb trail to God. It is interesting that among the "innumerable evidences" of God, Calvin mentions "astronomy, medicine, and all natural science," without any reference to philosophy. Focusing on God's manifest works rather than his ineffable essence, he follows a more empirical approach: exploring things that can "be easily observed with the eyes and pointed out with the finger." We should work inductively, from the facts all around us, rather than by deducing an idea of God from our own speculations. "We ought not to rack our brains about God; but rather we should contemplate him in his works." The goal is "not that knowledge which, content with empty speculation, merely flits in the brain, but that which will be sound and fruitful if we duly perceive it, and if it takes root in the heart."[20] We dare not "attempt with bold curiosity

---

[16] Ibid.
[17] Ibid., 1.3.3.
[18] Ibid.
[19] Ibid., 1.5.2.
[20] Ibid., 1.5.9.

to penetrate the investigation of his essence," but rather concentrate on God's works up close "whereby he renders himself near and familiar to us, and in some manner communicates himself."[21]

By seeking God where he has made himself known to us, we arrive at a knowledge that is practical in the fullest sense. It is not mere contemplation of the good, the true, and the beautiful that leads to awe, but the knowledge of our Creator and Redeemer that leads us to salvation. "Knowledge of this sort, then, ought not only to arouse us to the worship of God but also to awaken and encourage us to the hope of the future life."[22] We are the pinnacle of God's works in creation, God's own image and viceroy.[23] However, the grandeur of our species measures the depth of our depravity.

Everyone Suppresses the Truth in Unrighteousness

Given our fallen condition before God, Calvin says, whenever we encounter the slightest presence of the true God, our conscience is struck with fear so that we flee.[24] Instead of facing this confrontation, we fabricate an image of God (whether an idea or an object) that we can manipulate. There is enough in general revelation to assure us of the existence of a generous, just, wise, and powerful Creator. Yet sinful humanity is "struck blind in such a dazzling theater."[25]

The fall requires special revelation both because we willfully misinterpret God and ourselves even in natural terms and because it is only in the gospel that God announces his saving purposes to sinners. In Roman Catholic theology, general revelation is a stepping stone to redemption. In Calvin's view, it is the rope by which we hang ourselves. We start not with mere ignorance—an absence of knowledge of or relationship with God— but with a positive knowledge and experience that we intentionally warp, twist, and mangle into idolatry. To be sure, general revelation serves more positive purposes. We cannot suppress everything at the same time, and unbelievers still have remnants of the knowledge of God. The moral law written on the conscience is still evident in the relative justice and order in pagan societies. Nevertheless, apart from the gospel we turn this revelation into idolatry.

---

[21] Ibid.
[22] Ibid., 1.5.10.
[23] Ibid., 1.5.3.
[24] Ibid., 1.3.2.
[25] Ibid., 1.5.8.

Basically, this knowledge—both of God and of ourselves—is a revelation of the first use of the law; namely, to drive us out of idolatry and self-confidence so that we will flee to Christ.[26] "For we always seem to ourselves righteous and upright and wise and holy—this pride is innate in all of us—unless by clear proofs we stand convinced of our own unrighteousness, foulness, folly, and impurity."[27] As long as we confine our thoughts to the mundane matters of this life, "we flatter ourselves most sweetly, and fancy ourselves all but demigods."

> Suppose we but once begin to raise our thoughts to God, and to ponder his nature, and how completely perfect are his righteousness, wisdom, and power—the straightedge to which we must be shaped. Then, what masquerading earlier as righteousness was pleasing in us will soon grow filthy in its consummate wickedness. What wonderfully impressed us under the name of wisdom will stink in its very foolishness. What wore the face of power will prove itself the most miserable weakness.[28]

As in Paul's argument, this general revelation therefore leaves everyone "without excuse." As a revelation of God's power, justice, goodness, and majesty, it should expose our fallen hearts. Yet instead we project idols we can manage, with satisfactions that we devise. "They do not therefore apprehend God as he offers himself, but imagine him as they have fashioned him in their own presumption."[29] Calvin's piety turns on this absolute contrast between "as [God] offers himself" and "as they have fashioned him."

So despite this ineradicable knowledge of God, humans *deliberately befuddle themselves* in an effort to "shut [God] up idle in heaven . . . so that they may lust unpunished."[30] "For they think that any zeal for religion, however preposterous, is sufficient. . . . One can clearly see, too, how superstition mocks God with pretenses while it tries to please him."[31] Idolatry is no more obvious than in works-righteousness, whatever the form.

---

[26] In *Institutes* 2.7.6 Calvin defines this pedagogical use: "While it shows God's righteousness, that is, the righteousness alone acceptable to God, it warns, informs, convicts, and lastly condemns, every man of his own unrighteousness." In addition to this use, the law threatens civil punishments and also guides believers. These "three uses" were formulated first by Melanchthon and are confessed in art. 6 of the Formula of Concord.

[27] Ibid., 1.1.1.

[28] Ibid., 1.1.2.

[29] Ibid., 1.4.1.

[30] Ibid., 1.4.2, emphasis added.

[31] Ibid., 1.4.3.

Every culture, every religion, has at its heart regulations and rituals for appeasing the gods. "Nay, more, with greater license they sluggishly lie in their own filth, because they are confident that they can perform their duty toward him by ridiculous acts of expiation."[32] Tragically, this inclination of the fallen heart was evident on every hand in the medieval church. Most people in the medieval church had become accustomed to the stench: "Hardened by habit, they sit in their own excrement, and yet believe they are surrounded by roses."[33]

In Calvin's view, therefore, "religion is the beginning of all superstition"—our perversion of the "sense of divinity."[34] Idolatry alternates between deism and pantheism, shutting God up in his heaven or identifying the Creator with creation.[35]

> It is therefore in vain that so many burning lamps shine for us in the workmanship of the universe to show forth the glory of its Author. Although they bathe us wholly in their radiance, yet they can of themselves in no way lead us into the right path. Surely they strike some sparks, but before their fuller light shines forth these are smothered.[36]

Notice the active verbs. In Calvin's view, there is nothing neutral about the pursuit of truth. We are not friends waiting for evidence of our beloved, but enemies of God who are running from the plain truth that surrounds us on every hand. If "the Lord sings to the deaf as long as he does not touch inwardly their hearts," it is only because of our own perversity that we do not hear him.[37] While God's world is a "marvelous theater," our fallen hearts and minds are a "labyrinth"—Calvin's favorite metaphor for the maze of human folly. In this labyrinth of our sinful mind, "rashness and superficiality are joined to ignorance and darkness."[38]

From these comments we see that Calvin affirms general revelation no less than does Rome. He also teaches just as strongly the *natural* capacity of human beings to receive this revelation of God in nature. However, the major difference is to be found in his conviction that ever since the fall,

---

[32] Ibid., 1.4.4.
[33] Cited in Philip Benedict, *Christ's Churches Purely Reformed: A Social History of Calvinism* (New Haven, CT: Yale University Press, 2002), 86.
[34] Herman J. Selderhuis, *Calvin's Theology of the Psalms* (Grand Rapids: Baker Academic, 2007), 75.
[35] Calvin, *Institutes* 1.5.5.
[36] Ibid., 1.5.14.
[37] Calvin, *Commentary upon the Epistle of Paul the Apostle to the Romans*, in *Calvin's Commentaries*, vol. 19, trans. John Owen (Grand Rapids: Baker, 1996), 88.
[38] Calvin, *Institutes* 1.5.12, 14.

our *moral* capacity to understand and accept God's truth even in nature is thoroughly corrupted and warped. With a weakened view of the fall, Roman Catholic theology has confused this natural capacity with a moral ability to embrace the truth. This is why those who have never heard the gospel may nevertheless be saved by "doing what lies within them" (a common medieval maxim that is endorsed as recently as the new *Catechism of the Catholic Church*).[39] Grace helps us get back on our feet, strengthening our will to obey the revelation that we have. The natural mind may attain salvation by following the light of revelation as far as one sees it. This view has become largely assumed in modern Protestantism as well. In fact, Friedrich Schleiermacher appealed to Calvin's universal "sense of deity" to support his idea of a universal religious feeling that each particular religion expresses in its own way. Moving from general to special revelation is like turning a dimmer switch from lesser to greater light.

However, Calvin departs from this assumption in two respects. First, he does not believe that any of us since the fall interprets general revelation in a way that leads to the true God. Second, even if we did interpret it accurately, general revelation is not only a *dimmer* light but a *different* light than special revelation.

> The natural order was that the frame of the universe should be the school in which we were to learn piety, and from it pass over to eternal life and perfect felicity. But after man's rebellion, our eyes—wherever they turn—encounter God's curse. . . . For even if God wills to manifest his fatherly favor to us in many ways, yet we cannot by contemplating the universe infer that he is Father. Rather, conscience presses us within and shows in our sin just cause for his disowning us and not regarding or recognizing us as his sons. Dullness and ingratitude follow, for our minds, as they have been blinded, do not perceive what is true. . . .
>
> Therefore, although the preaching of the cross does not agree with our human inclination, if we desire to return to God our Author and Maker, from whom we have been estranged, in order that he may again begin to be our Father, we ought nevertheless to embrace it humbly. Surely, after the fall of the first man no knowledge of God apart from the Mediator has had power unto salvation.[40]

---

[39] This view is reiterated—in fact, expanded to include the salvation of non-Christians—in the declarations of the Second Vatican Council: "Those also can attain to salvation who through no fault of their own do not know the Gospel of Christ or His Church, yet sincerely seek God and moved by grace strive by their deeds to do His will as it is known to them through the dictates of conscience" (*Lumen Gentium* 16).

[40] Calvin, *Institutes* 2.6.1.

A serene sunset, colossal Alpine peaks, the terrifying power of an earthquake: even as interpreted properly, these creaturely signs may arouse our sense of God's majesty and power—even his goodness and love. However, there is no word of good news. Creation does not make any announcement about what God has decided to do with sinners after their rebellion. So even before Calvin has arrived at the summit of his argument, he feels obliged to anticipate it here:

> In this ruin of mankind no one now experiences God either as Father or as Author of salvation, or favorable in any way, until Christ the Mediator comes forward to reconcile him to us. . . . First, as much in the fashioning of the universe as in the general teaching of Scripture the Lord shows himself to be simply the Creator. Then in the face of Christ he shows himself the Redeemer. Of the resulting twofold knowledge [*duplex . . . cognitio*] of God we shall now discuss the first aspect; the second will be dealt with in its proper place.[41]

Directed by the shadows of the law and the prophetic promises, faith in Christ kept a remnant in Israel looking toward the future in hope.[42] God can only be considered the object of faith with the qualification that "unless God confronts us in Christ, we cannot come to know that we are saved." Calvin adds, "In this sense Irenaeus writes that the Father, himself infinite, becomes finite in the Son, for he has accommodated himself to our little measure lest our minds be overwhelmed by the immensity of his glory. . . . Actually, it means nothing else than that God is comprehended in Christ alone."[43]

Glory and the Cross

This last point that Calvin draws from the second-century church father Irenaeus introduces a crucial theme in the Reformer's piety. In his Heidelberg Disputation (1518), Martin Luther drew his famous contrast between the "theologian of glory" and the "theologian of the cross."[44] Climbing ladders of speculation, merit, and mystical experience, the naked soul seeks

---

[41] Ibid., 1.2.1.
[42] Ibid., 2.6.2–3.
[43] Ibid., 2.6.4.
[44] See Walther von Loewenich, *Luther's Theology of the Cross*, trans. Herbert J. A. Bouman (Minneapolis: Augsburg, 1976); A. E. McGrath, *Luther's Theology of the Cross: Martin Luther's Theological Breakthrough* (Oxford: Basil Blackwell, 1985); B. A. Gerrish, "To the Unknown God: Luther and Calvin on the Hiddenness of God," *Journal of Religion* 53 (1973): 263–92.

union with the naked God. As a theologian of glory, the monk tries to ascend to heavenly realms, away from this world—the body and its senses, in specific historical events. In such a presumptuous ascent, we miss God on his way down, descending to us in our world, in our flesh, lying in a manger and hanging on a cross. The theologian of glory judges by appearances: how things seem to look on the surface. However, the theologian of the cross trusts the promise of God that he hears in God's Word, even if it seems to be contradicted by how things appear. This contrast is decisive for interpreting the radical difference between Calvin's piety and many of the approaches with which we are familiar—even in evangelical circles.

Calvin shared Luther's contrast, interpreting idolatry as the quintessence of a theology of glory. As Herman Selderhuis observes, this is especially evident in Calvin's *Commentary on the Psalms*. The transcendent God of majesty descends to us. Even in general revelation, we should not "fly through the clouds."

> Those who seek to see him in his naked majesty are certainly very foolish. That we may enjoy the light of him, he must come forth into view with his clothing; that is to say, we must cast our eyes upon the very beautiful fabric of the world in which he wishes to be seen by us and not be too curious and rash in searching into his secret essence.[45]

Yet if we are to know this God as our Father, we must seek him where he has already found us: the eternal Son clothed *in our flesh*.[46] We try to ascend to heaven, expecting to find God in glory, when he is only to be found in the small and even despicable things—like the cursed cross. God is not tricking us by revealing himself where we are not looking. It is precisely because God is merciful that he makes himself known in the little things of this world and supremely in Christ. The theologians speak of "God" as the object of faith, forgetting that he can be known only in Jesus Christ whom he has sent.[47]

Ironically, the cold and abstract contemplation of God's sovereign majesty attributed by critics to Calvin is actually Calvin's criticism of Rome's teaching. "Our reason for praising God is found more clearly in his mercy than in his sheer power and justice," Calvin says (commenting on Ps.

---

[45] Selderhuis, *Calvin's Theology of the Psalms*, 19, quoting Calvin on Ps. 104:1.
[46] Ibid., 39.
[47] Calvin, *Institutes* 3.2.1.

118:1), but medieval spirituality displays "a cold and narrow view of his character."[48]

To be reconciled to God, "it was necessary to recognize God not only as Creator but also as Redeemer, for undoubtedly they arrive at both from the Word."[49] That knowledge of God the Redeemer in the gospel "alone quickens souls."[50] To know God and ourselves, we have to hear not just a doctrine here or a proof text there, but the whole story that reveals the identity of us both. The next chapter summarizes that story as Calvin understands it.

---

[48] Selderhuis, *Calvin's Theology of the Psalms*, 49. See Calvin on Ps. 118:1.

[49] Calvin, *Institutes* 1.6.1.

[50] Ibid., 1.6.1–3.

CHAPTER 4

ACTORS AND PLOT

If this world is a "marvelous theater," then the Bible is its script through which we come to know the central plot and characters. Bearing in mind our scope, Calvin on the Christian life, I offer the following simply as a brief summary leading up to the Reformer's pinpoint focus on Christ the Mediator. We are still following Calvin's own unfolding argument in the *Institutes* from the most general "awareness of God" to the specific object of our faith: God "in Christ as he is clothed in the gospel."

The Script

For Calvin, the doctrine of Scripture is never an independent article; *sola scriptura* (by Scripture alone) is always connected with the salvation that it communicates by grace alone, in Christ alone, through faith alone, to the glory of God alone.

To be sure, our minds need to be convinced that the Bible is God's Word, but Calvin emphasizes that, above all, our consciences need to be assured that salvation comes from God and not from ourselves. Although the human authors are God's ambassadors, Scripture ultimately is "not the word of the apostles but of God himself; not a voice born on earth but one descended from heaven."[1] Yet this God who speaks is three persons. Scripture is authoritative because it comes from the Father, but just as much

---

[1] Calvin, *Institutes of the Christian Religion*, ed. John T. McNeill, trans. Ford Lewis Battles (Philadelphia: Westminster, 1960), 4.11.1.

because the Son is its content and the Spirit is its perfecting agent.[2] For Calvin, Scripture is the Word of God because it comes from the Father, proclaiming the Son, and is inspired by the Spirit, who then illumines us to understand and embrace it.[3]

The pastoral and practical concern is uppermost in Calvin's mind. How could our hearts ever be assured of God's kindness and favor toward us in Christ, he asks, if we could not trust the communication of that promise and his fulfillment of it?[4] God descends to our capacity, since we cannot rise up. No more than salvation itself is Scripture to be attributed partly to God and partly to human beings. It is not the church that creates the Word, but the Word that creates the church. "So faith comes from hearing, and hearing through the word of Christ" (Rom. 10:17). To be sure, the church existed before the Bible—that is, the completed canon of written Scripture. Nevertheless, the word of God existed before both.[5] Thus, there is no need for further revelations to support a supposedly ongoing revelation through living apostles. "Hence the Scriptures obtain full authority among believers only when men regard them as having sprung from heaven, as if there the living words of God were heard."[6]

At the same time, God descends to us through creaturely means. Already we begin to discern at least implicitly the maxim "distinction without separation" that I mentioned in chapter 2. The Bible is distinct from God's essence, but the Spirit makes human words carriers of divine wisdom. In many places in his commentaries Calvin the rigorous exegete points up problems, apparent discrepancies, and other evidences of the human authors' limitations. Far from being an embarrassment, the thorough humanness of the text testifies to God's gracious accommodation. Revelation is always accommodated discourse, even "baby talk" in which God "must descend far beneath his loftiness," as Calvin puts it.[7] Not even in

---

[2] Ibid., 1.7.3.
[3] Calvin on 2 Tim. 3:15–16, in *Calvin's Commentaries*, vol. 21, trans. William Pringle (Grand Rapids: Baker, 1996), 248–49. Calvin observes that the authority of Scripture is generally acknowledged on all sides. Yet, he presses, "What if anyone give his whole attention to curious questions? What if he adheres to the mere letter of the law, and does not seek Christ? What if he perverts the natural meaning by inventions that are foreign to it? For this reason he directs us to the faith of Christ as the design, and therefore as the sum of the Scriptures." Yet the apostle adds that all of Scripture is God-breathed, through the agency of the Spirit. "This is a principle that distinguishes our religion from all others, that we know that God has spoken to us, and are fully convinced that the prophets did not speak at their own suggestion, but that, being organs of the Holy Spirit, they only uttered what they had been commissioned from heaven to declare."
[4] Calvin, *Institutes* 1.7.4.
[5] Ibid., 1.7.1–2.
[6] Ibid., 1.7.1.
[7] Ibid., 1.13.1; 3.11.20.

revelation does the believer "attain to [God's] exalted state," but one does receive truth "accommodated to our capacity so that we may understand it."[8] Scripture, "accommodating itself to our weak and limited capacity, speaks only after the manner of men."[9] Yet this weakness conceals a life-giving power: the theology of the cross—God's self-abasing descent in love. God speaks clearly and definitely, in words that we can understand, through the lips of prophets and apostles. Here, "not only does God teach the elect to look upon a god, but also shows himself as the God upon whom they are to look."[10]

The high-minded of our age are offended by the simplicity of God's speech to us, which addresses the learned and unlearned alike. It is true that Scripture does not satisfy our curiosity or answer all of our questions. Nevertheless, Calvin warns, "it is better to limp along this path than to dash with all speed outside it."[11] Just as we take offense at God's supreme self-revelation in the weakness of the incarnate Christ, we forget that the simplicity of Scripture is God's way of descending to us in humility and grace. In short, its humanity is perfectly consistent with its divine origin. As we see in the incarnation, weakness does not entail sinfulness; limitation does not imply error.[12]

The problem lies not in reason itself, but in the reasoners who use reason unreasonably to sit in judgment on the God who speaks. "What madness is it to embrace nothing but what commends itself to human reason? What authority will God's word have if it is not admitted any further than we are inclined to receive it?" It was precisely because of an unwillingness to accept at face value the plain teaching of Scripture at such points that many of the church's doctors "turned aside to a heathen philosophy" and extolled "free will" and "the righteousness of works."[13]

Yet Scripture is God's Word not only because it comes from the Father and speaks concerning the Son, but also because it is inspired by the Spirit, who illumines us to understand and embrace it. As in other places, Calvin emphasizes the person and work of the Spirit—not over against the external Word, but as its Lord and Giver, who operates through it. Indeed, it is the

---

[8] Ibid., 1.17.13.
[9] Calvin on Ps. 106:45, in *Calvin's Commentaries*, vol. 6, trans. James Anderson (Grand Rapids: Baker, 1996), 242.
[10] Calvin, *Institutes* 1.6.1.
[11] Ibid., 1.6.3.
[12] In addition to the previous references, see ibid., 1.6.2; 1.7.1–5; 4.8.8–9.
[13] Calvin on Ps. 105:25, in *Calvin's Commentaries*, 6:193.

Spirit's work that has made sinful creatures ambassadors whose testimony is preserved from error. And it is the Spirit who persuades us inwardly that what we are hearing is not merely the word of man, even of the church, but the Word of God.

> If we desire to provide in *the best way for our consciences*—that they may not be perpetually beset by the instability of doubt or vacillation, and that they may not also boggle at the smallest quibbles—we ought to seek our conviction in a higher place than human reasons, judgments, or conjectures, that is, in the secret testimony of the Spirit.[14]

In this context, Calvin is countering the assertion that the Bible is the church's book, produced and authorized by the magisterium. Only God himself can persuade us inwardly of the inspiration and authority of the external Word. Human testimony depends on divine authority, not vice versa. If we had nothing more than human testimony to confirm our faith, our consciences would have no peace.

Calvin is not suggesting that we tell unbelievers to wait for the secret testimony of the Spirit. Indeed, he goes on to add that when occasion calls, we refute the "despisers of God" with abundant arguments.[15] The Spirit uses these external arguments, in fact. Calvin is drawn especially to historical arguments: fulfilled prophecy, miracles, and especially Christ's resurrection and the resulting transformation of cowardly disciples into apostles.[16] Indeed, once Scripture's authority is based firmly on God alone, even the testimony of the church can come alongside to offer confirming proofs.[17]

Although he emphasizes the crucial role of the Spirit in convincing us of Scripture's truth, Calvin warns against any separation of the Spirit from the Word. The Spirit testifies inwardly to the truth of the external Word; he adds nothing in terms of content.[18] In fact, in his reply to Cardinal Sadoleto the Reformer wrote, "We are assailed by two sects, which seem to differ most widely from each other." "For what similarity is there in appearance between the Pope and the Anabaptists?" And yet, the weapon is the same.

---

[14] Calvin, *Institutes* 1.7.4, emphasis added.
[15] Ibid.
[16] Ibid., 1.8.2–13.
[17] Ibid., 1.8.12–13.
[18] Calvin on Ps. 119:18, in *Calvin's Commentaries*, 6:413–14.

For when they boast extravagantly of the Spirit, the tendency certainly is to sink and bury the Word of God, that they may make room for their own falsehoods. And you, Sadoleto, by stumbling on the very threshold, have paid the penalty of that affront which you offered to the Holy Spirit, when you separated him from the Word.[19]

Fanatics pit the Spirit against the external word, devising "some way or other of reaching God." Such people are "not so much gripped by error as carried away with frenzy." "For of late, certain giddy men have arisen who, with great haughtiness exalting the teaching office of the Spirit, despise all reading and laugh at the simplicity of those who, as they express it, still follow the dead and killing letter."[20] Calvin surely had figures like the radical Anabaptist Thomas Müntzer in mind at this point.[21] The Spirit's ongoing work is not that of adding to the deposit of revelation, says Calvin, "but of sealing our minds with that very doctrine which is commended by the gospel."[22] We "may embrace the Spirit with no fear of being deceived when we recognize him in his own image, namely, in the Word."[23]

Finally, the scope of Scripture—its central message—is Christ clothed in his gospel.[24] It directs faith to Christ—specifically, to "the sacrifice of Christ and, for the confirmation of his faith, at the Lord's Supper and baptism."[25] Wilhelm Niesel observes:

Reformed theology, just like Lutheran, knows that it is God's Word which addresses us from the Bible and produces faith and that this Word is Christ Himself. But this address does not become an experience within our control on the basis of which we can read through the Bible and test

---

[19] Calvin, "Reply by John Calvin to Cardinal Sadoleto's Letter," in *Selected Works of John Calvin: Tracts and Letters*, ed. Henry Beveridge and Jules Bonnet, 7 vols. (Grand Rapids: Baker, 1983), 1:36.

[20] Calvin, *Institutes* 1.9.1.

[21] Thomas Müntzer, "The Prague Protest," in *The Radical Reformation: Cambridge Texts in the History of Political Thought*, ed. and trans. Michael G. Baylor (Cambridge: Cambridge University Press, 1991), 2–7; see also, in the same volume, Müntzer, "Sermon to the Princes," 20.

[22] Calvin, *Institutes* 1.9.1.

[23] Ibid., 1.9.3.

[24] Herman J. Selderhuis, *Calvin's Theology of the Psalms* (Grand Rapids: Baker Academic, 2007), 126–27. Selderhuis points out the similarity here with Luther's hermeneutic: "Calvin is careful that he does not prematurely look for Christological meaning in the Old Testament. He studies each passage in the light of its immediate context as well as in the flow of redemptive history. "Nevertheless, he asserts that the texts of the Old Testament by themselves emphatically refer to Christ. The hermeneutical key that Calvin uses for the Christological interpretation of the text is this: that which did not come to fulfillment in the time of the Old Testament must indeed refer to Christ." This is hardly unique to Calvin—or to Luther, for that matter. See the Second Helvetic Confession, art. 5. It is standard in Reformed systems of Calvin's day and ever since to identify Christ as the scope of Scripture.

[25] Selderhuis, *Calvin's Theology of the Psalms*, 125, on Ps. 51:9.

whether it "sets forth Christ." Calvin read the whole Bible expecting to find Christ there.[26]

The Covenant Lord

Although everyone has a general awareness of God, only Scripture discloses the true God, who is not only one in essence, but also three in persons. "Unless we grasp these, only the bare and empty name of God flits about in our brains, to the exclusion of the true God."[27] Here too we must "play the philosopher soberly and with moderation," he advises, and "receive in brief form what is useful to know."[28]

Calvin underscores, with Western theologians like Augustine, the unity of the essence shared by the Father, the Son, and the Spirit. However, he is equally impressed with the emphasis of the Christian East on the distinctness of the persons. In every external work of the Godhead, Gregory of Nyssa says, the result "has its origin from the Father, and proceeds through the Son, and is perfected in the Holy Spirit."[29] Calvin repeats this formula frequently. The divine persons do not divide up the work of creation, redemption, and sanctification, but are engaged in every work though each in his distinct way.[30] While we affirm the unity of the divine essence, Calvin says that "it is not fitting to suppress the distinction that we observe to be expressed in Scripture." "It is this: to the Father is attributed the beginning of activity, and the fountain and wellspring of all things; to the Son, wisdom, counsel, and the ordered disposition of all things; but to the Spirit is assigned the power and efficacy of all that activity."[31] The rule here, as in so many other places, is "distinction without separation." "In this sense," he concludes, "the opinions of the ancients are to be harmonized, which otherwise would seem somewhat to clash."[32]

This formulation—"from the Father, in the Son, and through the Spirit"—reappears across the whole scope of Calvin's thinking, and even where it is not stated explicitly, it is assumed. We pray to the Father, in the Son as Mediator, by the indwelling Spirit. Every topic that Calvin considers

---

[26] Wilhelm Niesel, *Reformed Symbolics: A Comparison of Catholicism, Orthodoxy and Protestantism*, trans. David Lewis (Edinburgh: Oliver and Boyd, 1962), 229.

[27] Calvin, *Institutes* 1.13.2.

[28] Ibid.

[29] Gregory of Nyssa, "On 'Not Three Gods,' to Ablabius," in *A Select Library of Nicene and Post-Nicene Fathers of the Christian Church*, series 2, vol. 5, trans. S. D. F. Salmond (Grand Rapids: Eerdmans, 1973), 334.

[30] Calvin, *Institutes* 1.13.19.

[31] Ibid., 1.13.18.

[32] Ibid., 1.13.19.

is therefore framed by this dynamic exchange and cooperation between the divine persons. In short, the Trinity is for Calvin not simply a dogma to which we yield assent, but the heart of reality in which we live and move and have our being.

The Covenant Servant

Calvin freely praises the greatness and natural dignity of every person as God's image bearer: each is "a rare example of God's power, goodness, and wisdom, and contains within himself enough miracles to occupy our minds, if only we are not irked at paying attention to them."[33] As we saw in the previous chapter, Calvin believes that in Scripture God reveals what he is like—his attributes, not his hidden essence. The same is true in revealing us to ourselves. What it means to be human can be discerned only from the history of creation, fall, and redemption.

First, Calvin departs somewhat from the traditional restriction of the image of God to the soul—much less to a soul thought of as an eternal spark of divinity. It's remarkable how tenaciously this assumption hangs on us even to this day. Isn't the soul that part of us that makes us sort of divine, unlike the animals? Yet Calvin argues that not only the soul, with its reasoning capacity, but "the human body" and its senses also are "ingenious."[34] Seated in the soul, the image nevertheless "extends to the whole excellence" of humanity: clear reasoning, acute senses, and even bodily beauty.[35] He marvels at "the consummate artifice apparent in the structure of the human body."[36] In this wholeness, human beings are "the most illustrious ornament and glory of the earth."[37] The soul is not the divine part of man, by nature eternal and immortal. "Were God to withdraw his grace, the soul would be nothing more than a puff or blast, even as the body is dust."[38] Once more, "distinction without separation" is the rule. The body is distinct from the soul, even separated at death. However, only in reunion of both in the resurrection does the intermediate state yield to everlasting glory.

Second, beyond reintegrating soul and body in his understanding of

---

[33] Ibid., 1.5.3.
[34] Ibid., 1.5.2.
[35] Ibid., 1.15.3.
[36] Calvin on Ps. 139:6, in *Calvin's Commentaries*, 6:210.
[37] Calvin on Ps. 24:1, in *Calvin's Commentaries*, vol. 4, trans. James Anderson (Grand Rapids: Baker, 1996), 402.
[38] Calvin on Ps. 103:16, in *Calvin's Commentaries*, 6:138.

the image of God, Calvin reintegrates the self with others. Our identity is not only properly embodied, but also social. It may be overstating things to suggest that Calvin's interpretation represents "the birth of the relational imago."[39] However, there are reasons for the exaggeration. Calvin rejects the tendency, even in the Augustinian heritage to which he belongs, to identify the soul with the "upper world" and the body with the "lower world."[40] Our identity is to be found less in *what* we are—something that distinguishes us from everything else in the world—than in *who* we are in the covenantal drama. The "image" has more to do with the vocation given to humanity in Adam than with a faculty that he possessed. To put it differently, the image consists less in something *in* us than in a relationship *between* us (that is, with both God and fellow creatures). This is why the word that founds human nature and society in creation is God's law—the voice of conscience which is God's original claim on us that makes us responsible to him and to others.

Although the philosophers have something to teach us, we can know who we really are only from the narrative of covenantal history in Scripture. The true definition of the image of God "can be nowhere better recognized than from the restoration of his corrupted nature" in Christ, Calvin says. After the fall, Adam, Eve, and their posterity were alienated from God.

> Therefore, even though we grant that God's image was not totally annihilated and destroyed in him, yet it was so corrupted that whatever remains is frightful deformity. Consequently, the beginning of our recovery of salvation is in that restoration that we obtain through Christ, who also is called the Second Adam for the reason that he restores us to true and complete integrity.[41]

---

[39] Stanley Grenz, *The Social God and the Relational Self* (Louisville: Westminster John Knox, 2001), 162. He cites Paul Ramsey: "The image of God, according to this view, consists of man's position before God, or, rather, the image of God is reflected in man because of his position before him." But even more than Luther, Calvin stands out as the Reformer who gave "greater attention to the *imago dei* 'than any great theologian since Augustine,'" according to David Cairns. "Douglas Hall, in turn, cites Calvin as more important than Luther for the emergence of the relational understanding of the *imago dei*." Furthermore, Calvin develops an eschatological (future-anticipatory) approach.

[40] Calvin, *Institutes* 1.15.5. Here Calvin challenges Osiander's "infusionist" perspective. Despite his training and his early interests (viz., his refutation of "soul-sleep" in his first theological treatise, *Psychopannychia*), Calvin has surprisingly little interest in subtle excursions into the nature of the soul with respect to the divine image: "It would be foolish to seek a definition of 'soul' from the philosophers" (1.15.6). That is not to suggest that such philosophical discussion is to be utterly rejected. "But I leave it to the philosophers to discuss these faculties in their subtle way. For the upbuilding of godliness a simple definition will be enough for us" (ibid.). Eschewing "useless questions," he says it is sufficient for our purposes to recognize that the human soul consists of "understanding and will" (1.15.7).

[41] Calvin, *Institutes* 1.15.4.

This is what is meant in the command to "put on the new man, who has been created according to God" (Eph. 4:24).[42] Scripture tells us how it came to be that we are no longer as we once were—and how it will be that we are no longer as we are now, or even were before the fall. Christ is the image of God who has taken our humanity with him beyond Adam's probationary condition to everlasting glory. "Now we see how Christ is the most perfect image of God; if we are conformed to it, we are so re-stored that with true piety, righteousness, purity, and intelligence we bear God's image."[43] Again, we must look to Christ to really know both God and ourselves.

Created in a covenant with God, Adam had a mission to fulfill. Like Irenaeus, whom he often quotes, Calvin emphasizes that the original state of Adam and Eve was the beginning, not the goal. Endowed with righteousness, holiness, soundness of mind and body, love of God and neighbor, Adam our, covenant head, was entirely capable of fulfilling God's command and leading our race—indeed the whole creation—into the everlasting joy of God's own Sabbath rest.[44] Confirmed in righteous-ness and immortality, Adam would have won for his posterity the right to eat from the Tree of Life.

So on the one hand, there is no place in Calvin's thinking for an au-tonomous human nature. Whatever moral capacities we have are a gift, not a given. On the other hand, he dissents from Augustine's idea of a gift of grace added to nature to enable Adam to obey God.[45] With the superadded gift (*donum superadditum*), medieval theology taught, Adam could either raise himself above the realm of the body and its passions, following the image of God imprinted on his mind, or allow his lower nature to drag him down. These bodily passions were often described as the "kindling wood" that leads us into sin. If we would only follow our higher self—the intellect or soul—an ascending path away from the world and the body would lead to the beatific vision. It was this basically Platonist dualism between higher (spiritual) and lower (bodily) worlds that funded the spirituality of ascent endorsed by theologians of glory.

In Calvin's understanding, such a view necessarily attributes sin to a weakness in human nature as created by God.

---

[42] Ibid.
[43] Ibid.
[44] Ibid., 1.14.20.
[45] Ibid., 1.16.8.

> For not only did a lower appetite seduce [Adam], but unspeakable impiety
> occupied the very citadel of his mind, and pride penetrated to the depths
> of his heart. Thus it is pointless and foolish to restrict the corruption that
> arises thence only to what are called the impulses of the senses; or to call
> it the "kindling wood" that attracts, arouses, and drags into sin only that
> part which they term "sensuality."[46]

He adds, "Our destruction, therefore, comes from the guilt of our flesh, not
from God, inasmuch as we have perished solely because we have degener-
ated from our original condition."[47]

Calvin's high estimation of human nature as created serves also as a
defense of God's integrity as Creator. Not even Lucifer is naturally evil. "For
the depravity and malice both of man and of the devil, or the sins that arise
therefrom, do not spring from nature, but rather from the corruption of
nature."[48] This he distinguishes from the "Manichean error." "For if any
defect were proved to inhere in nature, this would bring reproach upon
[God]."[49] In fact, Calvin goes so far as to affirm:

> In this integrity man *by free will had the power,* if he so willed, *to attain*
> *eternal life.* Here it would be out of place to raise the question of God's
> secret predestination because our present subject is not what can happen
> or not, but what man's nature was like. Therefore Adam could have stood
> if he wished, seeing that he fell solely by his own will.[50]

The Shattered Image: Corrupted but Not Wholly Effaced

Why did God let Adam fall? We do not know, Calvin insists, and because
Scripture does not reveal the answer, "it manifests inordinate curiosity"
to speculate. "Let us accordingly remember to impute our ruin to depravity of nature, in order that we may not accuse God himself, the Author of
nature."[51] It is "blasphemy" to attribute evil to God.[52]

Although Adam had the moral capacity to attain everlasting joy—for us
as well as for himself—we have lost this ever since the fall.

---

[46] Ibid., 2.1.9.
[47] Ibid., 2.1.10.
[48] Ibid., 1.14.3. He adds in 2.2.11, "We only call this corruption "natural . . . in order that no man may
think that anyone obtains it through bad conduct, since it holds all men fast by hereditary right."
[49] Ibid., 1.15.1.
[50] Ibid., 1.15.8.
[51] Ibid., 2.2.11.
[52] Ibid., 3.23.4–5.

Hence the great obscurity faced by the philosophers, for they were seeking in a ruin for a building, and in scattered fragments for a well-knit structure. They held this principle, that man would not be a rational animal unless he possessed free choice of good and evil; also it entered their minds that the distinction between virtues and vices would be obliterated if man did not order his life by his own planning. Well reasoned so far—if there had been no change in man. But since this was hidden from them, it is no wonder they mix up heaven and earth![53]

In short, the "philosophers" failed to contrast the "distinguished and honorable estate" of human nature in creation with captivity "under a degrading and ignominious slavery."[54] They were not paying attention to the story! After all, for them the soul belonged to the realm of eternal being rather than historical becoming.

Like its original integrity, this corruption includes "the whole soul" as well as "the whole body."[55] In summary:

Because of the bondage of sin by which the will is held bound, it cannot move toward good, much less apply itself thereto; for a movement of this sort is the beginning of conversion to God, which in Scripture is ascribed entirely to God's grace. . . . Nonetheless the will remains, with the most eager inclination disposed and hastening to sin. For man, when he gave himself over to this necessity, was not deprived of will, but of soundness of will. . . . Therefore simply to will is of man; to will ill, of a corrupt nature; to will well, of grace.[56]

From what we hear on the street, Calvin was the architect of "total depravity," the most pessimistic view of human nature to have appeared in history. However, he is actually more affirming of human nature as created by God than the average medieval theologian, by rejecting the need for a gift of grace added to the good nature God had already given Adam. Luther spoke of the image being totally destroyed by the fall.[57] Anabaptists went even further, identifying human nature as "satanic" and referring to unbelievers

[53] Ibid., 1.15.8.
[54] Selderhuis, *Calvin's Theology of the Psalms*, 78, on Ps. 8:7.
[55] Ibid., 80, on Ps. 119:37.
[56] Calvin, *Institutes* 2.3.5.
[57] Martin Luther, *Lectures on Genesis Chapters 1–5*, in *Luther's Works*, American Edition, 55 vols., ed. Jaroslav Pelikan and Helmut T. Lehmann (Philadelphia: Fortress; St. Louis: Concordia, 1955–1986), 1:63–64. Calvin's difference from Luther at this point is one of definition. In fact, in his Genesis commentary, Calvin himself says that the image was lost. Here, by image of God he assumes (as Luther did) that moral excellence and ability to fulfill one's divine calling. Both agreed that this moral perfection was lost.

as "a great abomination" from whom "only abominable things" can come.[58] Instead, Calvin speaks of the image being "effaced," but "not destroyed."[59] In fact, he rebukes the Anabaptists for denying the Spirit's common grace, evident in the advances made even by pagans in the sciences and arts, philosophy and medicine, law and politics. Therefore, Calvin could speak almost glowingly of the "admirable light of truth shining in secular writers," teaching us that the human mind, "though fallen and perverted from its wholeness, is nevertheless clothed and ornamented with God's excellent gifts. . . . Let us, accordingly, learn by their example how many gifts the Lord left to human nature even after it was despoiled of its true good."[60] In fact, the remnants of our dignity—even moral excellence—prick our consciences, reminding us how willfully we have deserted the Giver.

Original Sin

As Calvin interprets it, the effects of the fall are twofold: Adam's guilt is imputed to us all, and consequently his corruption infects us all. "This is the inherited corruption, which the church fathers termed 'original sin,' meaning by the word 'sin,' the depravation of a nature previously good and pure."[61]

According to Rome's understanding of original sin, we all inherit Adamic corruption that, if acted on, leads to guilt and damnation. With Luther, though, Calvin reverses the order. He argues (especially on the basis of Romans 5) that the imputation of Adam's *guilt* to the whole race is the basis for its *corruption* and the penalty of death, just as the imputation of Christ's righteousness is the basis for our renewal rather than vice versa.[62] Calvin refuses to become mired in the finer historical debates over the transmission of the soul from one generation to another, content to assert with Scripture that Adam stood as the covenantal representative for the human race.[63] Original sin includes both guilt and corruption.[64]

Calvin acknowledges concerning the Roman Catholic theologians, "No doubt, they agree with us in holding the doctrine of original sin, but they

[58] *The Schleitheim Confession*, trans. John Howard Yoder (Scottdale, PA: Herald, 1973), 12.
[59] Calvin, *Institutes* 1.15.4. See Michael Horton, "A Shattered Vase: The Tragedy of Sin in Calvin's Thought," in *A Theological Guide to Calvin's Institutes: Essays and Analysis*, ed. David W. Hall and Peter A. Lillback (Phillipsburg, NJ: P&R, 2008), 151–63.
[60] Calvin, *Institutes* 2.2.15.
[61] Ibid., 2.1.5.
[62] Ibid., 2.1.6.
[63] Ibid., 2.1.7.
[64] Ibid., 2.1.8.

afterwards modify its effects, maintaining that the powers of man are only weakened, not wholly depraved."

> Their view, accordingly, is that man, being tainted with original cor-
> ruption, is in consequence of the weakening of his powers unable to
> act aright; but that, being aided by the grace of God, he has something
> of his own and from himself which he is able to contribute. We, again,
> though we deny not that man acts spontaneously and of free will when
> he is guided by the Holy Spirit, maintain that his whole nature is so im-
> bued with depravity that of himself he possesses no ability whatever to
> act aright.[65]

For Calvin, then, total depravity does not mean that we are as bad as we can possibly be, but that all of our best thoughts, feelings, willing, and actions fall short of God's glory. "None is righteous, no, not one" (Rom 3:10). Calvin takes issue with the popular notion that God simply holds out his hand in an offer of pardon to those who turn themselves toward him—and that this constitutes the grace of God in regeneration. Created with the ability to freely choose the good—indeed, inclined naturally toward it— our will is now bound by sin.[66] Again, it is not a question of *what* we are by nature, but *who* we are in the unfolding plot, as collective and individual rebels against God's kingdom. The will is not rendered inactive by sin, but is bound by sin until grace restores it in a one-sided, unilateral, and unas-sisted divine act.[67]

In his Romans commentary, Calvin follows Paul's logic closely, noting the "voluntary" self-deception of Gentiles in their depravity. Then chap-ter 2 "is directed against hypocrites, who dazzle the eyes of men by displays of outward sanctity, and even think themselves to be accepted before God, as though they had given him full satisfaction."[68] We consider some people more virtuous than others. "Yet we do not hesitate to include both under the universal condition of human depravity."[69] Therefore, in the court of

---

[65] Calvin, "The Necessity of Reforming the Church," in *Selected Works of John Calvin*, 1:159. As we are re-minded by modern theologian Henri de Lubac, this remains the teaching of the Church of Rome: "Human nature, she tells us at the outset, is certainly sick, infirm, but it is not totally depraved. Human reason is weak and wavering, but it is not entirely doomed to error, and it is not possible for the divinity to be entirely hidden from it." *Catholicism: Christ and the Common Destiny of Man*, trans. Lancelot C. Sheppard and Sister Elizabeth Englund (San Francisco: Ignatius, 1988), 283.

[66] Calvin, *Institutes* 2.3.10.

[67] Ibid., 2.3.14.

[68] Calvin, *Commentaries upon the Epistle of Paul the Apostle to the Romans*, in *Calvin's Commentaries*, vol. 19, trans. John Owen (Grand Rapids: Baker, 1996), 68–72.

[69] Calvin, *Institutes* 2.3.4.

human justice and opinion, there is great diversity. Yet before God's tribunal, all mouths are stopped.

Nor does Calvin find scriptural warrant for Rome's distinction between mortal (soul-killing) and venial (less deadly) sins. Calvin sees this as without any scriptural foundation. It is merely a way of lessening the severity of sin and therefore the complete dependence of sinners on Christ's merits. "Let the children of God hold that all sin is mortal," says Calvin.

> For it is rebellion against the will of God, which of necessity provokes God's wrath, and it is a violation of the law, upon which God's judgment is pronounced without exception. The sins of the saints are pardonable, not because of their nature as saints, but because they obtain pardon from God's mercy.[70]

Grace

The aim of Romans 1–3 is not simply to expose human perversity; "Paul's object was to teach us where salvation is to be found"—namely, "in the grace of God alone," in Christ rather than in us.[71] The targets of Calvin's polemics are "the Pelagians of our own age, that is, the Sophists of the Sorbonne."[72] Those who do not take the sinful condition seriously, and instead reduce it to sinful actions or tendencies that can be overcome by proper instruction and effort, will never flee to Christ.

> Paul contrasts the righteousness of the law with the righteousness of the gospel, placing the former in works and the latter in the grace of Christ (Rom. 10:5, etc.). He does not divide it into two halves, giving works the one, and Christ the other; but he ascribes it to Christ entirely, that we are judged righteous in the sight of God.[73]

The medieval church taught that a treasury of merit had been stored up by the saints; the pope managed this "central bank," with each priest overseeing a branch office. Of course, no one merits anything from God outright, apart from grace and Christ's merits.[74] Nevertheless, grace enables our meritorious efforts, and Christ's work makes it possible for God to

---

[70] Ibid., 2.9.59.
[71] Calvin, *Calvin's Commentaries*, 19:68.
[72] Calvin, *Institutes* 2.3.13.
[73] Calvin, "The Necessity of Reforming the Church," 161–62.
[74] Roman Catholic theology distinguishes between condign (pure) merit and congruent merit (God's agreement to reward good works with salvation).

accept our imperfect works as meritorious. Not only had the saints merited their own salvation in this view; their service went beyond the call of duty and created a surplus of credit. The church could draw upon this treasury—in effect writing checks that could be cashed by those who followed the priest's prescribed penance.

This dogma entirely vitiated the gospel. It is just one of the many inventions of recent times, Calvin says, summoning Augustine and Pope Leo I to testify against the late-medieval view.[75] None of our works—our best works—is free of sin and therefore meritorious. "But when once God has graciously adopted believers, he not only accepts and loves their persons, but their works also, and condescends to honor them with a reward."[76] In other words, justification actually makes our good works acceptable—not for justification but as rewarded by a generous Father. The faults clinging to them are "covered by the sacrifice of Christ," and they are accepted by the generosity of the Father only on account of Christ's merits.[77] While Rome teaches that Christ's satisfaction makes our merits possible, Calvin insists that it totally excludes them.

The Reformers disagreed with Rome not merely about the sufficiency of grace (*sola gratia*), but also over the nature of grace itself. In Roman Catholic theology, grace is viewed as a substance infused into the soul to heal it. By cooperating with this transforming grace, one can attain final salvation. The sacraments function much like an intravenous tube injecting this grace into a somewhat weakened soul. The more that one cooperates with this grace, the more grace one receives.

The Reformers saw a completely different definition of grace in Scripture. On a covenantal map, grace is not an impersonal substance but a gift that is given by one party to another. First and foremost, the gift is Christ himself, in whom all of the Father's treasures are hidden. Grace is the *favor* and *gift* of the Father, in the Son, communicated by the Spirit through the gospel. First of all God's favor toward those who deserve his wrath, it is also God's gift of justification and the indwelling Spirit who brings renewal and guarantees our resurrection unto immortal life. In Calvin's understanding, grace is given not as an aid to our spiritual ascent, so that we may attain to union with God; it is God's free gift of union with Christ by his Spirit.

---

[75] Calvin, "The Necessity of Reforming the Church," 164.
[76] Ibid., 164–65.
[77] Ibid., 165.

Providence

Even after rejecting the Trinity and miracles, including special revelation and redemption by the Son's incarnation and saving work, the radical Enlightenment sought to preserve the idea of a "benign providence." For Calvin, though, providence is not a general concept. Apart from experiencing God as our Father in the mediatorial office of his Son, Calvin argues, "the Supreme Majesty" or "Maker of heaven and earth" is merely an idol.[78]

In Calvin's view, God's providence is not just a doctrine to be affirmed but a lifeline that we cling to in adversity. We need to be persuaded that God cares for this world precisely because of its apparent chaos.[79] The Reformer's own daily experience of personal adversity and loss, threats, setbacks, and perpetual reports of distress and martyrdom drew him repeatedly to this subject. He held on to God, literally for dear life. God's providence was a lifeline not because Calvin assumed a world of steady calm, but because he felt like a tiny vessel being tossed constantly on the waves of ill circumstances. God cannot be charged with sin, but neither does it catch him by surprise.[80]

Especially in his *Commentary on the Psalms*, the Reformer emphasizes that life is short and those who have not tasted God's kindness in it are impoverished. The key benefit of the believer's understanding of providence is to recognize God as a generous Father. "Hence Calvin does not emphasize the tragedy of being lost without God so much as that of having lived without God," Selderhuis notes. They have never known God as Father.[81]

Love Wins

For Calvin—as for the world of the Bible—love is not antithetical to law and order. Love restores order where there is chaos, justice where self-interest reigns, and fellowship where exclusion and insecurity dominate. Calvin's basic presupposition about this world, therefore, is that it is founded in *love* (not violence), with the order of love (not violent chaos) as its fruit. This presupposition shapes his view not only of human relations, but also of natural investigation. God gifted the creation itself with its own propensi-

---

[78] Calvin, *Institutes* 2.6.4.
[79] See Calvin, *The Secret Providence of God*, ed. Paul Helm (Wheaton, IL: Crossway, 2010). The helpful study of Calvin's view may be found in Susan E. Schreiner, *Theater of His Glory: Nature and the Natural Order in the Thought of John Calvin* (Durham, NC: Labyrinth, 1991).
[80] Calvin, *Institutes* 1.18.4.
[81] Selderhuis, *Calvin's Theology of the Psalms*, 63; see Calvin's commentary on Pss. 89:47; 115:16; 104:31.

ties in the beginning: the command, "Let the earth bring forth . . ." (Gen. 1:24), as well as the fiat declaration, "Let there be . . ." (1: 3, 6, 14). "The earth brought forth vegetation" in all of its variety. "And God saw that it was good" (1:12). Although God sometimes works directly in miraculous wonders (of the "Let there be . . ." variety), he ordinarily works through providence—upholding all things in his Son as Mediator and by his Spirit at work within nature and history.

Order by no means equals sameness. "Nothing is more natural than for spring to follow winter; summer, spring; and fall, summer—each in turn," Calvin writes. "Yet in this series one sees such great and uneven diversity that it readily appears each year, month, and day is governed by a new, a special, providence of God."[82] There is no room for a deistic picture of a God who creates the world like a watch, winds it up, and then leaves it to itself.

The world is a gift, not a given, in Calvin's view. It is not self-caused or self-contained. The fact that God uses creaturely means in no way detracts from his providential care in upholding the universe. In striking detail, Calvin even breaks forth in wonder at nature and its processes.[83] God *could* act immediately and directly as the only cause in the daily affairs of nature and history. However, he has chosen to work through means. Yet the means are not the ultimate source. The creaturely means should direct us to God.

Thus, the mystical ascent away from earth to behold God directly is the wrong path. God is always revealing himself to us familiarly, in our world. Anyone "who wants to enjoy God's face, according to Calvin, should not look to heaven but to the earth." "In nature God's voice is heard indeed, but he who wants to understand the voice must go to church, where God speaks clearly and understandably. What is more, in nature God draws attention to his existence by frightening people, but in the church he invites people to him in a friendly way."[84] It is when we are gathered as God's children together, to receive his good and saving gifts, that we encounter a gracious Father even in the midst of our daily troubles.

Judging by appearances, a theologian of glory approves the works that appear holy. The moral assumption is that the righteous are justified and the guilty are condemned. Consequently, the difficult circumstances of God's providence frighten us with God's displeasure. However, behind the "mask" of God's apparent wrath is the true God whose purposes are unknown to

---

[82] Calvin, *Institutes* 1.16.2.
[83] Ibid.
[84] Selderhuis, *Calvin's Theology of the Psalms*, 71–72.

us. Only in God's word of promise—that is, in Christ as he is clothed in his gospel—do we come to know the true God. Selderhuis comments:

> Here Calvin utilizes a notion which is also used by Luther to explain that God represents himself to be different from what he truly is. . . . God is by nature merciful and propitious, and his severity is only accidental. When God is wrathful and vengeful, he speaks in an unusual way, actually assuming another character. He is naturally inclined to forgiveness by which he draws us to himself.[85]

Job's "friends" were paradigmatic theologians of glory in that respect. Remarking on Psalm 18:26, Calvin says that this is how we naturally interpret trials—relying on the outward appearance rather than the reality as interpreted by God's Word: "When God thunders in good earnest upon them, they transform him, through the blind terrors which seize upon them, into a character different from his real one, inasmuch as they conceive of nothing as entering into it but barbarity, cruelty, and ferocity."[86]

Regardless of how God may appear wrathful toward believers, this is impossible for the one who is now the Father of his children in Christ. We must cling to his promise and not judge our relationship with God by how things appear.[87] We do not have to travel to find God; he has traveled to find us. For God, it is the most natural thing to help the destitute.[88] "According to Calvin," notes Selderhuis,

> this lies in "God's character to redeem." . . . It belongs to God, Calvin says, "not only to lift up his servants from the mud but also to liberate them from the grave." The Reformer calls it God's proper work to bring the dead to life. Furthermore, it is typical of God to avenge injustice. . . . Calvin mentions God's beneficent disposition so frequently so as to reassure his readers.[89]

Our fallen hearts tend to blame God when things go wrong—as if he were the immediate cause—and then to ignore his involvement when things go well. Contrary to caricatures, Calvin does not believe that God is the only

---

[85] Ibid., 50.
[86] Calvin on Ps. 18:26, in *Calvin's Commentaries*, 4:287.
[87] Selderhuis, *Calvin's Theology of the Psalms*, 51.
[88] Calvin on Ps. 85:1, in *Calvin's Commentaries*, vol. 5, trans. James Anderson (Grand Rapids: Baker, 1996), 380–81.
[89] Selderhuis, *Calvin's Theology of the Psalms*, 54.

actor in history. Like Thomas Aquinas, he distinguishes between primary and secondary causes and argues that the blame for sin and guilt rest entirely on human beings.[90] Calvin calls it a "determinative principle" that "sometimes [God's providence] works through an intermediary, sometimes without an intermediary, sometimes contrary to every intermediary."[91] To attribute all glory to God is not to deny that both doctors and God heal us—one as the secondary or instrumental cause and the other as the primary or ultimate cause. The infant's conception, growth, and birth are natural, not miraculous. In his ordinary providence, God works through creaturely means and gives liberty to creatures to think, act, and will. All the while, God reigns over, in, and through the whole process—as the Father, the Son, and the Spirit.[92] We acknowledge his sovereignty not only when he acts directly in our lives and world, miraculously, but also when he cares for us providentially through layers—or "masks"—of creaturely mediation.

Calvin is not a fatalist who won't allow any talk of coincidence or luck. In fact, he says that "however all things may be ordained by God's plan, according to a sure dispensation, for us they are fortuitous, . . . since the order, reason, end, and necessity of those things which happen for the most part lie hidden in God's purpose, and are not apprehended by human wisdom." It is not just that they *seem* fortuitous; rather, they *are* fortuitous—but to us rather than to God. "For they bear on the face of them no other appearance, whether they are considered in their own nature or weighed according to our knowledge and judgment."[93]

The idea that God wills anything arbitrarily is "a diabolical blasphemy" that would render him the author of evil and reduce us to balls that he juggles in the air.[94] Calvin says that while all things are subject to God's decree, evil and sin are attributed to Satan and human beings.[95] "And we do not advocate the fiction of [God's] 'absolute power'; because this is profane, it ought rightly to be hateful to us. We fancy no lawless god who is a law unto himself." However, "we also deny that we are competent judges to pronounce judgment in this cause according to our own understanding."[96]

---

[90] Calvin, *Institutes* 3.23.7.
[91] Ibid., 1.17.1.
[92] Selderhuis, *Calvin's Theology of the Psalms*, 91.
[93] Calvin, *Institutes* 1.16.9.
[94] Ibid., 3.23.2, 4–5. See also Calvin, *Sermons on Job*, trans. Arthur Golding (Edinburgh: Banner of Truth, 1993), 415: "And undoubtedly whereas the doctors of the Sorbonne say that God hath an absolute or lawless power, it is devilish blasphemy forged in hell, for it ought not once to enter into a faithful man's head."
[95] Calvin, *Institutes* 2.4.2.
[96] Ibid., 3.23.2.

So it is not within God's ability to decree anything against justice, but it is also not within our ability to put God on trial.

In Calvin's many references to suffering, his exegesis, especially of the Psalms, often has an autobiographical flavor. He speaks from experience when he joins the psalmist in reckoning that we are "exposed to a thousand deaths and that his life hangs by a thread."[97] This was not the flourish of a poet striking a tragic pose, but the description of life—or at least one important aspect of it—as Calvin knew it intimately. However, it is just this precariousness of our creaturely (not to mention, fallen) existence that provokes the believer's conviction that God is always active. What is so astonishing is that people either live carelessly, "as if they were in a quiet nest," or are "ready to die for anguish" rather than entrusting themselves to God in all circumstances.[98]

This divine activism is a crucial emphasis in the Reformer's piety. Again it is crucial to see that Calvin's emphasis on God's sovereignty is intended to pacify rather than terrify the conscience. As Selderhuis points out, Calvin opposes the pagan view of the world as divided between an evil creator and a good god who redeems us from the created order. Rather, "the antithesis [is] between God and Satan, order and chaos, and fall and renewal"—in which God is always the victor over sin's corruption of nature. "Calvin's biggest fear is the idea that God and creation in one way or another could stand apart from each other."[99]

Like Luther in his arguments against Erasmus, Calvin calls the idea that God could be "idle in heaven" a new "Epicureanism" spreading like gangrene. The ancient Epicureans taught that the gods, if they exist, are oblivious to human concerns and uninvolved in the world's daily affairs. At the other extreme, the Stoics believed that everything in nature is divine and therefore everything that happens is a direct act of fate. The biblical doctrine of God's providence is also the antidote to Stoic fatalism: "For he who has set the limits to our life has at the same time entrusted to us its care; he has provided means and helps to preserve it; he has also made us able to foresee dangers; that they may not overwhelm us unaware, he has offered precautions and remedies." We are therefore bound to use them.[100] God has planned our future and is active in bringing it to pass. "Meanwhile,

---

[97] Calvin on Ps. 31:5, in *Calvin's Commentaries*, 4:502.
[98] Ibid.
[99] Selderhuis, *Calvin's Theology of the Psalms*, 86.
[100] Calvin, *Institutes* 1.17.4.

nevertheless, a godly man will not overlook the secondary causes."[101] Far from leaving us passive, then, God's providential use of secondary means arouses us to responsible action as his ambassadors. Calvin opposes both naturalism and fatalism.

Especially among humanists, there was the beginning of a naturalistic philosophy that would come to fuller expression in the deism of the radical Enlightenment. This growing sentiment, Calvin insists, can only lead to the complete eclipse of all piety in the world.[102] Nor does Calvin accept Aristotle's view of God as the "unmoved mover."[103] According to Calvin, "heaven is not a palace in which God remains idle and indulges in pleasures, as the Epicureans dream, but a royal court, from which he exercises his government over all parts of the world."[104] And yet, God is not only *sovereign over* creation, but also *present within* nature and history, like a caring parent. Recall that Calvin has in mind the Trinity: the Father over creation, the Son in whom creation holds together, and the Spirit working within creation to yield its "Amen!" to the divine plan. When the psalmist speaks of God as King (Ps. 74:12), Calvin notes, "It is quite clear that the title King, which is applied here to God, ought not to be restricted merely to his sovereignty." Even his sovereignty is "in order to preserve and maintain [his people] in safety."[105]

Of course, such confidence in God's providence provokes notorious objections. Yet for Calvin, the alternative—namely, to believe that the sorrows that befall us fall outside the purposes of a good and wise God—leaves us with a god to whom we cannot pray and to whom we cannot bring our tears, in whom we cannot place our trust. Calvin never treats God's providence as merely a doctrine, but as an anchor in life's storms. Like all doctrines, its aim is not to satisfy our intellectual curiosity but to assure us practically of God's faithfulness even when we cannot see it.

Far from ignoring tragedy in Stoic bliss, Calvin acknowledges that "the dreadful disorder that devastates man's life vehemently obscures the order of God's providence."[106] Though the sun shines, the clouds may obscure it. Our experience is real, but it is not competent to judge God's ways. Amid our anxieties, "we ought to be fully persuaded that it is God's peculiar office

---

[101] Ibid., 1.17.9.
[102] Selderhuis, *Calvin's Theology of the Psalms*, 92, on Ps. 121:3.
[103] Ibid., 91.
[104] Calvin on Ps. 33:13, in *Calvin's Commentaries*, 4:549.
[105] Calvin on Ps. 74:13, in *Calvin's Commentaries*, 5:173.
[106] Selderhuis, *Calvin's Theology of the Psalms*, 93, quoting Calvin on Ps. 92:6.

to come to the aid of the wretched and afflicted."[107] Again, there is no place for passivity in this account: because God is at work, we can do ours. In fact, God performs his work through us. Therefore, "they who know that God nurtures us until death or even until after death 'are not so distracted by fear as to cease from performing their duty.'"[108] "Those who aim to subvert the doctrine of providence even a little deprive God's children of their true contentment and harass their souls with wretched unrest."[109]

Avoiding the Labyrinth

Without providence, we're left with "a labyrinth," an "abyss." And yet, we wander into a labyrinth if we try to figure out God's secret will.[110] We will become theologians of glory who judge by appearances instead of by God's revealed Word. Instead of speculating or expecting private revelations, we should attend to the means that God has provided for our salvation (through Word and sacrament) and earthly welfare (vocations, friendship, and other common gifts that we share with unbelievers).[111] So we are directed to seek out God's will only in that which he has revealed: "in the law and the gospel," Calvin says. "Yet his wonderful method of governing the universe is rightly called an abyss, because while it is hidden from us, we ought reverently to adore it."[112] "And it would not even be useful for us to know what God himself . . . willed to be hidden."[113]

We must never forget that the place where the triumph of evil seemed so obvious and God's saving care seemed most hidden was at the cross.[114] God's sovereign rule over nature and history in general cannot be separated from his *saving* purpose. Just as we find God in the "low places" of this world—in a dirty feeding trough in Bethlehem; on the road to Jerusalem, weary; and on the cross, crying out in dereliction—we trust that he is most present in our lives precisely where he seems most hidden.

In the face of suffering, the default setting of the godly is often to wonder, "What did I do?" "Why is God punishing me?" Precisely because he has revealed the meaning of this central event of our redemption, we must

---

[107] Ibid., 94, quoting Calvin on Ps. 10:1.
[108] Ibid., 95, quoting Calvin on Ps. 31:5.
[109] Ibid., 113, quoting Calvin on Ps. 107:42.
[110] Ibid., 117–18.
[111] Calvin, *Institutes* 1.18.4.
[112] Ibid., 1.17.2.
[113] Ibid., 1.14.1.
[114] Ibid., 3.8.1.

not interpret trials as divine "payback." Nor is prosperity a confirmation of God's favor. Instead of judging by appearances—what we see on the surface of things—we need to give ear to God's promised mercy in the gospel, come what may.[115]

Calvin emphasizes that suffering is never a sign of God's wrath toward us, much less a sign that we are not elect.[116] Trials are the workshop of a Father, not the threats of a Judge. The arrow that looks as if it were targeting our heart is actually aimed at the sin that clings to us, so that we may be loosened from its grip.[117] "Sometimes even when God delivers us from calamities, it is at the last moment, so that we can only cast ourselves upon him—and what an experience of growth this produces!"[118] In fact, Calvin says, "Properly speaking, God is not angry with his elect, whose diseases he cures by afflictions as it were by medicines." Christ has propitiated God's wrath against us, so any trials that God sends our way are entirely for our good and should not be seen as an act of retribution for our sins.[119]

We may never know how a particular trial served as God's strong medicine. Indeed, we may never know whether the suffering was sent directly by God, but it is enough to know that he works even pain and evil together for our good and his glory. God would never allow a wound that he couldn't heal. Furthermore, as Calvin notes, "The Son of God doth suffer not only with us, but also in us," bearing us up and provoking within us by his Spirit the cry "Abba, Father," even in our misery.[120]

This understanding of providence restrains us from blaming not only God, but also those who have wronged us. Joseph was able to show kindness to his brothers because, despite their treacherous motives, God's purpose in his calamity prevailed, turning evil to good. "To sum up, when we are unjustly wounded by men, let us overlook their wickedness (which would but worsen our pain and sharpen our minds to revenge), remember to mount up to God, and learn to believe for certain that whatever our enemy has wickedly committed against us was permitted and sent by God's just dispensation."[121] Therefore, we do not live in resentment of wrongdoers—not because we're above it all, but because we know who is.[122]

---

[115] Selderhuis, *Calvin's Theology of the Psalms,* 102, quoting Calvin on Ps. 91:15.
[116] Ibid., 105, on Ps. 41:2.
[117] Ibid., 101.
[118] Ibid., 106, quoting Calvin on Ps. 27:5.
[119] Calvin on Ps. 74:1, in *Calvin's Commentaries,* 5:161.
[120] Calvin, *Commentary Upon the Acts of the Apostles,* vol. 2, trans. Henry Beveridge (Grand Rapids: Baker, 1974), 297.
[121] Calvin, *Institutes* 1.17.8.
[122] Calvin on Ps. 26:3, in *Calvin's Commentaries,* 4:439–41.

PART 2

LIVING IN GOD

CHAPTER 5

CHRIST THE MEDIATOR

We live *coram Deo*—before God—as the creatures he made according to his image and likeness. Yet the goal of our creation is greater: namely, to live *in* God, being united to him as much as is possible for a creature. Yet how can that ever happen if God is transcendent in his majesty and we are finite? What's more, if God is holy and we are sinful? God is dangerous. Ignoring this danger—and the difference between a holy God and sinful creatures— radical mystics boldly ascended upward by turning inward, as if to discover God within. "True, he is called a Redeemer" in medieval piety, "but in a manner which implies that men also, by their own free will, redeem themselves from the bondage of sin and death. True, he is called righteousness and salvation, but so that men still pursue salvation for themselves, by the merit of their works."[1]

No, Calvin replies; Jesus is not just a rung on the ladder of our ascent to God. He *is* the Ladder![2] "The situation would surely have been hopeless had the very majesty of God not descended to us, since it was not in our power to ascend to him," Calvin says. He adds:

> Hence, it was necessary for the Son of God to become for us "Immanuel, that is, God with us," and in such a way that his divinity and our human nature might by mutual connection grow together. Otherwise the near-

---

[1] Calvin, "The Necessity of Reforming the Church," in *Selected Works of John Calvin: Tracts and Letters*, ed. Henry Beveridge and Jules Bonnet, 7 vols. (Grand Rapids: Baker, 1983), 1:192.
[2] Calvin on John 1:51, in *Calvin's Commentaries*, vol. 17, trans. William Pringle (Grand Rapids: Baker, 1996), 80–81.

ness would not have been near enough, nor the affinity sufficiently firm, for us to hope that God might dwell with us. . . .

Therefore, relying on this pledge, we trust that we are sons of God, for God's natural Son fashioned for himself a body from our body, flesh from our flesh, bones from our bones, that he might be one with us.[3]

The object of faith is not merely "God," Calvin argues, but the *triune* God. Yet this still is not the bull's-eye at which saving faith aims. The triune God is *revealed in Christ*.[4] This, however, is still not definite enough: not only Christ as the facilitator of union with God or one among many intercessors or as the supreme example to follow in order to become united with God, but as the saving God incarnate *as he is clothed in his gospel*.[5]

A saving union with God occurs only through union with Christ, who is *God with us* and also *us with God*. To be in Christ is to live *in* God, not just *before* him, because Christ is the divine Lord and human servant of the covenant. "Ungrudgingly, he took our nature upon himself to impart to us what was his, and to become both Son of God and Son of man in common with us."[6] United to him, we now enter into that familiar relationship that he enjoys with the Father and with the Spirit.

Christ's Person and Office

Calvin brings together the person and work of Christ by considering his threefold office. "For he was given to be prophet, king, and priest."[7] Through this threefold office of Christ, the ultimate aim of our redemption is completed: namely, our being re-created in the consummated image of Christ. Already we pick up in Calvin's thinking the echo of ancient church teaching, especially the emphasis of the second-century church father Irenaeus, on recapitulation (literally, "re-headshiping"). As Adam fell not only for himself, but for his posterity, Christ "did not rise for himself alone; for he came that he might restore everything that had been ruined in Adam."[8]

As Prophet, Jesus reveals the Father like no other prophet before him, because he was with the Father in eternity and shares the same divine na-

---

[3] Calvin, *Institutes of the Christian Religion*, ed. John T. McNeill, trans. Ford Lewis Battles (Philadelphia: Westminster, 1960), 2.12.1–2.
[4] Ibid., 3.2.1.
[5] Calvin, *Institutes* 3.2.32.
[6] Ibid., 2.12.2.
[7] Ibid., 2.15.1.
[8] Calvin on 1 Cor. 15:21, in *Calvin's Commentaries*, vol. 20, trans. John Pringle (Grand Rapids: Baker, 1996), 25.

ture. In fact, it is to him that all of the prophets pointed.[9] Jesus Christ is also the King, although for now this kingdom is spiritual rather than geo-political, as it was in the old covenant.[10] Once more, Calvin cautions us to go beyond a general sovereignty of God to locate this lordship specifically in Christ—and in Christ not only as God but also in his humanity: "We acknowledge, it is true, God as the ruler, but it is in the face of the man Christ."[11] He is the only Head of the church, and that which may be accurately identified as the church finds its unity in his sole headship.[12] For now, this kingdom of Christ is always opposed, often with brutal intensity, but its conquest is already secured by the victory of its king.[13]

As important as Christ's prophetic and royal ministry are for his service to us, Calvin believes that Scripture places the spotlight especially on his priestly ministry. "Let us therefore bear in mind that the entire gospel consists mainly in the death and resurrection of Christ."[14] However, Calvin also reminds us that Christ's saving work does not begin at the cross. His incarnation and thirty-plus years are not merely a prerequisite for his atoning death. Assuming our humanity and fulfilling all righteousness in his active obedience are essential to our redemption.[15] "In short, from the time when he took on the form of a servant, he began to pay the price of liberation in order to redeem us."[16]

Christ's Person: "Distinction without Separation"

The most profound controversies among Protestants, both the Reformers and the radicals, may be traced to differences over christology—interpretations of Christ's person. Given its importance, I will summarize the differences all too briefly. At its heart is the Chalcedonian maxim "distinction without separation," which is scattered across Calvin's entire theology. The dangers of downplaying the humanity of Christ (docetism and Gnosticism), separating the two natures (Nestorianism), or confusing them (monophysitism) were confronted at Chalcedon (AD 451), and Calvin recalls this ecumenical creed for meeting the errors of his own day. It may

[9] Calvin, *Institutes* 2.15.2.
[10] Ibid., 2.15.3.
[11] Calvin, *Calvin's Commentaries*, 20:32.
[12] Calvin, *Institutes* 2.15.3.
[13] Ibid.
[14] Calvin, *Calvin's Commentaries*, 20:19.
[15] Calvin, *Institutes* 2.12.3.
[16] Ibid., 2.16.5.

seem like fine print, but the implications of Calvin's christology are decisive for his view of the Christian life.

The first danger that Calvin seeks to avoid is the Anabaptist tendency to
separate Christ's deity from his humanity by denying the reality and saving
efficacy of the latter. Influenced by Greek philosophy, the early heresy of docetism (from the verb meaning "to appear") taught that Jesus only appeared to
be a true human being. Similar to Irenaeus's *Against Heresies*, Calvin's whole
treatment of Christ's person in the *Institutes* is preceded by a lengthy summary of the history of redemption leading up to the incarnation—so eager is
he to ground the person of Christ in the story of Israel.

That the Anabaptist movement was indebted to a Greek dualism between spirit and matter is acknowledged even by Anabaptist scholars.[17]
"Total personal renewal, where 'all creaturely desires are rooted out and
smashed,'" was central to their piety and view of salvation.[18] "This grace
divinized people so fully that they passed beyond 'the creaturely.'"[19] Given
this assumption, it is not surprising that the identification of God with "the
creaturely" would meet with difficulty. The Polish Reformed leader John à
Lasko discerned this problem in the writings of Menno Simons (founder of
the Mennonites), and Calvin added his own critique of this "docetic" view of
Christ's person.[20] According to Menno, the Son assumed a "celestial flesh"
without taking his humanity from the Virgin Mary. Menno assumes that
human nature is essentially corrupt, but Calvin counters that this confuses
sinfulness with humanness as such.[21] Did God truly descend all the way
down to us? Can we say truly that Jesus not only represents but in fact actually is "God with us"? Calvin embraced the ancient maxim "What he did
not assume he did not heal."[22] If Christ does not possess the same human
nature with us, then he cannot be the covenant Head of his church, he has

[17] Thomas N. Finger, *A Contemporary Anabaptist Theology: Biblical, Historical, and Constructive* (Downers Grove, IL: InterVarsity, 2004), 563.
[18] Ibid., 563.
[19] Ibid., 474.
[20] Calvin, *Institutes* 2.13.4. Against Reformed leader John à Lasko, Menno Simons wrote that "there is no letter to be found in all the Scriptures that the Word assumed our flesh . . . ; or that the divine nature miraculously united itself with our human nature" ("The Incarnation of Our Lord," in *Complete Works of Menno Simons*, trans. L. Verduin, ed. J. C. Wenger [Scottsdale, PA: Herald, 1956], 829). Verduin (transla-tor of that text) observes, "Menno Simons, following Melchior Hofmann, had abandoned the orthodox view concerning the incarnation" (Leonard Verduin, *The Reformers and Their Stepchildren* [Grand Rapids: Eerdmans, 1964], 230). It is not integral to Anabaptist christology. However, "it was from Hofmann that Menno Simons, perhaps the most influential writer in the camp of the Stepchildren, appropriated this docetic strain. Principally by way of Menno, it entered the stream of Anabaptist thought more or less widely." However, the orthodox view is held widely by most Anabaptists today (253).
[21] Calvin, *Institutes* 2.13.4.
[22] Ibid., 2.13.3–4. See Gregory of Nazianzus, "Letter 101," in *Nicene and Post-Nicene Fathers*, series 2, vol. 7 (Edinburgh: T&T Clark, 1989), 440.

not "expiated [our sins] in our flesh," and there is no resurrection of the dead.[23] Calvin emphasizes that Jesus was "descended from the Jews" and was "subject to hunger, thirst, cold, and other infirmities of our nature."[24]

While pointing out that this view was not generally held by subsequent followers, Anabaptist scholar Leonard Verduin observes that Menno received it from other Anabaptist leaders, especially Melchior Hofmann. Verduin argues that the Reformed reaction indicates deeper differences. Anabaptist leaders thought that Calvin and other Reformed leaders—no less than Rome and the Lutherans—identified God with creation, and the regenerate believers with the fallen church and society of "Christendom." So Menno was simply emphasizing "discontinuity in the area of Christology," Verduin argues.[25] He is wrong about Calvin and the Reformed view more generally. Nevertheless, he does put his finger on the "discontinuity" between God and creaturely reality that is evident also in relating spirit and matter, soul and body, church and state, invisible and visible church, God's saving work and the external means of grace. In short, the bond between God and the world is broken.

There is even a dualistic tendency in Zwingli's thinking, although he does not take it as far as the Anabaptists. Loading all of saving efficacy on the deity of Christ, Zwingli exhibits a Nestorian tendency to separate Christ's deity from his humanity.[26] Consequently, this dualistic tendency in christology drives his assumption that spiritual grace cannot be communicated through creaturely means.[27] So Calvin is as opposed as Luther to any *separation* of Christ's two natures.

"On the other hand," Calvin adds, "we ought not to understand the statement that 'the Word was made flesh' [John 1:14] in the sense that the Word was turned into flesh or confusedly mingled with flesh." Rather, "the Son of God became the Son of man—not by confusion of substance, but by unity of person. For we affirm his divinity so joined and united with his humanity that each retains its distinctive nature unimpaired, and yet these two natures constitute one Christ."[28] Though he does not make the identi-

---

[23] Ibid., 2.13.1–2.
[24] Ibid., 2.13.1.
[25] Verduin, *The Reformers and Their Stepchildren*, 256.
[26] Ulrich Zwingli, *The Theology of Hyldrich Zwingli*, ed. W. P. Stephens (New York: Oxford University Press, 1988), 204: "We must note in passing that Christ is our salvation by virtue of that part of his nature by which he came down from heaven, not of that by which he was born of an immaculate virgin, though he had to suffer and die by this part."
[27] Ibid. Zwingli concludes that faith "draws us to the invisible and fixes all our hopes on that. For it dwelleth not amidst the sensible and bodily, and hath nothing in common therewith."
[28] Calvin, *Institutes* 2.14.1.

fication explicitly, Calvin here surely has in mind Luther's view—or at least the view that his followers increasingly defended. In this view, known as ubiquity (meaning "ability to be everywhere"), Christ can be present bodily in and with the bread and wine in Communion because his divine attributes (such as omnipresence) penetrate his human nature. So Calvin also opposes any *confusion* of the two natures.

"Distinction without separation" is the rule. Scripture repeatedly attributes both human and divine characteristics to the *one person*, Jesus Christ.[29] So we wholeheartedly affirm that "'God purchased the church with his blood' [Acts 20:28], and 'the Lord of glory was crucified' [1 Cor. 2:8]" and "'the Word of life was handled' [1 John 1:1]."[30] Mary is the mother of God, since her child is in fact God incarnate.[31] "Away with the error of Nestorius, who in wanting to pull apart rather than distinguish the nature of Christ devised a double Christ!"[32] Nevertheless, Scripture nowhere speaks of the attributes of *one nature* being communicated to *the other*. Calvin is simply affirming with the Council of Chalcedon that "the distinction of natures [is] by no means taken away by the union, but rather the property of each nature [is] preserved," not only "without division" but also "without confusion." Calvin is concerned that in different ways Anabaptists and Lutherans have undermined the true humanity of Christ—either by dualistic separation or by confusion of his two natures. Pushing Luther's christology to an extreme that Lutherans considered heterodox, Osiander taught that the deity of Christ swallows his humanity and undermines the reality of creaturely existence.[33]

Calvin emphasizes that God's transcendence is not *distance* but *difference* from us. While the Son wholly united himself to our humanity in the incarnation, he remains forever transcendent according to his deity. Calvin summarizes the matter this way: "Here is something marvelous: the Son of God descended from heaven in such a way that, without leaving heaven, he willed to be born in the virgin's womb, to go about the earth, and to hang upon the cross; yet he continuously filled the world even as he had done from the beginning!"[34] Although some Lutherans dubbed such language

[29] Ibid., 2.14.3.
[30] Ibid., 2.14.2.
[31] See Calvin on Luke 1:34, 43; 11:27, in *Calvin's Commentaries*, vol. 16, trans. William Pringle (Grand Rapids: Baker, 1996), 40–41, 49–50.
[32] Calvin, *Institutes* 2.14.4.
[33] Ibid., 2.12.6.
[34] Ibid., 2.13.4.

the "Calvinistic extra" (*extracalvinisticum*), this statement is a nearly verbatim citation of Athanasius (*On the Incarnation of the Word* 3.17) and Basil (*On the Holy Spirit* 8.18).

Why such a detour into the finer points of christology? Besides being important in its own right, christology establishes the coordinates with which one is working with regard to a host of topics. Separating the divine from the human-creaturely—worse still, setting them against each other—leads us away from the God who comes to us in Christ, the external Word, and the sacraments. Consequently, we ascend into the heavens or into the depths of our own spirit to find him where he has not promised to meet us in peace. At the other extreme, there is the danger of simply collapsing the divine into the creaturely. Roman Catholic theology does this by teaching, for example, that the sacraments themselves effect regeneration and justification (*ex opere operato*: "by doing it, it is done").

It is precisely because of his emphasis on the true humanity of Christ that Calvin sees as central to the gospel itself the continuity between Christ's resurrection and ours. If the humanity of the glorified Christ is discontinuous with ours—that is, swallowed up in divine attributes—then the body loses its connection to its risen Head. Ironically, whether by collapsing his humanity into his deity or by highlighting his deity over his humanity, Luther and Zwingli at least in this respect arrived at a similar conclusion by different routes. Both views tended to undermine Christ's saving humanity that is united to but distinct from his divine nature.

As we will see in later chapters, the Chalcedonian maxim "distinction without separation" guides Calvin's reflection not only on the sacraments but across the whole field of Christian faith and life. Only *God* can save us. And yet, only the *incarnate* God can save us wholly.[35]

Christ's Saving Work

At its heart, the gospel is *solo Christo* (by Christ alone). Rome has always maintained that Christ is the *necessary* ground of our salvation; what the *solo* adds is that he is also the *sufficient* ground of our salvation. There is no blessing or merit, no basis for hope that can be found outside of Christ, even in the Father or the Holy Spirit. In one of his most eloquent summaries of the whole gospel, Calvin nearly breaks into song on this point.[36] So there

---

[35] Ibid.
[36] Ibid., 2.16.19.

is no moving on from Christ, as he is clothed in his gospel, to a higher truth or way of ascent. God has descended all the way to us and accomplished everything we need in his Son. "The apostle does not say that he was sent to help us attain righteousness but himself to be our righteousness," Calvin reminds us.[37]

Calvin combines the conquest imagery with vicarious substitution. It is not only Christ's triumphant resurrection that displays his victory over the powers of death and hell, but also the cross itself is a kind of throne: "There is no tribunal so magnificent, no throne so stately, no show of triumph so distinguished, no chariot so elevated, as is the gibbet on which Christ has subdued death and the devil."[38]

Far from ignoring the other aspects—such as Christ's victory over the powers of death and Satan, and cosmic renewal—Calvin sees Christ's bearing of our curse as the *basis* for these wider effects. Indeed, "All the wisdom of believers is comprehended in the cross of Christ."[39] Calvin even interprets the "descent into hell" as Christ's sin-bearing on the cross—"of no little importance to the accomplishment of our redemption."[40] "And certainly had not his soul shared in the punishment, he would have been the Redeemer of our bodies only."[41] Not only in his flesh but also "in his soul he bore the torture of condemned and ruined man."[42] In Christ's death we find not only expiation (atonement), but a free, final, and sufficient *propitiation* of God's wrath as well.[43] It is not only a necessary condition, making it possible for God to save us if we cooperate with grace; it is the sufficient basis. In other words, Christ's death and resurrection accomplished our salvation.[44]

The horizon of Christ's work encompasses both the incarnation and the ascension. In fact, Christ's ascension occupies a greater place in Calvin's thinking and piety than it does in the writings of other Reformers. After all, it reaffirms the indissoluble connection between Christ and his coheirs. Indeed, he "truly inaugurated his kingdom only at his ascension into heaven."[45] It is not simply an addendum or exclamation point on the resurrection, but a new event in redemptive history. At the same time, it

---

[37] Ibid., 3.15.5.
[38] Calvin on Col. 2:15, in *Calvin's Commentaries*, vol. 21, trans. William Pringle (Grand Rapids: Baker, 1996), 191.
[39] Calvin, *Calvin's Commentaries*, 20:74.
[40] Calvin, *Institutes* 2.16.8.
[41] Ibid., 2.16.12.
[42] Ibid., 2.16.10.
[43] Ibid., 2.12.3.
[44] Ibid., 2.12.5.
[45] Ibid., 2.16.14.

means that although we are united to him, Christ is now absent from the earth in the flesh until he returns.[46]

Yet Calvin does not stop there. Not only did the two angels promise the disciples at Christ's ascension that he would return at the end of the age in the same way that he departed (Acts 1:11), but Jesus also promised them that he would be with them—and us—even to the end of the age (Matt. 28:20). How is this possible? It is accomplished only by the power of the Spirit, who unites us with the ascended Christ. In this way, Christ is personally present on the earth in power and through the mighty working of the Holy Spirit, dividing the spoils of his victory. One day he will return to the earth to judge and to reign over the whole earth forever.[47]

Right now, however, Christ's supreme reign is not visible in the daily news; we live by promise, on the basis of already-accomplished events.[48] We live in an intermission in which the powers of the age to come break in upon us by the Spirit's mysterious work, and yet it is this very fact that arouses the flesh to battle on a personal as well as global scale. We live in an ambiguous tension between the "already" and the "not yet." That tension lies at the heart of Calvin's spirituality, and his emphasis on the ascension is a key factor in placing us there, at the busy and precarious intersection of the two ages.

United to Christ

The eternal Son has united himself to us forever by his incarnation. In our flesh, he has undone Adam's treason and fulfilled all righteousness; he has born our guilt and was raised the victor over sin and death. Yet as wonderful news as it is that God has become one with us, we receive the benefits only by being united to him. Calvin explains:

> As long as Christ remains outside of us, and we are separated from him, all that he has suffered and done for the salvation of the human race remains useless and of no value for us. Therefore, to share with us what he has received from the Father, he had to become ours and dwell within us. For this reason, he is called "our Head" [Eph. 4:15], and "the first-born among many brethren" [Rom. 8:29].[49]

---

[46] Ibid.
[47] Ibid.
[48] Ibid., 2.16.17.
[49] Ibid., 3.1.1.

Calvin's way of expounding the richness of our union with Christ remains one of the most enduring treasures for our piety today.

Luther is famous for emphasizing the "marvelous exchange" of debts and riches in marital union with Christ. And he even recognizes that he was not an innovator here. He notes in his treatise *Against the Antinomians*, "This doctrine is not mine, but St. Bernard's. What am I saying? St. Bernard's? It is the message of all of Christendom, of all the prophets and apostles."[50] Luther's advance on Bernard turned upon his recognition that this marriage is first judicial—the imputation of our sin to Christ and his righteousness to sinners—and then (as a consequence) a growing relationship of trust, love, and good works in which the union is realized subjectively more and more.[51]

Far from rejecting the believer's actual righteousness (sanctification), Luther says that Christ's imputed righteousness "is the basis, the cause, the source of all our own actual righteousness."[52] In *The Freedom of a Christian*, he writes:

> We conclude, therefore, that a Christian lives not in himself, but in Christ and his neighbor. Otherwise he is not a Christian. He lives in Christ through faith, in his neighbor through love. By faith he is caught up beyond himself into God. By love he descends beneath himself into his neighbor. Yet he always remains in God and in his love.[53]

Faith not only suffices for justification, but also is the constant source of the believer's renewal and service toward others. Faith not only justifies; it also "unites the soul with Christ as a bride is united with her bridegroom," says Luther. "At this point a contest of happy exchanges takes place. . . . Is that not a happy household, when Christ, the rich, noble, and good bridegroom, takes the poor, despised, wicked little harlot in marriage, sets her free from all evil, and decks her with all good things?"[54] Not only justification, but sanctification, too, is granted in our union with Christ.

In the relevant section in the *Institutes*, Calvin also displays his debt to

---

[50] Martin Luther, "Against the Antinomians," in *Luther's Works*, American Edition, 55 vols., ed. Jaroslav Pelikan and Helmut T. Lehmann (Philadelphia: Fortress; St. Louis: Concordia, 1955–1986), 47:110.

[51] The prominence of the union motif in Luther is evident, for example, in his treatise, "The Freedom of a Christian," in *Luther's Works*, 31:351.

[52] Martin Luther, "Two Kinds of Righteousness," in *Luther's Works*, 31:298.

[53] Ibid., 371; cf. Cornelis P. Venema, "Heinrich Bullinger's Correspondence on Calvin's Doctrine of Predestination," *Sixteenth Century Journal* 17, no. 4 (1986): 435–50.

[54] Luther, "Two Kinds of Righteousness," 351.

Bernard—with at least twenty-nine direct quotes.[55] Bernard's insight was far from unique, however, and Calvin freely drew on other sources. Besides Augustine, Bernard, and Luther, he expressed gratitude to colleagues like Peter Martyr Vermigli for helping him to understand this rich scriptural teaching. The most distinctive emphasis of Calvin on this topic, which he shared with Vermigli among others, may be found in his interest in the decisive role of the ascension and Pentecost in this union.

The apostle Paul urges:

> If then you have been raised with Christ, seek the things that are above, where Christ is, seated at the right hand of God. Set your minds on things that are above, not on things that are on earth. For you have died, and your life is hidden with Christ in God. When Christ who is your life appears, then you also will appear with him in glory. (Col. 3:1–4)

For Calvin, this is not an exhortation to mystical contemplation. Rather, the apostle is directing our attention to the ascended Christ who has glorified our flesh. Paul is directing our hearts to heaven, where Christ our pioneer has gone before us in our flesh, reigning in grace until he comes in glory.[56] The eternal Son who descended to save us has sent his Spirit to raise us up with Christ and seat us with him in heavenly places. As Philip Walker Butin observes, "Calvin's approach at this point thus complements and completes the 'downward' Lutheran emphasis on incarnation with an equal 'upward' emphasis on resurrection and ascension."[57] And, we might add, Pentecost—since, it is the Spirit's work especially that Calvin highlights in discussing how we are united to Christ as coheirs with him of the Father's estate. Contemplating Christ with his gifts is the joy of the Christian life. It is to that inheritance that we turn next.

---

[55] Calvin, *Institutes* 3.20.1. On the number of references to Bernard, see François Wendel, *Calvin: Origins and Development of His Religious Thought*, trans. Philip Mairet (New York and London: Harper & Row, 1963), 127n43. For a thorough study of the influence of Bernard on Calvin, see Dennis J. Tambarillo, *Union with Christ: John Calvin and the Mysticism of St. Bernard* (Louisville: Westminster John Knox, 1994).
[56] Calvin on Col. 3:1–3, in *Calvin's Commentaries*, 21:205–7.
[57] Philip Walker Butin, *Revelation, Redemption, and Response: Calvin's Trinitarian Understanding of the Divine-Human Relationship* (New York: Oxford University Press, 1995), 118.

CHAPTER 6

GIFTS OF UNION
WITH CHRIST

Why have we been spending so much time exploring Calvin's doctrinal emphases in a book on the Christian life? Once again, we have to appreciate that in his view these truths are not simply facts that we assent to and then move on to higher and more practical interests. For Calvin, the Christian life is a daily feeding upon these riches. We never move on from the gospel, but grow more deeply into its nourishing soil, thereby bearing the fruit of love and good works.

The supreme gift in this union is Christ himself, but he brings his gifts with him. As Calvin explores the benefits in the *Institutes*, he does not begin with election. Of course, he understands election as God's gracious decision in eternity. Nevertheless, his concern is always pastoral and practical rather than speculative theory. The gospel is brought to everyone, and through it sinners are called, justified, renewed, and glorified. Why then do some believe while others don't?[1] That is where Calvin discusses election. So we will follow Calvin's order of treatment.

Effectual Calling and the Gift of Faith

The point at which the Spirit unites us to Christ is effectual calling or regeneration. Calvin understands the new birth as pure gift, including even the

---

[1] Calvin, *Institutes of the Christian Religion*, ed. John T. McNeill, trans. Ford Lewis Battles (Philadelphia: Westminster, 1960), 2.24.4, 6.

faith to embrace it. We are not born again because we believe; we believe because we receive new life from above.

Over against the Anabaptist "enthusiasts" who separated the external Word and the Spirit, Calvin teaches just as emphatically as Luther that the Spirit freely binds his work to the external Word. However, like Augustine, he sees in Scripture a clear distinction between the external call and the internal or effectual call.[2] Recall again the maxim "distinction without separation." God binds his Word to creaturely means, while retaining his sovereign freedom. The gospel, proclaimed to everyone, is the means through which the Spirit regenerates his elect, but it would fall on deaf ears apart from the Spirit's work in our hearts, liberating our minds and wills from captivity to sin and death. The preaching of the gospel isn't magic; it does not work automatically. Rather, the Spirit regenerates sinners through it when and where he chooses.

Calvin never uses the term "irresistible grace." Rather, he speaks of it as effectual, since God's Word never fails to accomplish its intended purpose. Left to ourselves, we would always resist, but when the Spirit regenerates us, we come willingly, our will being liberated rather than coerced.[3] Thus, salvation is from beginning to end the result of God's work (monergism), not of cooperation between God and human beings (synergism).

Justification

The original Greek word for justification is a strictly forensic (courtroom) term, meaning the legal verdict that one is righteous before the law. The Latin Vulgate, Jerome's fourth-century translation of the Bible, unfortunately rendered the Greek verb *iustificare*, "to *make* righteous." Erasmus pointed out this error, as have contemporary Roman Catholic scholars. For a variety of reasons, dogma has not followed better exegesis, and Rome understands justification as a process of gradually becoming righteous. Nor did the Anabaptists depart from such synergistic thinking; in fact, they often went further in affirming the believer's personal holiness as justifying. Anabaptist scholars differ over whether their forebears ignored justification or found it "simply unacceptable," but the focus was on following Jesus's example and the process of the soul's union with God.[4]

---

[2] Ibid., 3.24.8. See Augustine, "To Simplician—On Various Questions," in *Augustine: Earlier Writings, Selected and Translated with an Introduction*, ed. John H. S. Burleigh (London: SCM, 1953), 395.
[3] This point is emphasized throughout chapter 24 of book 3, as elsewhere.
[4] Thomas N. Finger, *A Contemporary Anabaptist Theology: Biblical, Historical, Constructive* (Downers Grove, IL: InterVarsity, 2004), 109.

According to official Roman Catholic teaching, the *first justification* is by grace alone, and it occurs in baptism with the washing away of original sin. Although concupiscence (the tendency to lust) remains, this is not itself sinful until acted upon. An *increase in justification* occurs as you accept implicitly the church's teachings and follow the prescribed penances and satisfactions imposed for particular sins. You hope to attain *final justification* by grace-enabled works, but it is considered presumptuous to claim assurance of your election and final justification. In any case, the best of us will have to suffer temporal punishments in purgatory before being welcomed into God's presence.

In summary, justification according to Rome is a process of becoming holy—in other words, sanctification. According to Romans 4:5, God justifies the *ungodly*. But in Roman Catholic teaching, this is impossible; God can only declare righteous those who have been made righteous. They can be righteous before God not by an alien righteousness imputed—credited—but only by an inherent righteousness imparted and improved by obedience.

By contrast, the Reformers *distinguished* justification from sanctification *without separating* them. Condemned by the righteousness of God revealed in the law, we are clothed in Christ's righteousness revealed in the gospel, as a free gift. Our sins are credited to Christ and his righteousness is credited to us. Commenting on Romans 4:7, Luther says, we must be united to Christ, since "all our good is outside us, and that good is Christ."[5] Simultaneously justified and sinful, the believer is assured now that there is no condemnation. The verdict of the last day has already been rendered in the present, so it is not presumption but true faith to rest in the confidence that there is no penalty—temporal or eternal—that has not been borne already by Christ, no obedience that has not been performed by Christ, and no indwelling sin that has not been already covered by the righteousness of Christ. We live in freedom and assurance *from* a present and perfect justification, not *toward* it as a goal.

Calvin declares, "There is nothing intermediate between . . . being justified by faith and justified by works."[6] Elsewhere he adds, "Whatever mixture men study to add from the power of free will to the grace of God is only a corruption of it; just as if one should dilute good wine with dirty water."[7] "Therefore, we explain justification simply as the acceptance with which

---

[5] Martin Luther, *Lectures on Romans*, in *Luther's Works*, American Edition, 55 vols., ed. Jaroslav Pelikan and Helmut T. Lehmann (Philadelphia: Fortress; St. Louis: Concordia, 1955–1986), 25:267.
[6] Calvin on Ps. 143, in *Calvin's Commentaries*, vol. 6, trans. James Anderson (Grand Rapids: Baker, 1996), 251.
[7] Calvin, *Institutes* 2.5.15.

God receives us into his favor as righteous. And we say that it consists in the remission of sins and the imputation of Christ's righteousness."[8] By this definition Calvin excludes from justification any moral transformation of the believer, much less his or her merits. In my view, the richest veins of his teaching on justification are to be found in his commentaries, where his close attention to passages remains very much in play even in recent debates. He also finds support in the church fathers, while conceding that they were not always consistent. Yet the basic lines of Calvin's thinking were evident already in Luther's 1519 sermon-tract *Two Kinds of Righteousness* (more fully developed in his 1535 Galatians commentary).

This cannot be dismissed as an academic debate; it's the most relevant concern to every believer. In his Psalms commentary, Calvin feels David's anxiety. When our hearts are terrified by the weight of our sins, "cold speculations" will not help. Instead of clinging to "what faith discovers in the written word"—namely, "the unspeakable riches of grace that have been manifested to us in Christ"—we "tremble or waver." Those who think faith is easy have never experienced this anxiety. Indeed, "there is nothing in which we find greater difficulty than to acknowledge that He is merciful to us."[9] Terrors of conscience break in. "There is no certainty, no security. What shall I think? In what shall I confide? To what shall I have recourse?"[10] The Devil does not seek to seduce us from worship, but only encourages us "to seek another God" or to convince us that this God "must be appeased after another manner, or else that the assurance of his favor must be sought elsewhere than in the Law and the Gospel."[11]

Without this assurance of justification, even appearing in God's presence through prayer "becomes something like placing wood on the fire."[12] Preaching fear actually empties the world of all true piety.[13] "In short, the realization of God's judgment without the hope of forgiveness creates a fear that will automatically turn into hate."[14] We need to hear the promises continually; otherwise "we would certainly find ourselves in a miserable condition if we had to again be afraid all of the time that God's grace could all of a sudden not be there for us anymore!"[15]

---

[8] Ibid., 3.11.2.
[9] Calvin on Ps. 103:8, in *Calvin's Commentaries*, 6:133.
[10] Calvin on Ps. 116:11, in *Calvin's Commentaries*, 6:368.
[11] Calvin on Ps. 44:20, in *Calvin's Commentaries*, vol. 5, trans. James Anderson (Grand Rapids: Baker, 1996), 166–67.
[12] Herman J. Selderhuis, *Calvin's Theology of the Psalms* (Grand Rapids: Baker Academic, 2007), 270.
[13] Ibid.
[14] Calvin, quoted in ibid., 271.
[15] Calvin, quoted in ibid.

Yet justification tells us how God can remain just while declaring the guilty righteous (Rom. 3:26). Apart from this imputation of an alien righteousness, we are left in doubt about whether God is truly gracious *toward us*. For anyone, like Calvin, who experiences this doubt and anxiety, justification cannot be just one doctrine among many. Rome teaches that Christ's sacrifice remits the guilt but not the punishment of sins, Calvin observes. How can this be good news to sinners?[16]

Calvin repeatedly speaks of Christ having *merited* our salvation. We are indeed saved by works—that is, by perfect obedience to God's law—but it is Christ's, not ours. He not only bore our guilt in our place on the cross, but fulfilled all righteousness in our place by his life. Not only as the God who commands, but so too as the servant who fulfills the mandate of our creation is Jesus our Savior.[17] Thus, Rome's charge that the Reformation doctrine of justification constitutes a legal fiction was unfounded: Christ discharged the office of covenant Head, claiming by meritorious right that status of perfect justice, which he shares with his body. To say that we are righteous in Christ by imputation is no more a legal fiction than to say that we are guilty in Adam by imputation, or that Christ was made sin for us by our sins being imputed to him (2 Cor. 5:21).

The Reformation debate is not simply over the mechanism of justification, but also over the broader definition of grace, as we have seen. The Reformers also disagreed with Rome over the definition of faith. For Rome, faith is assent to everything that the church teaches (implicit faith). Therefore, it is not fully justifying until it is formed (or perfected) by love. Just as justification is collapsed into sanctification, faith becomes a virtuous work when it is formed by love. To this day, Roman Catholic theology affirms "justification by faith" only by defining justifying faith as obedient love. Calvin counters that faith is not blind assent to everything that the church teaches. "It would be the height of absurdity to label ignorance tempered by humility 'faith'!"[18] Rather, faith is knowledge of the gospel, assent to its message, and trust in Christ alone.

It is this faith that receives God's justifying verdict apart from offering any love or good works, simply as an open hand embracing Christ. "With respect to justification, faith is a thing merely passive, bringing nothing

---

[16] Calvin, *Institutes* 3.4.30.

[17] François Wendel, *Calvin: Origins and Development of His Religious Thought*, trans. Philip Mairet (Durham, NC: Labyrinth, 1987), 260. I elaborate Calvin's argument on this point in *Lord and Servant: A Covenant Christology* (Louisville: Westminster John Knox, 2006).

[18] Calvin, *Institutes* 3.2.3.

of our own to conciliate the favor of God, but receiving what we need from Christ."[19] Apart from any virtues or actions that might improve our inherent moral condition, "faith adorns us with the righteousness of another, which it seeks as a gift from God."[20] The faith by which we are justified *is* also active in love, but *not in the act of justifying.*

> Faith then is not a naked knowledge either of God or of his truth; nor is it a simple persuasion that God is, that his word is the truth; but a sure knowledge of God's mercy, which is received from the gospel, and brings peace of conscience with regard to God, and rest to the mind. The sum of the matter then is this,—that if salvation depends on the keeping of the law, the soul can entertain no confidence respecting it, yea, that all the promises offered to us by God will become void: we must thus become wretched and lost, if we are sent back to works to find out the cause or the certainty of salvation . . . for as the law generates nothing but vengeance, it cannot bring grace.[21]

Like Luther, Calvin believes that faith *is* assurance. To believe in Christ is to be assured objectively not only of God's mercy and grace in general, but also of his favor toward me (*pro me*) in particular. Through faith in Christ, I know that I am elect and already declared just before his tribunal on the last day. What Rome calls presumption, the Reformers call faith. Faith is defined in the Geneva Catechism as "a sure and steadfast knowledge of the fatherly goodwill of God toward us, as he declares in the gospel that for the sake of Christ he will be our Father and Savior."[22] Faith is directed not merely to God, or even to his Word in general.[23] Rather, saving faith is "receiving Christ as he is clothed in the gospel."[24] For Calvin, as Joel Beeke points out, "The grace of faith is from the Father, in the Son, and through the Spirit, by which, in turn, the believer is brought into fellowship with the Son, by the Spirit and consequently is reconciled to, and walks in fel-

---

[19] Ibid., 3.13.5.

[20] Calvin, *Commentaries upon the Epistle of Paul the Apostle to the Romans*, in *Calvin's Commentaries*, vol. 19, trans. John Owen (Grand Rapids: Baker, 1996), 159.

[21] Ibid., 171.

[22] Geneva Catechism, 1536, in *Selected Works of John Calvin: Tracts and Letters*, ed. Henry Beveridge and Jules Bonnet, 7 vols. (Grand Rapids: Baker, 1983), 2:132: Faith is "a firm and certain knowledge of God's benevolence toward us, founded upon the truth of the freely given promise in Christ, both revealed to our minds and sealed upon our hearts through the Holy Spirit." See also Calvin, *Institutes* 3.2.7: "[Faith] is a steady and certain knowledge of the Divine benevolence towards us, which, being founded on the truth of the gratuitous promise in Christ, is both revealed to our minds and confirmed to our hearts by the Holy Spirit."

[23] Calvin, *Institutes* 3.2.1.

[24] Ibid., 3.2.32.

lowship with, the Father."[25] "God has made Himself 'little in Christ,' Calvin strikingly states, so that we might comprehend and flee to 'Christ alone who can pacify our consciences.'"[26]

However, our subjective experience of this assurance waxes and wanes. "How can I, a sinner, be accepted by a holy God?" is a question that believers ask in moments of doubt and anxiety throughout their lives.[27] In fact, Calvin recognizes that "unbelief is . . . always mixed with faith" in every Christian.[28] He frequently reminds us that it is not the quality of faith, but the object of faith, that justifies. "Our faith is never perfect; . . . we are partly unbelievers."[29] The promise is solid and secure, but our apprehension of it varies.[30] "Nothing prevents believers from being afraid and at the same time possessing the surest consolation," Calvin adds. "Fear and faith dwell in the same mind.'"[31] As Beeke summarizes, "It does not hesitate, yet can hesitate. It contains security, but may be beset with anxiety. The faithful have firm assurance, yet waver and tremble." It's a distinction between faith itself and the believer's experience.[32] Though God's assurance of his goodwill to us is objective and certain, our subjective experience varies.[33] Yet God must always have the last word. We cling to the gospel no matter what. This is why the objective promise and its ratification by the sacraments are so important for us throughout our pilgrimage.[34]

"Then what about rewards?" Calvin's critics demanded, to which the Reformer replies that "it is an absurd inference to deduce merit from reward."[35] Calvin is aware of the medieval exegesis of Romans 2:13: "For it is not the hearers of the law . . . but the doers of the law who will be justified." Yet he replies, "They who pervert this passage for the purpose of building up justification by works deserve most fully to be laughed at even by children." It is obvious from Paul's argument that the purpose is to show that his readers

---

[25] Joel R. Beeke, "Calvin and Spirituality: Making Sense of Calvin's Paradoxes on Assurance of Faith," in *Calvin Studies Society Papers, 1995, 1997: Calvin and Spirituality; Calvin and His Contemporaries*, ed. David Foxgrover (Grand Rapids: CRC Product Services, 1998), 23.
[26] Ibid., 24.
[27] Ibid., 13n2: "Though Luther's struggles in attaining faith and assurance, documented copiously by himself and others, are well-known, J. H. Merle D'Aubigne provides evidence that Calvin's 'chamber became the theatre of struggles as fierce as those in the cell at Erfurt.'"
[28] Calvin, *Institutes* 3.2.4.
[29] Calvin on Mark 9:24, in *Calvin's Commentaries*, vol. 16, trans. William Pringle (Grand Rapids: Baker, 1996), 325.
[30] Calvin, *Institutes* 3.2.4, 15.
[31] Ibid., 3.2.23.
[32] Beeke, "Calvin and Spirituality," 18.
[33] Ibid., 14–24.
[34] Ibid., 19.
[35] Calvin, *Calvin's Commentaries*, 19:90.

were in fact under the law's curse along with the Gentiles for failing to do what the law requires, "so that another righteousness must be sought."[36] Not only the ceremonies but the whole law—including the moral law—is included when Paul opposes the law to faith as the way of justification.[37] "For if there be any righteousness by the law or by works, it must be in men themselves; but by faith they derive from another what is wanting in themselves; and hence the righteousness of faith is rightly called imputative."[38]

A theology of glory judges by appearances. Intuitively, we believe that good people go to heaven and bad people go to hell; that God cannot declare someone righteous who is at that moment inherently unrighteous. However, the gospel is counterintuitive. With Abraham, faith clings to a promise, against all human "possibilities":

> All things around us are in opposition to the promises of God: He promises immortality; we are surrounded with mortality and corruption: He declares that he counts us as just; we are covered with our sins: He testifies that he is propitious and kind to us; outward judgments threaten his wrath. What then is to be done? We must with closed eyes pass by ourselves and all things connected with us, that nothing may hinder or prevent us from believing that God is true.[39]

To be sure, God renovates us by his Spirit, but this is not justification, which is lodged exclusively in the free remission of sins and the imputation of righteousness.[40] No more than the careless unbeliever does "the Pharisee" know this peace with God through justification.[41] There are no "preparations" of our own that can give us "access" to God.[42] And there is no renovation—even by the grace of the Holy Spirit—that can make us worthy of justification.[43]

Sanctification

Many see the choice between Rome and the Reformation as a dispute over whether one prefers justification or sanctification. However, it is only the

---

[36] Ibid., 95–96.
[37] Ibid., 151.
[38] Ibid., 155.
[39] Ibid., 180.
[40] Ibid., 186.
[41] Ibid., 187.
[42] Ibid., 188.
[43] Ibid., 186.

Reformers' interpretation that embraces both. United to Christ by faith, we receive the imputation of Christ's righteousness for justification and the impartation of Christ's righteousness for sanctification. The Reformers are at one on this point. Calvin could not be clearer about the importance he gives to justification: it is "the principle article of the Christian faith," "the main hinge on which religion turns," "the principal article of the whole doctrine of salvation and the foundation of all religion," and "the sum of all piety."[44] "Whenever the knowledge of it is taken away, the glory of Christ is extinguished, religion abolished, the Church destroyed, and the hope of salvation utterly overthrown."[45] In his response to Cardinal Sadoleto, Calvin wrote that justification is "the first and keenest subject of controversy between us."[46]

At the same time, he emphasizes that we are united with Christ for both justification and sanctification. However, this is no different from Luther, as early as his *Sermon on the Double Righteousness* (1519). Also like Luther, Calvin follows Paul in discussing union with Christ in Romans 6 as the answer to those who charge that we can be justified without being sanctified.[47] His response is Paul's: ". . . for it is beyond any question that we put on Christ in baptism, and that we are baptized for this end—that we may be one with him." In baptism, then, there is not only a remission of sins "but also the putting to death and the dying of the old man" as we are raised with Christ in newness of life.[48]

Antinomianism and legalism conspire in forcing us to make a false choice: Is salvation a matter of God's forgiveness or is it moral transformation? This is a trick question from the Reformers' point of view. Calvin reasons, "Surely those things which are connected do not destroy one another!"[49] Forensic justification through faith alone is not the enemy but the basis of sanctification.[50] Again we meet "distinction without separation":

---

[44] Calvin, *Institutes* 3.2.1; 3.11.1; sermon on Luke 1:5–10 in *Corpus Reformatorum: Johannis Calvini opera quae supersunt omnia*, 46.23; and *Institutes* 3.15.7.

[45] Calvin, "Letter to Cardinal Sadoleto," in *Calvin's Tracts and Treatises*, trans. Henry Beveridge, vol. 1 (Grand Rapids: Eerdmans, 1958), 41.

[46] Ibid.

[47] Calvin on Romans 6, in *Calvin's Commentaries*, 19:218–31.

[48] Ibid., 220, on Rom. 6:3. There are differences between Calvin and Luther, especially on whether grace can be lost, but there is no basis for making the one a theologian of union and the other a theologian of justification. Both see union with Christ as the source for all spiritual blessings and at the same time see sanctification as logically dependent on justification. On this point, see especially Richard Muller, *Calvin and the Reformed Tradition: On the Work of Christ and the Order of Salvation* (Grand Rapids: Baker Academic, 2012), esp. 202–43, 281; cf. J. V. Fesko, *Beyond Calvin: Union with Christ and Justification in Early Modern Reformed Theology* (Göttingen: Vandenhoeck & Ruprecht, 2012).

[49] Calvin, *Institutes* 3.2.25.

[50] For more on this topic (especially in relation to Calvin's debate with Osiander), see Michael Horton, *Covenant and Salvation: Union with Christ* (Louisville: Westminster John Knox, 2007), 143–44.

Although we may distinguish them, Christ contains both of them inseparably in himself. Do you wish, then, to attain righteousness in Christ?
You must first possess Christ; but you cannot possess him without being
made partaker in his sanctification, because he cannot be divided into
pieces [1 Cor. 1:13]. Since, therefore, it is solely by expending himself that
the Lord gives us these benefits to enjoy, he bestows both of them at the
same time, the one never without the other. Thus it is clear how true it is
that we are justified not without works yet not through works, since in
our sharing in Christ, which justifies us, sanctification is just as much
included as righteousness.[51]

There are not two acts of faith or two stages of the Christian life. Every
believer clings to Christ for justification and sanctification.[52] "You cannot
grasp this [justification] without at the same time grasping sanctification
also."[53]

For in Christ he offers all happiness in place of our misery, all wealth in
place of our neediness; in him he opens to us the heavenly treasures that
our whole faith may contemplate his beloved Son, our whole expectation
depend upon him, and our whole hope cleave to and rest in him. This,
indeed, is that secret and hidden philosophy which cannot be wrested
from syllogisms.[54]

Calvin adds, "This alone is of importance: having admitted that faith and
good works must cleave together, we still lodge justification in faith, not
in works. We have a ready explanation for doing this, provided we turn
to Christ to whom our faith is directed and from whom it receives its full
strength."[55]

Calvin bathes in the Bible's organic as well as legal analogies for this
union. All those who are justified in Christ the Tree of Life become his fruit-
bearing branches. We are familiar with the emphasis in evangelical circles
on following Christ's example, asking, "What would Jesus do?" This was a
central theme in medieval piety as well, as illustrated in the popularity of
Thomas à Kempis's fifteenth-century work *The Imitation of Christ*. This piety
lay at the heart especially of the Brethren of the Common Life, to which I

---

[51] Calvin, *Institutes* 3.16.1. See also 3.11.1.
[52] Ibid, 3.11.1.
[53] Ibid., 3.16.1.
[54] Ibid., 3.20.1.
[55] Ibid., 3.16.1.

referred in chapter 2. It is evident also in the Wesleyan-Holiness stream of teaching that dominates much of contemporary evangelical spirituality.

Calvin took at face value biblical exhortations to follow Christ's example. However, he recognized that by itself this is the law without the gospel. Calvin comments that in Romans 6,

> Let us know that the Apostle does not simply exhort us to imitate Christ, as though he had said that his death is a pattern which all Christians are to follow; for no doubt he ascends higher, as he announces a doctrine with which he connects an exhortation; and his doctrine is this: that the death of Christ is efficacious to destroy and demolish the depravity of our flesh, and his resurrection, to effect the renovation of a better nature, and that by baptism we are admitted into a participation of this grace. This foundation being laid, Christians may very suitably be exhorted to strive to respond to their calling.

This is true of everyone who is united to Christ, not just to a superior class, he adds.[56] Thus, this "ingrafting is not only a conformity of example, but a secret union."[57] One might add by way of analogy that while a little brother or sister certainly looks up to and even imitates an older sibling, the deeper reality is their familial bond.

Christ is not only our hero, model, or pattern, but also our vine—and we are branches. He is the Head of his body of which we are members; the firstfruits of the whole harvest to which we belong. Calvin says that we are "in Christ (in Christo) because we are out of ourselves (extra nos)," finding our sanctification as well as our justification not by looking within but by clinging to Christ.[58] Commenting on John 17, Calvin explains that we are "one with the Son of God; not because he conveys his substance to us, but because, by the power of the Spirit, he imparts to us his life and all the blessings which he has received from the Father."[59] "But Christ dwells principally on this, that the vital sap—that is, all life and strength—proceeds from himself alone." Therefore, not only in justification, but also in sanctification, faith receives every good from Christ alone as the source; "if you contemplate yourself, that is sure damnation."[60]

---

[56] Calvin on Rom. 6:4, in *Calvin's Commentaries*, 19:221.

[57] Ibid., 222, on Rom. 6:5.

[58] Calvin, quoted in Mark A. Garcia, *Life in Christ: Union with Christ and Twofold Grace in Calvin's Theology* (Milton Keynes, UK: Paternoster, 2008), 116.

[59] Calvin, *Commentary on the Gospel According to John*, in *Calvin's Commentaries*, vol. 17, trans. William Pringle (Grand Rapids: Baker, 1996), 183–84.

[60] Ibid., 107.

Just as Calvin goes beyond Augustine and the medieval tradition in identifying the whole person (body as well as soul) with the image of God, so too he adds, "The spiritual connection which we have with Christ belongs not merely to the soul, but also to the body."[61] This is why he attaches significance to the Supper not only for the soul's communion with Christ but also for the life-giving energies communicated to our whole humanity from our glorified and life-giving Head. "The mystical union subsisting between Christ and his members should be a matter of reflection not only when we sit at the Lord's Table, but at all other times."[62]

Sanctification is a matter of getting used to both our justification and our broader union with Christ in all of its dimensions—judicial *and* organic. This union is not the *goal* (as in Roman Catholic and some Protestant pieties), but the *source* of the Christian life. We are not just following Christ, but living in Christ and, by his Spirit, he is living in us.

While both are given in union with Christ, Calvin sees justification as the logical basis for sanctification, "for since we are clothed with the righteousness of the Son, we are reconciled to God, and renewed by the power of the Spirit to holiness."[63] "Sanctification, for Calvin, grows out of justification," Selderhuis explains, "and the glory of Christ's perfect righteousness may never be obscured, not even for a moment." "Therefore, justification is the cause and sanctification is the effect."[64] He adds:

> In Calvin's view the believer never rises above the status of *simul iustus et peccator*. . . . Calvin's description of the regenerate man's struggle against sin explains that a believer is *declared* righteous without actually *becoming* righteous. Sanctification is the internal struggle to tame the carnal inclinations which rule us by nature. It is a fight with one's self. . . . The more someone progresses in sanctification throughout life, the more he or she realizes the distance by which he or she has fallen short of the righteousness of God, and all that is left is to trust in God's mercy.[65]

While this is certainly true, Calvin also exults in the newness that flows from being united to Christ. The Spirit is at work in us, enabling us more and more to struggle against indwelling sin and to yield the fruit of

---

[61] Calvin, *Commentary on the First Epistle to the Corinthians*, in *Calvin's Commentaries*, vol. 20, trans. John Pringle (Grand Rapids: Baker, 1996), 217.
[62] Calvin on Ps. 63:2, in *Calvin's Commentaries*, 5:435.
[63] Calvin, *Institutes* 3.11.17.
[64] Selderhuis, *Calvin's Theology of the Psalms*, 195.
[65] Ibid., 197–98.

the Spirit. While we dare not lodge our justification in sanctification, we should be on guard against imagining that the justified are left in the same spiritual condition that they were in under the reign of sin and death.

Passivity and perfectionism are twin dangers to be avoided in the Christian life, according to the Reformer. Of course, we are merely recipients of God's good gifts, including sanctification. We hear the Word and receive Christ in baptism and Communion. In this, faith is "a purely passive action" (actio mere passiva).[66] Yet the point of being recipients of God's grace is to be active distributors of his love to others. We receive from God and give to others. Grace not only gives; it also activates our giving—not to God, but to our neighbors. Since grace liberates nature, it is opposed not to our activity, but to our merit. That's the way it is throughout our life. We are always passive receivers of salvation, but we are active in our living out of that daily conversion—dying to ourselves and living to God in Christ. With faith lodged only in Christ, we are far from passive in putting to death indwelling sin. And we are therefore called repeatedly in Scripture to press on, to grow up, to train ourselves, to bear the fruit of the Spirit in our relationships with others, and to strive with all of our might to say no to sin and yes to righteousness. All of this we can do, though imperfectly, because we are already united to Christ and are indwelled by his Spirit.

Christ died for us, but he does not repent and believe for us. Repentance and faith are gifts that he gives us by his Word and Spirit, but we exercise them as a deliberate act of the will.[67] Let us not downplay the difficulty of this struggle. Every believer fights against insurgents within and without, the remnants of a defeated foe. This growth is not automatic. We may quench the Spirit by refusing his promptings. When we fail to avail ourselves of the means of grace, we shrivel on the vine. Furthermore, if we don't communicate with our Father and if we abandon the fellowship of our brothers and sisters, we become drifters instead of pilgrims. The gospel gives us a secure place to stand as we fight this battle with all our might and main.

Paradoxically, it is the acknowledgment that we are simultaneously justified and sinful that fuels our commitment to press on in the race.[68] "Far removed from perfection, we must move steadily forward, and though

---

[66] Calvin, Institutes 4.14.26.
[67] Ibid., 2.12.6.
[68] Ibid., 3.3.10.

entangled in vices, daily fight against them."[69] Sanctification is real, but it is not complete. "Christ by his Spirit does not perfectly renew us at once, or in an instant, but he continues our renovation throughout life."[70] Sin's dominion has been toppled, but still indwells believers.[71] This orientation stood in sharp contrast not only with Rome, but with the radical Protestants as well. "Certain Anabaptists of our day conjure some sort of frenzied excess instead of spiritual regeneration," thinking that they can attain perfection in this life.[72]

Not only at the beginning, but throughout our Christian life, we derive all of our righteousness from Christ, not from ourselves.[73] Ironically, those who are preoccupied with raising their standing in God's estimation end up offending God, deepening their guilt, and doing nothing for their neighbors. The monk was the ideal portrait of this confused spirituality. As Calvin explained to Cardinal Sadoleto, it is the one who is assured of God's favor in Christ alone who is free to love his or her neighbors simply for their own sake and for God's glory, rather than for one's own self-improvement and self-justification.[74] There is another role for the law in the Christian life, as we will see, but it no longer has any power to condemn us.

> Removing, then, mention of law, and laying aside all consideration of works, we should, when justification is being discussed, embrace God's mercy alone, turn our attention from ourselves, and look only to Christ. . . . If consciences wish to attain any certainty in this matter, they ought to give no place to the law.[75]

So when we consider ourselves, there is nothing but despair; when we consider ourselves *in Christ*, there is faith, which brings hope and love in its train. Works-righteousness is the enemy of genuine holiness by cutting the tree at its root, but the gospel creates faith in Christ, which puts forth branches of love and bears the fruit of good works. This gospel is the deathblow to antinomianism and legalism alike.

---

[69] Ibid., 3.3.14.
[70] Calvin on 1 John 3:5, in *Calvin's Commentaries*, vol. 22, trans. John Owen (Grand Rapids: Baker, 1996), 209.
[71] Calvin, *Institutes* 3.3.11.
[72] Ibid., 3.3.14.
[73] Ibid., 3.12.3.
[74] Calvin, *A Reformation Debate: Sadoleto's Letter to the Genevans and Calvin's Reply*, ed. John C. Olin (Grand Rapids: Baker, 1966), 56.
[75] Calvin, *Institutes* 3.19.2.

Adoption

Another important gift of our union that Calvin frequently emphasizes with delight is adoption. B. B. Warfield, among others, concluded that God's fatherhood is more pervasive in Calvin's piety even than God's sovereignty. It is an astonishing claim only to those who have never read the Reformer closely. As Selderhuis notes, "The purpose of election is God's fatherhood. . . . In his theology of the doctrine of God, the Reformer often returns to this idea again and again." In fact, "it is evident that he views God first and foremost as a father."[76] The Father chose a people to be his children, a bride for his Son, and a living temple for his Spirit. Believers are the family that comes into being as a result of the mutual exchange of love between the persons of the Trinity.

Even justification is important not as an end in itself, but because it secures that filial relationship that the Godhead willed from all eternity. The point of sanctification is not simply the moral improvement of individuals, but also the setting apart of children, transforming enemies into heirs. The goal is a family. It is one thing to assent to the doctrine of God's fatherhood and another to experience his loving adoption and "fatherly love." Calvin underscores the psalmist's reference to "the light of [God's] face" (Ps. 44:3): the parental smile that compensates for whatever losses we encounter in the world.[77] God's love for us, not ours for him, is always the source of this relationship, and because of Christ's merits there is no threat that we might revert to God as our Judge rather than our Father. Because we are united to Christ, we enjoy the same privileges, favor, and access to the Father as Christ does himself.[78]

The Christian Life as a Banquet

The Christian life is a struggle, but it is also a lavish banquet with a generous Father, a faithful elder Brother, and an active and indwelling Holy Spirit who binds us to Christ and therefore to each other. In fact, B. A. Gerrish has argued that Calvin's entire theology may be summarized as "Eucharistic"—a life of gratitude, marked by feasting with the triune God and each other. "The holy banquet is simply the liturgical enactment of the theme of grace and gratitude that lies at the heart of Calvin's entire theology."[79] Selderhuis

---

[76] Selderhuis, *Calvin's Theology of the Psalms*, 247.
[77] Calvin on Ps. 4:6–7, in *Calvin's Commentaries*, vol. 4, trans. James Anderson (Grand Rapids: Baker, 1996), 48–49.
[78] Calvin on Ps. 79:9 in *Calvin's Commentary*, 5:291.
[79] B. A. Gerrish, *Grace and Gratitude: The Eucharistic Theology of John Calvin* (Minneapolis: Augsburg Fortress, 1993), 20, 13.

also notes, "Calvin points to the example in Psalm 104 that, although man has water to drink according to his needs, God has additionally given wine to make us cheerful."[80] Indeed, it is striking how frequently Calvin stresses the liberal generosity of the Father toward us in his Son. It was Rome that turned the banquet into a fearful courtroom and Anabaptists who saw the Christian life as a heavy yoke. Yet for Calvin the Christian life is a pilgrimage with a banquet spread in the wilderness for weary travelers. We have passed from the courtroom to the family room.

Pilgrimage and banquet: these two motifs are woven together frequently in Calvin's teaching. While the banquet motif highlights the present joys of that salvation that we possess already in Christ, pilgrimage suggests patient endurance. We know where we are going, and we already have a foretaste of the feast's rich fare, but we have not yet arrived at the wedding supper of the Lamb.

We experience the gifts of the triune God in that tension of the "already" and the "not yet." Believers are already elected, redeemed, called, justified, and adopted. They are being sanctified, and they will one day be glorified. This already–not yet paradox lies at the heart of Calvin's recurring metaphors for the Christian life as pilgrimage and banquet. A pilgrim has not yet arrived, nor is he or she an aimless wanderer or tourist, but someone called away with the throng to the City of God based on a promise. Along the way, God spreads a table in the wilderness to refresh his people in anticipation of the wedding feast with the Bridegroom in glory.

As the image of God in creation is social as well as individual, so also is its restoration in Christ. Of course, there is a place for private prayer and meditation on Scripture. However, Calvin does not think of a lonely pilgrim or diner at a table for one. That is why most of Calvin's discussions of sanctification occur in the context of the church, the family, and our callings in the world. Monastic spirituality concentrated on private disciplines, as if detaching oneself from "the world" (i.e., society) might make one holier. Anabaptist piety was similar in that regard. However, Calvin thought of sanctification as a family affair. How could one learn loving humility, patience, wisdom, and forgiveness in isolation from others? We discover our need to continually confess our sins and pursue godliness more in the daily trials and joys of church fellowship, friendships, marriage, and child rearing than we do on our own. Since the law calls us to

---

[80] Selderhuis, *Calvin's Theology of the Psalms*, 150, on Ps. 104:15.

love our neighbors, what could be more of an obstacle to sanctification than withdrawing from others—especially the fellowship of saints—in pious seclusion?

Election

"We shall never be clearly persuaded, as we ought to be, that our salvation flows from the wellspring of God's free mercy until we come to know his eternal election."[81] Predestination is not the center of Calvin's "system"; nor does he add anything to the doctrine that was unknown to other Augustinian Catholics, including Thomas Aquinas. However, he does bring it out of the room of philosophical speculation and set it before the Christian faithful as an article of gospel joy. Like Luther in his debate with Erasmus, Calvin sees the doctrine of election as pulling up synergism and spiritual pride at its root. "God once established by his eternal and unchangeable plan those whom he long before determined once for all to receive into salvation, and those whom, on the other hand, he would devote to destruction."[82]

Calvin never addresses this subject apart from some pastoral question or concern, especially when he comes to particular passages that clearly teach it. Why do some believe and others not believe? How can I know that I have persevering faith, rather than the sort of faith that is choked by the weeds? How can I know that I'm in a state of grace? Medieval piety had already intensified these anxious questions, and when the God of justice and wrath is more real than the God of mercy and justifying grace, predestination is a terrifying doctrine. However, when seen in gospel light, it is assuring comfort. "When one comes to election," Calvin says, "there mercy alone appears on every side."[83]

The doctrine is only comforting when we remain within the bounds of God's Word, specifically the gospel, and refuse our speculative urges.

> Human curiosity renders the discussion of predestination, already somewhat difficult of itself, very confusing and even dangerous. No restraints can hold it back from wandering in forbidden bypaths and thrusting upward to the heights. If allowed, it will leave no secret to God that it will not search out and unravel. . . .

---

[81] Calvin, *Institutes* 3.21.1.
[82] Ibid., 3.21.7.
[83] Ibid., 3.24.1.

> . . . [The curious] will not succeed in satisfying his curiosity and he
> will enter a labyrinth from which he can find no exit. For it is not right
> for man unrestrainedly to search out things that the Lord has willed to
> be hid in himself.[84]

Here, as elsewhere, Calvin's rule is clear: "When the Lord closes his holy
lips, he also shall at once close the way to inquiry."[85]

Like any attempt to ascend to the hidden God of majesty, any strategy
to discover our election in God's secret chamber will lead to despair. We
only find God's goodness and grace where he has revealed it, in Christ and
his gospel. If we set out "to penetrate to God's eternal ordination," Calvin
warns, "that deep abyss will swallow us up." We must not seek to "flit about
above the clouds," but must be "restrained by the soberness of faith . . . in
his outward Word."

> For just as those engulf themselves in a deadly abyss who, to make their
> election more certain, investigate God's eternal plan apart from his Word,
> so those who rightly and duly examine it as it is contained in his Word
> reap the inestimable fruit of comfort.[86]

The danger lies on both sides: saying either less or more than Scripture
teaches.[87]

The key is to locate our election *in Christ.*

> First, if we seek God's fatherly mercy and kindly heart, we should turn
> our eyes to Christ, on whom alone God's Spirit rests. . . . No matter how
> much you toss it about and mull it over, you will discover that its final
> bounds still extend no farther. . . . If we have been chosen in him, we shall
> not find assurance of our election in ourselves; and not even in God the
> Father, if we conceive him as severed from his Son. Christ, then, is the
> mirror wherein we must, and without self-deception may, contemplate
> our own election.[88]

Calvin is aware that even a doctrine designed by God for assurance can
be used badly when we seek God and his predestination outside of Christ.
Calvin calls this "seeking outside the way."

---

[84] Ibid., 3.21.1.
[85] Ibid., 3.21.3.
[86] Ibid., 3.24.3–4.
[87] Ibid., 3.21.2.
[88] Ibid., 3.24.5.

Satan has no more grievous or dangerous temptation to dishearten believers than when he unsettles them with doubt about their election, while at the same time he arouses them with a wicked desire to seek it outside the way. I call it "seeking outside the way" when mere man attempts to break into the inner recesses of divine wisdom and tries to penetrate even to highest eternity, in order to find out what decision has been made concerning himself at God's judgment.[89]

Elsewhere he offers this prayer:

Grant, Almighty God, . . . that having cast away and renounced all confidence in our own virtue, we may be led to Christ only as the fountain of thy election, in whom also is set before us the certainty of our salvation through thy gospel, until we shall at length be gathered into that eternal glory which He has procured for us by his own blood. Amen.[90]

Since we discover our election not in God's secret decree but in his revealed Word, the good news is for every person. "The gospel is preached indiscriminately to the elect and the reprobate; but the elect alone come to Christ, because they have been 'taught by God.'"[91] It is not right for us to identify even vicious enemies of the gospel as reprobate.

Renée, Princess of France and Duchess of Ferrara, once asked Calvin if she could hate her son-in-law, the Duke of Guise. Surely this cruel exterminator of the Reformed believers in France was reprobate. Calvin says he prayed often that God would show the duke mercy—but if not, that God would then "lay his hand on him" to save "the poor church." "To pronounce that he is damned, however, is to go too far. . . . For there is none can know but the Judge before whose tribunal we have all to render an account." Even though the duke may not be considered "a member of the Church," Calvin adds, "I pray for the salvation of every person."[92] "And as we cannot distinguish between the elect and the reprobate," he says elsewhere, "it is our duty to pray for all who trouble us; to desire the salvation of all people; and even to be careful for the welfare of every individual."[93]

If speculating beyond Scripture is one danger, then for Calvin ignor-

[89] Ibid., 3.24.4.

[90] Calvin, "Prayer," in *Commentary on Zechariah–Malachi*, in *Calvin's Commentaries*, vol. 15, trans. John Owen (Grand Rapids: Baker, 1996), 482.

[91] Calvin on Isa. 54:13, in *Calvin's Commentaries*, vol. 8, trans. William Pringle (Grand Rapids: Baker, 1996), 146.

[92] Calvin, "To the Duchess of Ferrara" (Geneva, January 24, 1564), in *Selected Works of John Calvin*, 7:355.

[93] Calvin on Ps. 109:16, in *Calvin's Commentaries*, 6:283.

ing clear passages is the other. Scripture unmistakably teaches that before the world was created, the Father chose a people and gave them to the Son as their trustee and Mediator, to be united to the Son by the Spirit in due course. Calvin interprets this election of a church from a sinful human race as individual, not just collective, unconditional rather than based on foreseen faith or obedience, and the cause rather than the effect of holiness in those chosen. Like Paul, he anticipates the likely charge of injustice (for which, by the way, any sound exegesis of Romans 9 has to account). Far from beginning with a neutral condition in which God issues arbitrary decrees, Calvin says, "As all of us are vitiated by sin," it is not from "tyrannical cruelty but by the fairest reckoning of justice" that all of us would be condemned unless God has chosen to save some.[94] Calvin says that the reprobate will be compelled to recognize on the last day that "the cause of condemnation" lies "in themselves."[95] Later he adds, "Accordingly, we should contemplate the evident cause of condemnation in the corrupt nature of humanity—which is closer to us—rather than seek a hidden and utterly incomprehensible cause in God's predestination."[96]

The final gift of our union with Christ that Paul mentions in Romans 8 is *glorification*. In union with Christ we discover our eternal election as well as our historical redemption, calling, justification, and adoption. Irrevocable, these gifts belong to the "already" of our salvation. From this same union we are being sanctified. This process straddles the "already" of sin's toppled dominion and the "not yet" of complete holiness. Yet it also looks forward to the future glory that awaits us, when we are changed in a moment to share in the resurrection beauty that belongs already to our living Head. I explore Calvin's treatment of that subject in the final chapter.

---

[94] Calvin, *Institutes* 3.23.3.
[95] Ibid.
[96] Ibid., 3.23.8.

PART 3

LIVING IN THE BODY

CHAPTER 7

HOW GOD DELIVERS
HIS GRACE

We know God (and ourselves) only in Christ as he is clothed in the gospel, which announces his all-sufficient, objective, and completed work for us, outside of us, in the past. Yet if we are actually to benefit from this saving work, the Spirit must unite us to Christ here and now and keep us there. But how does he do this? Calvin asks this next in the *Institutes'* unfolding argument, under the subheading "The Way in Which We Receive the Grace of Christ." With that question we have reached the busiest intersection of this study. Here meet theory and practice, redemption accomplished and applied, union with Christ and communion with his church.

This is the place where we often stumble. Even when faith is directed to Christ alone for justification, we can easily conceive the rest of the story—the Christian life—as a self-obsessed, inward-focused, feverishly busy schedule of spiritual programs. Judging by the Christian-living and spirituality sections of Christian bookstores, as well as many sermons and conferences, guides to spiritual growth are usually in the self-help vein. They focus on what we do and, furthermore, what we do by ourselves and for ourselves.

Calvin knew this sort of piety very well. In this view, first the arrow of activity was from us to God. By following a prescribed rule or steps and procedures defined by a noted mystic, one could achieve union with God. The image of ascending a ladder, rung by rung, was dominant, as in Walter

Hilton's popular fourteenth-century classic *The Ladder of Perfection*. The law of love, following Christ's example, was the method of making this ascent.[1] Second, the nature of the activity was striving upward by turning inward in solitude and contemplation. This could be done in community (the monastic approach), but many found that they could accomplish more going it alone (the hermetic approach). There were medieval debates over whether the contemplative life (solitude and prayer) or the active life (good works toward others, especially the poor) was to be preferred, and a similar cleavage appears in contemporary evangelicalism. In either case, though, we begin at the wrong place: with us and our gifts that we offer to God or to our neighbors. Many Anabaptists followed a similar pattern, turning the whole community into a monastic refuge from the world. If anything, the perfectionistic impulse, with its strict disciplines, was even more pronounced in these groups. Many Christians today also assume that God in Christ has made salvation possible, but now it's up to us to ascend to heaven or descend into the depths to "appropriate" it for ourselves. It is perhaps not surprising that evangelicals have frequently turned to medieval spirituality for spiritual resources.

The contrast with Reformation piety is profound. In the Reformed view, first the arrow of activity points downward as God descends to us. Calvin turned repeatedly to Paul's argument in Romans 10.[2] "God does not command us to ascend into heaven, but, because of our weakness, he descends to us." Theologies of glory ascend to heaven with humanly devised methods for bringing Christ down or for descending into the depths to make him living and real to us, but a theology of the cross receives him in the humble and weak form of those creaturely means that he has ordained.[3]

Second, the nature of the activity is not striving for union through love and good works, but receiving the gift of union through faith alone. The law of love is not the path *to* God's favor, but the highway *from* it that leads out into the world. Medieval piety reversed the direction of the flow of gifts. The order was love → good works → justification. For the Reformers, it was the opposite: the Word creates the faith that receives justification in Christ and then produces the fruit of love and good works. Consequently,

[1] See David Lyle Jeffrey, *The Law of Love: English Spirituality in the Age of Wyclif* (Grand Rapids: Eerdmans, 1988), ix, 2.

[2] Calvin on Romans 10, in *Calvin's Commentaries*, vol. 19, trans. John Owen (Grand Rapids: Baker, 1996), 381–407.

[3] Herman J. Selderhuis, *Calvin's Theology of the Psalms* (Grand Rapids: Baker Academic, 2007), 203, on Pss. 42:2 and 24:7.

we bring our good works not to God to gain favor, but to our neighbors to show God's love. God's gifts come *to* us, and then *through* us, out to others. God is glorified, we are saved, and our neighbors are served. Reverse the flow, and nobody benefits. God is offended, we deepen our guilt, and our neighbors are ignored.

Third, the Father has sent his Son and his Spirit to form a communion of forgiven and renewed sinners. In medieval piety, one could avoid the church and the world. The recommended methods were best followed either in private or with fellow monks outside of the public gathering of the covenant community for the ordinary means of grace. The monks dedicated their whole lives to acts of devotion and service on behalf of the rest of the body that engaged in secular life. No, said the Reformers. God finds us in peace where he has promised to meet us, with the whole covenant assembly, through the methods that he has appointed for delivering Christ with all of his benefits. The whole force of this sort of piety is to drive us outside of ourselves so that we will look up to God in faith and out to our neighbors in love. It's neither our quietism nor our activism that makes us Christians, but the activity of the triune God that makes us recipients of saving grace and active distributors of his love and service to others.

Modern individualism deepens the tendency to be turned in on ourselves. We trust what happens within us, what we experience and do, what we can manage and measure. Genuine faith is not only personal, but private. We're suspicious of any notion of God's grace coming to us from outside ourselves, through public, ordinary, creaturely means.

Once again we meet Calvin's invocation of the maxim "distinction without separation." On the one hand, Roman Catholic theology failed to distinguish between the free work of the Spirit and the creaturely means he employs. The word of the church is simply the Word of God. Baptism regenerates simply by being administered (*ex opere operato*), and, after the priestly consecration in the Mass, the signs of bread and wine no longer exist, but are simply transformed into the body and blood of Christ. On the other hand, Anabaptists separated the Spirit from these external means.

In Calvin's view, the creaturely signs of preaching, water, bread, and wine are distinguished but never separated from the saving reality. The Spirit is free, but he freely binds himself to these means as his ordinary method of operation. The basis for this union of sign and reality in all "sacramental" cases is the incarnation. The same logic that would simply collapse the humanity of Christ into his deity would also collapse the sign into the reality: preaching and the sacraments in this case would simply cause salvation. The same logic that would separate Christ's two natures, downplaying the saving significance of his humanity, cannot affirm the union of creaturely signs with their saving reality.

Coming to Scripture with our Gentile (Greek) assumptions, we correlate the Spirit and his work with that which is invisible and internal—over against that which is physical. Yet throughout the biblical drama, the Spirit is always working with and through the stuff of creation. The Spirit hovers over the waters in the beginning, leads his people through the pillar and cloud, takes up residence in the tabernacle and then the temple, and separates his people unto himself through circumcision and the Passover meal. And yet the Spirit is free to work as he will through—or even, in extraordinary cases, apart from—these means. He can indwell the temple without being imprisoned in it. According to Calvin, Rome binds God to earthly means, while the Anabaptists disallow that God can freely bind us to himself through them.[4]

Though he did not take it as far as the Anabaptists, Zwingli also assumed a dualism between sign and reality, spirit and matter, God's work and the church's ministry. "For faith springs not from things accessible to sense nor are they objects of faith," he insisted.[5] However, Calvin had early on rejected the contrast between "flesh" and "Spirit" understood as equivalent to "matter" and "spirit."[6] In short, he saw the physical aspect as the means chosen by God for delivering and strengthening the spiritual communion with Christ.[7]

Not all who were circumcised or shared in the Passover feast believed the promise. In the wilderness, many failed to look upon the brass serpent with faith in God's promise. Not all who hear the gospel, are baptized, and take Communion embrace the reality—Christ with all of his benefits. Yet when the Spirit does give the elect faith and ratifies the Father's promise in Christ, it is through these means.

To convey the efficacy of the means of grace, Calvin often uses the verb

[4] Calvin, *Institutes of the Christian Religion*, ed. John T. McNeill, trans. Ford Lewis Battles (Philadelphia: Westminster, 1960), 4.1.5.
[5] Ulrich Zwingli, *Commentary on True and False Religion*, ed. Samuel Macauley Jackson and Clarence Nevin Heller, trans. Samuel Macauley Jackson (Durham, NC: Labyrinth, 1981), 214. Of course, if one followed this view consistently (which, happily, Zwingli did not), one wonders how faith could come by *hearing* (Rom. 10:17).
[6] Calvin on Rom. 6:6, in *Calvin's Commentaries*, 19:224–25.
[7] Willem Balke, *Calvin and the Anabaptist Radicals*, trans. William J. Heynen (Grand Rapids: Eerdmans, 1981), 53.

exhibēre, which means "to present, confer, or deliver."[8] The same view is summarized later in the Westminster Standards, which refers to the sacraments as "effectual means of salvation."[9]

The Preached Word

Like the other Reformers, Calvin understands the *word of God* in three senses. Only Jesus Christ is the eternal Word in his very essence. Only Scripture is God's inerrant and normative Word. However, preaching is the "sacramental Word"—that is, the word as the means of God's work of judging, justifying, renewing, and conforming us to Christ's image. Through his Word, God is truly present in the world.[10]

In evangelical circles we typically think of preaching as teaching and exhorting. Of course, Scripture informs, instructs, explains, asserts, and commands. Yet for the Reformers, the preaching of the Word is more than a preacher's thoughts, encouragements, advice, and impassioned pleas. Through the lips of a sinful preacher, the triune God is actually judging, justifying, reconciling, renewing, and conforming sinners to Christ's image. God created the world by the words of his mouth and by his speech also brings a new creation into being. In other words, through the proclamation of his Word, God is not just speaking about what might happen if we bring it about but is actually speaking it into being. Hence, Calvin calls preaching the *sacramental word*: the word as a means of grace. Faith comes by hearing the Word—specifically, the gospel (Rom. 10:17). Thus, the church is the creation of the Word (*creatura verbi*).

There has been a tendency over the last century to set propositional truth over against personal encounter. However, this is a false choice. B. A. Gerrish observes, "Calvin felt no antagonism between what we may call the 'pedagogical' [teaching] and the 'sacramental' functions of the word."[11] "God's word, for Calvin, is not simply a dogmatic norm; it has in it a vital efficacy, and it is the appointed instrument by which the Spirit imparts illumination, faith, awakening, regeneration, purification, and so on. . . .

---

[8] Calvin's view is nicely summarized in answer 65 of the Heidelberg Catechism: "The Holy Spirit produces [faith] in our hearts by the preaching of the holy gospel [Ro 10:17; 1 Pet 1:23–25] and confirms it through our use of the holy sacraments [Mt 28:19–20; 1 Cor 10:16]." *Ecumenical Creeds and Reformed Confessions* (Grand Rapids: CRC Publications, 1988).

[9] Westminster Confession of Faith, 27; Shorter Catechism, 91–93; Larger Catechism, 161–64.

[10] Selderhuis, *Calvin's Theology of the Psalms*, 134.

[11] B. A. Gerrish, *Grace and Gratitude: The Eucharistic Theology of John Calvin* (Minneapolis: Augsburg Fortress, 1993), 84–85. Gerrish refers here especially to Calvin's *Petit tracté de la sancta Cene* [1541], *Opera Selecta* (hereafter *OS*) 1:504–5, and the *Institutes* 4.14.4; cf. 3.2.6–7; 3.2.28–30.

Calvin himself describes the word as *verbum sacramentale*, the 'sacramental word,'" that gives even to the sacraments themselves their efficacy.[12] Gerrish adds, "It is crucial to Calvin's interpretation that the gospel is not a mere invitation to fellowship with Christ, but the effective means by which the communion with Christ comes about."[13] In proclaiming God's Word, the minister is not merely describing a new creation and exhorting us to enter into it; through this proclamation, Christ himself is speaking a new creation into being.

In the words of the Second Helvetic Confession, "The preached Word is the Word of God."[14] The biblical canon is the completed foundation, but the preached Word is the primary means of the Spirit's ongoing building project. Even in this present evil age we "taste of the goodness of the word of God and the powers of the age to come" (Heb. 6:5). Faith is not the act of the church or the act of the believer merely *in response to* God's Word, but is created by the Spirit *through* that Word. We find faith not by looking within or by blind obedience to everything the church teaches, but by the regular proclamation of Christ. When we lose a sense of this miraculous power of God's proclaimed Word, we begin to look for God's presence and power in other places, through our own activities that we have devised.

The Reformers translated the Scriptures so that everyone could have the Bible in his or her own language. Reading and meditating on Scripture in private, family, and group study became an important aspect of piety. Nevertheless, they emphasized the priority of *hearing* the Word preached publicly. Peace treaties are not only read in private, but announced in public—for the new state of affairs that they create concerns the whole body politic. The eye scans, dissects, and selects, but the ear receives, submits and attends to what someone else is saying. No medium is more suited to God's objective promise making than preaching. Furthermore, the public preaching of the Word creates a public community of hearers, not simply private readers. This is why the Westminster Larger Catechism adds, "The Spirit of God maketh the reading, *but especially the preaching* of the Word, an effectual means of enlightening, convincing, and humbling sinners, of *driving them out of themselves*, and drawing them unto Christ."[15] It is not only the message but also the method that *drives us out of ourselves*, which

---

[12] Gerrish, *Grace and Gratitude*, 85, referring to Calvin, *Institutes* 4.14.4.

[13] Gerrish, *Grace and Gratitude*, 84. His references to Calvin are from the *Institutes* 3.5.5.

[14] The Second Helvetic Confession, chap. 1, in the *Book of Confessions* (Louisville, PCUSA General Assembly, 1991).

[15] Westminster Larger Catechism, 155.

of course an "inner word" cannot do. By this Word the Holy Spirit drives us out of ourselves to God in faith and to our neighbors in love.

"For Calvin the word is equivalent to God's promises, and therefore the emphasis is more on the preached word than on the written word in the Bible."[16] John Leith observes, "For Calvin as for Luther, 'The ears alone are the organ of the Christian.'"[17] Leith elaborates, "The justification for preaching is not in its effectiveness for education or reform. . . . The preacher, Calvin dared to say, was the mouth of God." It was God's intention and action that made it effective. The minister's words, like the physical elements of the sacraments, were united to the substance: Christ and all of his benefits. Therefore, the Word not only describes salvation, but conveys it. "Calvin's sacramental doctrine of preaching enabled him both to understand preaching as a very human work and to understand it as the work of God."[18] Indeed, "Calvin interpreted the Reformation as the result of the power of God's word. The fact that in such a short time so many people could be brought under the dominion of Christ was 'solely due to the voice of the gospel, and this happened in spite of the opposition of the whole world.'"[19]

This emphasis on the external Word as the medium of God's saving action is the line that separates the Reformers from what they regarded as the "enthusiasm" (from "God-within-ism") common to Rome and the radical Protestants. The Reformers rejected the belief that the living voice of the Spirit through popes, prophets, or private individuals made the otherwise dead letter of Scripture relevant, direct, and contemporary. We do not make God's Word "living and active"; this is what it is in itself. Following the logic of Romans 10, Calvin emphasizes that we must refuse any contrast between the outer and inner word.[20] In fact, Paul "not only makes himself a co-worker with God, but also assigns himself the function of imparting salvation."[21] Without the work of the Spirit, the Word would fall on deaf ears, but the Spirit opens deaf ears *through* the external Word.[22] The same view is found in the Second Helvetic Confession, written by Bullinger.

---

[16] Selderhuis, *Calvin's Theology of the Psalms*, 119. See Calvin's commentary on Ps. 119:49.
[17] John H. Leith, "Doctrine of the Proclamation of the Word," in Timothy George, ed., *John Calvin and the Church: A Prism of Reform* (Louisville: Westminster John Knox, 1990), 212.
[18] Ibid., 210–11.
[19] Selderhuis, *Calvin's Theology of the Psalms*, 121, on Ps. 110:3.
[20] Calvin, *Institutes* 4.1.5–6.
[21] Ibid., 4.1.6.
[22] Calvin, *Commentary on the Gospel of John, The Gospel According to John*, vol. 1:1–10, trans. T. H. L. Parker, Calvin's New Testament Commentaries 4, ed. David W. Torrance and Thomas F. Torrance (Grand Rapids: Eerdmans, 1959–1972), on John 15:27.

We consider "the Word itself which is preached . . . , not the minister that preaches; for even if he be evil and a sinner, nevertheless the Word of God remains still true and good."[23] At a time when we place so much weight on the charisma, personality, and even the exegetical skills and godliness of the messenger, this is a good reminder. Not only the message, but the medium too is considered foolish in the eyes of the world; indeed, ministers are but frail vessels carrying a weighty treasure.

It is not only preaching, but the preaching of the Word—and not only the preaching of the Word, but the preaching of the *gospel*—that is assigned the special role as a means of grace. Especially from Paul, assisted by Augustine's *Spirit and the Letter*, Luther came to distinguish the law and the gospel as the two ways in which God speaks to us.[24] This emphasis is just as clear in Calvin (as well as his Reformed colleagues and theological heirs).[25]

Calvin points out that for Paul, "faith through the word of the gospel" is the proper formula. When Paul specifically refers to "the word of faith that we proclaim" (Rom. 10:8), he means the gospel.[26] "Faith is not produced by every part of the Word of God, for the warnings, admonitions and threatened judgments will not instill the confidence and peace requisite for true faith."[27] Sometimes God's speech brings judgment, disaster, fear, warning, and dread, Calvin reminds us.[28] While everything that God says is true, useful, and full of impact, not everything that God says is *saving*. Scripture repeatedly identifies this saving power of the Word with the gospel (for example, Rom. 1:16; 10:6–17; 1 Pet. 1:23–24). "For although faith believes every word of God, it rests solely on the word of grace or mercy, the promise of God's fatherly goodwill," which is only realized in and through Christ.[29] "For in God faith seeks life," says Calvin, "which is not to be found

---

[23] The Second Helvetic Confession, chap. 1.

[24] Martin Luther, *The Proper Distinction between Law and Gospel: Thirty-Nine Evening Lectures*, trans. W. H. T. Dau: "Hence," wrote Luther, "whoever knows well this art of distinguishing between the Law and the Gospel, him place at the head and call him a doctor of Holy Scripture." See the Apology to the Augsburg Confession (1531), art. 4. Art. 5 of the Formula of Concord adds, "We believe, teach, and confess that the distinction between the Law and the Gospel is to be maintained in the Church with great diligence." *Triglot Concordia: The Symbolical Books of the Evangelical Lutheran Church*, ed. and trans. F. Bente and W. H. T. Dau (St. Louis: Concordia, 1921).

[25] Wilhelm Niesel observes, "Reformed theology recognises the contrast between Law and Gospel, in a way similar to Lutheranism. We read in the Second Helvetic Confession: 'The Gospel is indeed opposed to the Law. For the Law works wrath and pronounces a curse, whereas the Gospel preaches grace and blessing'" (Wilhelm Niesel, *Reformed Symbolics: A Comparison of Catholicism, Orthodoxy and Protestantism*, trans. David Lewis [Edinburgh: Oliver and Boyd, 1962], 217.) See Michael Horton, "Calvin and the Law-Gospel Hermeneutic," *Pro Ecclesia* 6, no. 1 (1997): 27–42; Horton, "Law and Gospel, with Response by Mark Garcia," in *The Confessional Presbyterian* 8 (2012).

[26] Calvin on Rom. 10:8, in *Calvin's Commentaries*, 19:389–91.

[27] I. John Hesselink, *Calvin's Concept of the Law* (Allison Park, PA: Pickwick, 1992), 28.

[28] Calvin, *Institutes* 3.2.7, 29.

[29] Ibid., 3.2.28–30.

in commandments or the pronouncement of penalties, but in the promise of mercy—and only a free promise."[30]

The only safe route, therefore, is to receive the Father through the incarnate Son. Christ is the saving content of Scripture, the very substance of its unified message.[31] "This is the true knowledge of Christ: if we take him as he is offered by the Father, namely, *clothed with his gospel*. For as he himself has been designated the goal of our faith, so we shall not run straight to him unless the gospel leads the way."[32] Without the clear and regular proclamation of the gospel, faith shrivels along with its fruit.

Once this sacramental aspect of God's Word is embraced, we are able also to affirm that it teaches us truths to be believed and exhorts us to obey its commands. It not only creates and sustains our faith, but also regulates our doctrine and life.

Preaching and Preachers

Aside from special events with visits from famous preachers, sermons were rare before the Reformation.[33] Especially after he returned to Geneva with a clear mandate for reform, Calvin emphasized—and exemplified—what it meant to preach the Scriptures, from Genesis to Revelation, in their ordinary sense. As W. Robert Godfrey observes, Calvin said that no matter how flattered, entertained, or attracted people are, the purpose of preaching is the *edification* of the saints. He said:

> "If I do not procure the edification of those who hear me, I am a sacrilege, profaning God's Word." Edification is central to proper preaching: "For God will have his people edified. . . . When we come together in the name of God, it is not to hear merry songs and to be fed with wind, that is vain and unprofitable curiosity, but to receive spiritual nourishment."[34]

Calvin asked Cardinal Sadoleto, "Do you remember what kind of time it was when our Reformers appeared, and what kind of doctrine candidates for the ministry learned in the schools?" Surely Calvin could speak to this from his own memory. "With what skill, I ask, did they edify the Church?"

---

[30] Ibid., 3.2.29.
[31] Ibid., 1.13.7.
[32] Ibid., 3.2.6, emphasis added.
[33] Scott M. Manetsch, *Calvin's Company of Pastors: Pastoral Care and the Emerging Reformed Church, 1536–1609* (New York: Oxford University Press, 2012), 147.
[34] W. Robert Godfrey, *John Calvin: Pilgrim and Pastor* (Wheaton, IL: Crossway, 2009), 67.

"Nay, what one sermon was there from which old wives might not carry off more whimsies than they could devise at their own fireside in a month?" The first half was devoted to "those misty questions of the schools which might astonish the rude populace, while the second contained sweet stories or amusing speculations by which the hearers might be kept awake." Calvin adds, "Only a few expressions were thrown in from the Word of God, that by their majesty they might procure credit for these frivolities."[35]

Calvin thought that sermons were to follow the humanist rule of "brevity and simplicity," with rhetoric serving rather than obscuring the content of what was proclaimed. The Company of Pastors determined that church services should not exceed one hour.[36] In edifying preaching, "teaching and exhortation 'must be conjoined, and they must never be separated,'" Calvin exhorted.[37] Furthermore, as Scott Manetsch notes, "Calvin the preacher almost never spoke of his personal affairs from the pulpit."[38] To be sure, this reticence came more easily to Calvin than to most, given his private personality. Nevertheless, he was truly convinced that the preacher's calling is to make Christ, not himself, known; the preacher is simply an ambassador, never the King.

To underscore this priority of the ministry of Christ over the personality of the minister, Geneva's pastors and city council approved Calvin's rule that ministers (including himself) rotate among the different parishes. Manetsch explains:

> The preacher was not the proprietor of a pulpit or the captain of his congregation: it was Christ who presided over his church through the Word. At least in theory, ministers of the Christian gospel were interchangeable. So too, the rotation system probably encouraged collegiality between ministers as they worked with different colleagues in different parish churches during the week and sometimes had the opportunity to hear one another preach.[39]

There is an irony in contemporary ministry, where even among churches committed to expository preaching there is a tendency to attach greater importance to the preacher than to the Word itself. We often speak

---

[35] Calvin, "Reply by John Calvin to Cardinal Sadoleto's Letter," in *Selected Works of John Calvin: Tracts and Letters*, ed. Henry Beveridge and Jules Bonnet, 7 vols. (Grand Rapids: Baker, 1983), 1:40.
[36] Manetsch, *Calvin's Company of Pastors*, 153.
[37] Ibid., 161, from Calvin's commentary on 1 Tim. 4:12–13.
[38] Ibid., 162.
[39] Ibid., 150.

of "So-and-So's church." Calvin not only discouraged the cult of celebrity; he sought to structure the ministry in such a way that the region's pulpits belonged to Christ and his Word rather than to any pastor.

The Word of God is proclaimed not only in the sermon, but also throughout the liturgy: from the invocation to the benediction. Paul instructs Timothy, "Devote yourself to the public reading of Scripture," as well as teaching and exhortation (1 Tim. 4:13). Indeed, the Word is spoken to the people and back to God from the people even in the sung prayers and praises (Col. 3:16). It is spoken throughout the service, from the invocation and God's greeting all the way to the benediction. Especially important as an element in regular services were confession and absolution.

Confession and Absolution

The Roman Catholic system of penance involves a series of steps as conditions for receiving God's forgiveness or absolution: (1) sorrow, (2) private confession of each sin to a priest, (3) making satisfaction or restitution as determined by the priest, and (4) sincere intention never to commit the sin again. Upon fulfilling these obligations one can be absolved of particular sins. According to Calvin, this system of penance is a travesty of New Testament repentance and forgiveness.[40] The Anabaptists also carried this legalistic rigor into their discipline. Both failed to see confession and absolution in a sufficiently evangelical light, Calvin argues.

It is indeed true that God's mercy is sincerely invoked with repentance, Calvin acknowledges.

> But we added at the same time that repentance is not the cause of forgiveness of sins. Moreover, we have done away with those torments of souls which they would have us perform as a duty. We have taught that the sinner does not dwell upon his own compunction or tears, but fixes both eyes upon the Lord's mercy alone. We have merely reminded him that Christ called those who "labor and are heavy-laden," when he was sent to publish the good news to the poor, to heal the broken-hearted, to proclaim release to the captives, to free the prisoners, to comfort the mourners.[41]

---

[40] Calvin, *Institutes* 3.4.2: "But I would have my readers note that this is no contention over the shadow of an ass, but that the most serious matter of all is under discussion: namely, forgiveness of sins. . . . Unless this knowledge remains clear and sure, the conscience will have no rest at all, no peace with God, no assurance or security; but it continuously trembles, wavers, tosses, is tormented and vexed, shakes, hates, and flees the sight of God. But if forgiveness of sins depends on these conditions which they attach to it, nothing is more miserable or deplorable for us."

[41] Ibid., 3.4.3.

Calvin had no intention of starting over from scratch, but instead sought to reform the liturgy in an evangelical direction. Like other Reformed leaders, he did not see absolution as a third sacrament, as Luther did, but saw it as part of the regular ministry of the Word in public and in private.

First, these elements were stripped of their works-righteousness. Repentance is included in daily conversion. "But the perpetual rule of Christ . . . is that conscience must not be brought into bondage," Calvin insists. "Besides, the law on which our opponents insist is one which can only torture souls, and ultimately destroy them." The frivolous are confirmed in their hypocrisy and indulgence, while the serious-minded believer is led to despair.[42] *God* does not need confession as a good work we perform in order for him to absolve us; rather, *we* need to confess our sins and to receive the assurance of pardon from our merciful Father.

Second, confession and absolution began the regular *public* service in the ancient church, as seen especially in the liturgy of John Chrysostom (AD 390). Little in the medieval service was intelligible to the average layperson; confession and absolution were done in private, one-on-one. Even baptism was buried in superstitious rites and was usually performed in private, with only the family and godparents. All of these rites were revised by the Reformers in an evangelical direction and were now performed in the public service. Although baptism is received only once, its effects avail for our whole life, and we receive its benefits whenever we gather. The Lord does not merely "admit us into the Church" by forgiving our sins, "but by the same means He preserves and defends us in it." Every godly person knows that it would not be sufficient to experience this absolution only once, in the beginning, "for there is none who is not conscious, during his whole life, of many infirmities which stand in need of divine mercy." With good reason, then, God "orders the same message of reconciliation to be daily delivered to them." "Wherefore, as during our whole lives we carry about with us the remains of sin, we could not continue in the Church one single moment were we not sustained by the uninterrupted grace of God in forgiving our sins."[43]

---

[42] Calvin, "The Necessity of Reforming the Church," in *Selected Works of John Calvin*, 1:179. See also Calvin, "Articles Agreed Upon by the Faculty of Sacred Theology of Paris, with Antidote (1542)," in *Selected Works of John Calvin*, 1:79. He points out here that auricular confession (much less satisfaction) was not required before Innocent III in 1213, and he quotes Chrysostom's explicit statements against its necessity for forgiveness.

[43] Calvin, *Institutes* 4.1.20.

Calvin followed Bucer's form with few alterations. Facing the people, the minister leads the congregation in singing the Ten Commandments, with the *Kyrie eleison* (the publican's plea, "Lord, have mercy") sung after each commandment. There followed a public confession of sin, words of comfort from various passages (John 3:16; 1 Tim. 1:15; etc.), and then the absolution: "So in His Name do I pronounce forgiveness unto you of all your sins, and I declare you to be loosed of them in earth so that ye may be loosed of them also in heaven and in all eternity. Amen." This is also the form found in the Book of Common Prayer, which Bucer helped Cranmer revise.

There is great assurance in being gathered by the triune God to confess our sins and receive Christ's forgiveness as an official public act through the lips of a fellow believer called to proclaim Christ's Word in his name. "And indeed, we see this custom observed with good result in well-regulated churches. . . . In short, with this key a gate to prayer is opened both to individuals in private and to all in public."[44]

Third, although all believers are priests, absolution was especially the duty of the minister by virtue of his office and calling to exercise the keys of the kingdom. He joins the congregation in confession and speaks the word of pardon in Christ's name, binding and loosing in accordance with Matthew 16:19; 18:9–18; and John 20:23. "When you hear that this is attributed to them, recognize that it is for your benefit."[45]

Fourth, Calvin also encouraged those struggling with anxieties and doubts to avail themselves of private confession and absolution. Abuses do not justify dispensing with such a useful and scriptural remedy: "Namely, that, for his relief, he should use private confession to his own pastor . . . whose duty it is, both publicly and privately, to comfort the people of God by the gospel teaching." "But," Calvin adds, "he should always observe this rule: that where God prescribes nothing definite, consciences be not bound with a definite yoke." Believers should avail themselves of this opportunity as they sense the need and "neither be forced by any rule nor be induced by any trick to recount all their sins." By exercising this aspect of their calling, he says, "faithful pastors" will "avoid tyranny in their ministry and superstition in the people."[46] Here, as other places, we see Calvin's conservative pastoral instincts—reforming corrupted practices while recognizing the biblical and evangelical core that had been obscured.

---

[44] Ibid., 3.4.11.
[45] Ibid., 3.4.12.
[46] Ibid.

Holy Baptism: A Gift That Keeps on Giving

"Christ communicates his riches and blessings to us by his word," writes Calvin, "so he distributes them to us by his sacraments."[47] The Spirit creates faith through the Word, says Calvin. "But the sacraments bring the clearest promises."[48] "For baptism attests to us that we have been cleansed and washed; the Eucharistic Supper, that we have been redeemed."[49] Ironically, Calvin saw in both Roman Catholic and Anabaptist views a common tendency to treat sacraments as human works. However, Calvin argues, "In Sacraments God alone properly acts; men bring nothing of their own."[50] God is the promise maker. "Baptism testifies to us our purgation and ablution; the Eucharistic supper testifies our redemption. Water is a figure of ablution [washing], and blood of satisfaction."[51] The sacraments are first and foremost God's testimony to us, and secondarily "serve our confession before men."[52]

Anabaptists lodged the efficacy of baptism in the believer's act of promising. What Calvin calls the secondary benefit they made the primary—indeed, entire essence—of the sacrament. Zwingli also tended in this direction, comparing the sacraments to a badge or insignia worn by a soldier. However, Calvin says that

> those who regarded baptism as nothing but a token and mark by which we confess our religion before men, as soldiers bear the insignia of their commander as a mark of their profession, have not weighed what was the chief point of baptism. It is to receive baptism with this promise: "He who believes and is baptized will be saved" [Mark 16:16].[53]

All of the Reformed confessions, even the one written by Zwingli's successor, Heinrich Bullinger, explicitly reject the view that sacraments are merely badges of our Christian profession.

God is the active agent in baptism and what he outwardly represents he actually gives. As in the preached Word, baptism is not just a symbol teaching us about God's saving grace, but also a means of grace. God himself is

---

[47] Calvin, "Form for Administration of the Sacraments," in *Selected Works of John Calvin*, 2:115.
[48] Calvin, *Institutes* 4.14.5.
[49] Ibid., 4.14.22.
[50] Calvin, "Antidote to the Council of Trent," in *Selected Works of John Calvin*, 3:176.
[51] Calvin, *Institutes* 4.14.22.
[52] Ibid., 4.15.1.
[53] Ibid.

acting through the sacrament. In baptism Christ attests that he has forgiven our sins, triumphed over Satan, and made us sharers in Christ's death and resurrection. "These things, I say, he performs for our soul within as truly and surely as we see our body outwardly cleansed, submerged, and surrounded with water. . . . And he does not feed our eyes with a mere appearance only, but leads us to the present reality and effectively performs what it symbolizes."[54] Calvin says that "our faith receives from baptism the advantage of its sure testimony to us that we are not only engrafted into the death and life of Christ, but so united to Christ himself that we become sharers in all his blessings." Hence, we are baptized in the name of Christ. "For all the gifts of God proffered in baptism are found in Christ alone." "Yet this cannot take place," he adds, "unless he who baptizes in Christ invokes also the names of the Father and the Spirit. . . . For this reason we obtain and, so to speak, clearly discern in the Father the cause, in the Son the matter, and in the Spirit the effect of our purgation and our regeneration."[55] "Baptism, viewed in regard to us, is a passive work . . . and all that belongs to it is laid up in Christ."[56]

Everyone is born in original sin, so there is no "age of accountability." "Through baptism, believers are assured that this condemnation has been removed and withdrawn from them . . . by imputation only, since the Lord of his own mercy considers them righteous and innocent."[57]

Obviously, if baptism is the believer's act of faith and repentance, children cannot be included.[58] The horizon for Calvin's understanding of the sacraments is the covenant of grace, in which God pledges his mercy to believers and their children. God's promise comes before ours. In fact, his promise creates our response. As heirs of the same Abrahamic promise—the one covenant of grace—the children of believers are to receive the sign of God's pledge. So "baptism has taken the place of circumcision to fulfill the same office among us."[59] Calvin points to examples of household baptisms in the New Testament and the continuation of the practice in the post-apostolic church. There is simply no gap in history where infant baptism was suddenly introduced.[60]

---

[54] Ibid., 4.15.14.
[55] Ibid., 4.15.6.
[56] Calvin on Galatians, in *Calvin's Commentaries*, vol. 21, trans. William Pringle (Grand Rapids: Baker, 1996), 150.
[57] Ibid., 4.15.10.
[58] Calvin defends the baptism of covenant children at length in *Institutes* 4.16.1–29.
[59] Ibid., 4.16.4.
[60] Ibid., 4.16.8.

Accordingly, let those who embrace the promise that God's mercy is to be extended to their children deem it their duty to offer them to the church to be sealed by the symbol of mercy, and thereby to arouse themselves to a surer confidence, because they see with their very eyes the covenant of the Lord engraved upon the bodies of their children. On the other hand, the children receive some benefit from their baptism: being engrafted into the body of the church, they are somewhat more commended to the other members. Then, when they have grown up, they are greatly spurred to an earnest zeal for worshiping God, by whom they were received as children through a solemn symbol of adoption before they were old enough to recognize him as Father.

Furthermore, it is a warning to those who despise God's promise and refuse to embrace Christ through faith.[61]

As the sign and seal of the gospel itself, baptism is not effective merely for the past, so that some new sacrament or act of rededication is required. Only a weak view of baptism could account for the addition of sacraments like penance. "But we must realize that at whatever time we are baptized, we are once for all washed and purged for our whole life. Therefore, as often as we fall away, we ought to recall the memory of our baptism and fortify our mind with it, that we may always be sure and confident of the forgiveness of sins."[62] Its efficacy is "not destroyed by subsequent sins," but on the contrary, gives us a place to stand in lifelong faith and repentance.[63]

The Lord's Supper: Communion with Christ and His Body

In the Supper our Lord spreads a lavish table in the wilderness to sustain our pilgrim journey. It is a tragedy that different interpretations of the sacrament of union with Christ and communion with his body have occasioned so much division. Yet, as J. Gresham Machen observed, worse than the differences among the churches of the Reformation is the indifferentism of our age, where debates like this don't even matter.[64] Christians who take the Supper seriously enough to disagree over it have more in common with each other than they do with many today who ignore or trivialize it. All of the Reformers agreed among themselves and with Rome on the point

---

[61] Ibid,, 4.16.9.
[62] Ibid., 4.15.3.
[63] Ibid.
[64] J. Gresham Machen, *Christianity and Liberalism* (1923; repr., Grand Rapids: Eerdmans, 1946), 50–51.

that the Supper lies at the heart of the person of Christ, the Christian life, and the nature of the church.

We are redeemed by the *historical* body of Christ, given for us on the cross and raised in indestructible life. The bread and wine in the Supper give us his *eucharistic* body. United to Christ through faith, we constitute together Christ's *mystical* body, the church. So, along with the Word and baptism, the Supper stands at the intersection of our union with Christ and communion with his body. As some Roman Catholic theologians have argued in recent decades, late medieval theology had tended to collapse the mystical into the eucharistic body, with the result that the Mass became an end in itself rather than leading to the ultimate miracle and mystery: namely, the mystical union of Head and members in one body.[65] Calvin was concerned to distinguish these references without separating them.

Calvin confirms the observation that the medieval church had reduced the Lord's Supper to a shadow of its former self. "For, provided men went once a year to the Lord's Table, they thought it enough, for all the remainder of that period, to be spectators of what was done by the priest, under the pretext, indeed, of administering the Lord's Supper, but without any vestige of the Supper in it."[66] Laypeople never received the cup, but only the bread. Where Jesus bid his disciples to eat the bread and drink the wine, now all that was left was "the vulgar gazing upon them in stupid amazement."[67]

By contrast, Calvin says that in evangelical services believers receive "the body and blood of Christ." "Nor do we thus teach that the bread and wine are symbols, without immediately adding that there is a truth [reality] which is conjoined with them and which they represent."[68] I have discussed the sixteenth-century debates over the Supper in detail elsewhere.[69] Here I will only summarize Calvin's view briefly in that context.

Luther rejected the Roman Catholic doctrine of transubstantiation. Instead of the reality annihilating and replacing the signs, Christ joins himself to the signs—bodily, in and with the elements of bread and wine. Therefore, everyone who receives the signs eats and drinks the body and

---

[65] See especially Henri de Lubac, *Corpus Mysticum: The Eucharist and the Church in the Middle Ages*, trans. Gemma Simmonds, CJ (South Bend, IN: University of Notre Dame Press, 2007).

[66] Calvin, "The Necessity of Reforming the Church," 167.

[67] Ibid., 168.

[68] Ibid., 169.

[69] Michael Horton, *People and Place: A Covenant Ecclesiology* (Louisville: Westminster John Knox, 2008), 99–152; cf. Horton, *The Christian Faith: A Systematic Theology for Pilgrims on the Way* (Grand Rapids: Zondervan, 2011), 751–827.

blood of Christ. This can happen because Christ's divine nature so penetrates his human nature that he can be even physically omnipresent. Zwingli held that this view of Luther's was exegetically strained: Jesus did not say, "This body is present with the wine," so Luther himself is not as literal as he pretends. Furthermore, nobody imagines that Jesus spoke literally when he called himself a door, a gate, a cornerstone, and a ladder.[70] More importantly, turning Jesus Christ into an omnipresent or ubiquitous body leads to a "monstrous phantasm" rather than the glorified Savior who walked the earth and will return at the end of the age. Instead, Zwingli argued, since Christ's omnipresent divinity is saving anyway, there is no need to be united to his flesh. In the Supper we remember the work of Jesus Christ, long for his return, and testify to the world that we belong to him.

Luther and Zwingli met at Marburg in 1529. They agreed on fourteen of fifteen points, but the brick wall was Christ's presence in the Supper. Luther's associate, Philipp Melanchthon, counseled no further concessions to Zwinglians. To Zwingli, Luther's view of Christ was monophysite: the heresy of *confusing* Christ's natures. For his part, Luther thought that Zwingli was a Nestorian: one who *separated* the two natures. While rejecting Luther's notion of Christ's bodily omnipresence, Bucer and other Reformed leaders distanced themselves from Zwingli's view, and considerable agreement was achieved in the Wittenberg Concord in 1536.

Calvin stepped into this maelstrom and made no secret of his disagreements with Zwingli. He even told Bullinger that if a comparison had to be made, "you yourself know how much Luther is to be preferred."[71] To another colleague he wrote that Zwingli's view of the Supper is "wrong and pernicious."[72] "It would be extreme madness to recognize no communion of believers with the flesh and blood of the Lord," he asserts in the *Institutes*.[73]

First, the Genevan Reformer rejects all spirit-matter dualism. Where Zwingli can only force a choice between God's action and creaturely action, Calvin says, "Whatever implements God employs, they detract nothing from his primary operation."[74] Christ must be truly present in the Supper,

[70] Huldrych Zwingli, "On the Lord's Supper," in *Zwingli and Bullinger*, ed. G. W. Bromiley (Philadelphia: Westminster, 1963), 188–89.
[71] Calvin, quoted in T. H. L. Parker, *John Calvin* (Tring, UK: Lion, 1975), 154.
[72] Calvin, "Letter to Andre Zebedee, May 19, 1539," in *Letters of John Calvin*, ed. Jules Bonnet, trans. Marcus Robert Gilchrist, vol. 4 (Philadelphia: Presbyterian Board of Publications, 1858), 402.
[73] Calvin, *Institutes* 4.17.9.
[74] Ibid., 4.14.17.

giving himself together with all of his benefits. Otherwise, faith becomes a "mere imagining" of Christ's presence.[75]

Second, Calvin reproves Zwingli's tendency to separate Christ's two natures and thus downplay the saving significance of his humanity. "For in his flesh was accomplished man's redemption."[76] Furthermore, "The gift is Jesus Christ himself," not only his divinity but the whole Christ; his gifts are inseparable from his person. When we receive the bread and the wine, says Calvin, "let us no less surely trust that the body itself is also given to us."[77] The signs are "guarantees of a present reality: the believer's feeding on the body and blood of Christ."[78] Carl Trueman is not going too far to suggest that Zwingli and Calvin represent two different understandings of the incarnation.[79] Our salvation depends on our union with *Christ*—the whole Christ, his humanity as well as his divinity.

In his *Short Treatise on the Holy Supper*, which Luther reportedly approved, Calvin wrote, "All the benefit which we would seek in the Supper is annihilated if Jesus Christ be not given to us as the substance and foundation of all."[80] Zwingli does not understand why we must be united to Christ's flesh, because he so emphasizes his deity alone as saving. Yet, especially drawing on the Eastern fathers, Calvin writes, "The flesh of Christ is like a rich and inexhaustible fountain that pours into us the life springing forth from the Godhead into itself. Now who does not see that communion of Christ's flesh and blood is necessary for all who aspire to heavenly life?"[81] The bread and wine neither *become the gift*, as in Rome's view, nor simply *remind us of the gift*, as Zwingli implied; rather, *the Spirit gives us Christ* when we receive the bread and the wine as his saving pledge.[82]

On this point—namely, *what* we receive in the Supper—Calvin agrees fully with Luther.[83] Especially in the *Institutes* 4.17.6, Calvin underscores

---

[75] Ibid., 4.17.5–6.

[76] Calvin, *The Gospel According to John*, 167.

[77] Calvin, *Institutes* 4.17.10.

[78] Gerrish, *Grace and Gratitude*, 165.

[79] Carl Trueman, "The Incarnation and the Lord's Supper," in *The Word Became Flesh: Evangelicals and the Incarnation*, ed. David Peterson (Carlisle, UK: Paternoster, 2003), 227–50.

[80] Calvin, "Short Treatise on the Holy Supper," in *Selected Works of John Calvin*, 2:170.

[81] Calvin, *Institutes* 4.17.9.

[82] Calvin, *De la Cene*, OS 1:508; *Theological Treatises* 2:170; cf. *Confessio fidei de eucharistia* (1537), OS 1:435–36 (Library of Christian Classics 22:168–69; 4.17.7, 9).

[83] Gerrish, *Grace and Gratitude*, 8. "Later, after Marburg," as Gerrish points out, "it was repeatedly argued that the point at issue between the Lutherans and the Reformed was no longer whether, but only how, the body and blood of Christ were present in the Sacrament. Calvin himself so argued." Since even Bullinger (Zwingli's successor) came to embrace the sacramental union of sign and signified, the focus was on *what* is received (Christ and all of his benefits) in the Supper, rather than on the *manner* of eating—in other words, presence as such.

this point that "the Supper is a gift; it does not merely remind us of a gift." As with receiving the gospel through the preached Word, in the sacrament we are receivers: it is "an *actio mere passiva* (a 'purely passive action')."[84] "From the very first," notes Gerrish, Calvin "was convinced that Zwingli was wrong about the principal agent in both baptism and the Lord's Supper. A sacrament is first and foremost an act of God or Christ rather than of the candidate, the communicant, or the church."[85] Calvin adds, "And we ought carefully to observe, that the chief, and almost the whole energy of the sacrament, consists in these words, 'It is broken for you: it is shed for you.'"[86] In other words, Communion is not the church's sacrifice—either of atonement or of praise. Rather, it is God's act of ratifying his promise to each person who receives Christ in the sacrament by faith. The human response to a gift is thanksgiving, says Calvin, which is why it is called the Eucharist (from the Greek word meaning "I give thanks"), in opposition to the sacrifice of the Mass offered by the priest on behalf of the people. "The sacrifice differs from the Sacrament of the Supper as widely as giving differs from receiving," Calvin says.[87]

Luther, however, in his explanation of *how* Christ can be present in every eucharistic celebration, introduced a novel and problematic element into the doctrine of Christ's person. Jesus prepared his disciples for his bodily ascension and taught clearly that he would return in the same way at the end of the age. He is therefore not bodily present on earth in his historical body until he returns. If his body is everywhere, then it is nowhere.[88] He ascended in exactly the same way in which he will return (Acts 1:11). Until then, he is not present physically on the earth, but he reigns over all things, fills all things by his active energies, and has sent his Spirit to unite us to himself.[89]

Luther and Zwingli were stuck over whether Christ can be present bodily *on earth* (at the altar) prior to his return in glory. Each yielded, respectively, an equally emphatic yes! and no! If Zwingli was right, then Christ is a distant memory until he returns, and we are not united to him here and now. However, Luther's solution threatens the integrity of Christ's humanity: that very bond that we share with him. Of course, Christ is glori-

---

[84] Calvin, *Institutes* 4.14.26.
[85] Gerrish, *Grace and Gratitude*, 204.
[86] In this paragraph I am summarizing his argument especially in chapter 17 of the *Institutes*, book 4.
[87] Calvin, *Institutes* 4.18.7.
[88] Ibid., 4.17.7.
[89] Ibid., 4.14.9, 12.

fied. But if our humanity is radically different from his, then how can we entertain the hope that we will be like him, that he is the firstborn from the dead, the firstfruits of the harvest? How can we affirm Jesus's own teaching that he would physically ascend and would return bodily only at the end of the age? And how can Jesus say at the same time that he is present with his church to the end of the age? These are not philosophical speculations, but questions provoked by numerous and explicit texts of Scripture. Furthermore, the most crucial question of all is at stake: our salvation. After all, if there is no true communion with Christ's body and blood in the Supper, then there cannot be any true union with Christ.

The real question, Calvin argues, is whether Christ can be present *in the sacrament* without being present *at the altar* or table. The bread and wine are "not empty symbols," Calvin insists, "but communicate the reality they signify." How? By Christ coming down bodily to every altar where the Supper is celebrated or by the believer's intellectual ascent? No, but by the energy of the *Holy Spirit* who unites us to the ascended and glorified Christ.

Everything that Calvin says about communion with Christ in the Supper assumes his treatment of union with Christ. We are clearly told that the Spirit has "raised us" spiritually and "seated us with Christ in heavenly places" (Eph. 2:6). We cannot be united merely to Christ's spirit, his divinity, or even the Holy Spirit, but must be united to the *whole Christ*. Calvin rejects Zwingli's contention that it is "tortured exegesis" to see the Supper in the marriage analogy of Ephesians 5. "'We are bone of his bone and flesh of his flesh' (Gen. 2:23) not [merely] because, like ourselves he has a human nature, but because, by the power of his Spirit, he makes us a part of his body, so that from him we derive our life."[90] Indeed, Paul confesses, "This mystery is profound" (Eph. 5:32). "Those who refuse to admit anything on this subject beyond what their own capacity can reach act an exceedingly foolish part." For his own part, Calvin says he will join the apostle "in acknowledging at once my ignorance and my admiration. . . . Let us therefore labor more to feel Christ living in us than to discover the nature of that communion."[91] So far was Calvin from being a rationalist that he could say that the mystery of the Supper is "a secret too sublime for my mind to understand or words to express. I experience it rather than understand it."[92]

[90] Calvin on Eph. 5:30–31, in *Calvin's Commentaries*, 21:323.
[91] Ibid., 324–25.
[92] Calvin, quoted in G. R. Potter and M. Greengrass, *John Calvin* (London: Edward Arnold, 1983), 34.

Calvin never describes his view as "spiritual presence." Christ is truly present in the Supper, not just in our imagination or memory. Yet it is the Holy Spirit who unites us to him so that we feed on his body and blood unto everlasting life. "The Spirit makes things which are widely separated by space to be united with each other, and accordingly causes life from the flesh of Christ to reach us from heaven."[93] It is the Spirit who mysteriously brings about the sacramental union of sign and reality.[94] Christ is neither enclosed in the bread and the wine nor separate from them. Our participation in Christ now is real, but it is not yet that fully realized experience we will have when he returns to consummate his kingdom. From Calvin's perspective, Luther's view of Christ's bodily presence on earth is an over-realized eschatology, while Zwingli's is under-realized, and the therapy for both is a robust doctrine of the Holy Spirit.

Calvin also believed that this gift is presented to everyone who receives the Supper, believer and unbeliever alike. Just as the Word of God remains what it is regardless of whether people embrace Christ, unbelief cannot render a sacrament ineffective. "The integrity of the Sacrament, which the whole world cannot violate," says Calvin, "lies in this: that the flesh and blood of Christ are no less truly given to the unworthy than to God's elect believers."[95] At the same time, the reality is embraced only through faith. "The sacramental word is not an incantation," Gerrish summarizes, "but a promise." "The eucharistic gift therefore benefits those only who respond with the faith that the proclamation itself generates."[96]

Interpreting Christ's words, "This is my body," Paul does not say that the bread and cup are *empty signs*; nor that they *are converted into* Christ's body and blood; nor that Christ's body and blood are *in, with, and under* the bread and cup. Rather, he says that the bread and wine are "*a participation in*" the body and blood of Christ (1 Cor. 10:16).[97] Calvin also quotes a raft of church fathers, from Irenaeus to Cyprian, Fulgentius, and Augustine, for support. He adds that the part of the ancient Communion liturgy invoking the Spirit and calling the congregation to lift up its heart to the Lord presupposes the doctrine he has elaborated.[98]

If, unlike Zwingli, we affirm that the substance of the sacrament is

---

[93] Calvin, "The Best Method of Obtaining Concord," in *Selected Works of John Calvin*, 2:578.
[94] Calvin, *Institutes* 4.17.12.
[95] Ibid., 4.17.33.
[96] Gerrish, *Grace and Gratitude*, 139; see Calvin, *Institutes* 4.14.4; 4.17.15.
[97] Calvin, *Institutes* 4.17.22.
[98] Calvin, "The Necessity of Reforming the Church," 83–85.

Christ's true and natural body, Calvin wonders, "What could be more ridiculous than to split the churches and stir up frightful commotions" over *how* this happens?[99] The only pious conclusion, he says, is "to break forth in wonder at this mystery, which plainly neither the mind is able to conceive nor the tongue to express."[100]

To Luther's emphasis on the descent of Christ to us, Calvin adds the equally Pauline emphasis also on the Spirit's work of seating us with Christ in heavenly places. As Philip Walker Butin explains concerning Calvin's view:

> There is "a manner of descent by which he lifts us up to himself." Not only does Christ (in the Spirit) condescend to manifest himself to believers by means of visible, tangible, created elements; at the same time by the Spirit, the worshiping church is drawn into the heavenly worship of the Father though the mediation of the ascended Christ, who is seated with the Father in the heavenlies. For Calvin, this accentuates, rather than diminishes, the true humanity of Christ.[101]

With such a robust view of the efficacy of the Supper, Calvin offered a sustained plea that the Supper should be celebrated whenever the Word is preached, "or at least once a week."[102] This was one argument that Calvin lost in his many skirmishes with Geneva's magistrates. Yet he insisted on including Communion in his regular liturgy to show that it belonged in every service. "I have taken care to record publicly that our custom is defective," he said, "so that those who come after me may be able to correct it more freely and easily."[103]

Union with Christ and the Communion of Saints

United to Christ, we are simultaneously united to his body. Because we truly feed on Christ in the Supper, we are drawn "both to purity and holi-

---

[99] Calvin, *Defensio doctrinae de sacramentis*, OS 2:287.
[100] Ibid.
[101] Philip Walker Butin, *Revelation, Redemption and Response: Calvin's Trinitarian Understanding of the Divine-Human Relationship* (New York: Oxford University Press, 1995), 118.
[102] Calvin, *Institutes* 4.17.44–46. In fact, only a year after the city of Geneva officially embraced the Reformation, Calvin's *Articles for Organization of the Church and Worship at Geneva* (1537) stated, "It is certain that a Church cannot be said to be well ordered and regulated unless in it the Holy Supper of our Lord is always being celebrated and frequented." "Articles concerning the Organization of the Church and of Worship at Geneva Proposed by the Ministers at the Council, January 16, 1537," in *Calvin: Theological Treatises*, ed. and trans. J. K. L. Reid (Philadelphia: Westminster, 1954), 48.
[103] Cited in Godfrey, *John Calvin*, 72.

ness of life, and also to charity, peace, and concord" with each other, as Paul argues in 1 Corinthians 10:14–17. Although each of us receives Christ personally, no one receives him privately. Just as we are made part of his new creation together through the public preaching of the Word, we feed on Christ's body and blood together as coheirs of a common estate. "Christ, presenting himself to us, not only invites us by his example to give and devote ourselves mutually to each other, but inasmuch as he makes himself common to all, [he] also makes us all to be one in him." From the fellowship with Christ in the Supper,

> we will take care that none of our brethren is hurt, despised, rejected, injured, or in any way offended, without our, at the same time, hurting, despising, and injuring Christ; that we cannot have dissension with our brethren, without at the same time dissenting from Christ; that we cannot love Christ without loving our brethren; that the same care we take of our own body we ought to take of that of our brethren, who are members of our body; that as no part of our body suffers pain without extending to the other parts, so every evil which our brother suffers ought to excite our compassion.[104]

Grace leads to gratitude—a thanksgiving toward God that turns us outward to our brothers and sisters and then also out to our neighbors, whoever they may be.

Luther observed that God does not need our good works, but our neighbors do. Similarly, for Calvin, "The only way to serve God well is to serve our fellow believers. Since our good deeds cannot reach God anyway, he gives us instead other believers unto whom we can do good deeds. The one who wants to love God can do so by loving the believers."[105]

The Word and the sacraments are central in Calvin's understanding of the Christian life. As Richard Gamble summarizes his view, "Entrance into the church by baptism grants to believers all that Christ has for them. After baptism and through careful attention to the preaching of the Word and attendance at the Lord's Supper, the believer is enabled to serve the Lord."[106]

---

[104] Calvin, *Institutes* 4.17.38.
[105] Selderhuis, *Calvin's Theology of the Psalms*, 235.
[106] Richard Gamble, "Calvin and Sixteenth-Century Spirituality: Comparison with the Anabaptists," in *Calvin Studies Society Papers, 1995, 1997: Calvin and Spirituality; Calvin and His Contemporaries*, ed. David Foxgrover (Grand Rapids: CRC Product Services, 1998), 33. Gamble's conclusion itself is a summary of Howard Hageman's survey in "Reformed Spirituality," in *Protestant Spiritual Traditions*, ed. Frank C. Senn (New York: Paulist, 1986), 60–72.

Because God serves us, we can serve our neighbors. Martha L. Moore-Keish is exactly right when she says, "This may be the most valuable and the most challenging thing we can learn from Calvin's ecclesiology today: that the church is not something that we form of our own accord. It is not a product of our reaching out to God, but a gift of God reaching out to us."[107]

---

[107] Martha L. Moore-Keish, "Calvin, Sacraments and Ecclesiology: What Makes a Church a Church," accessed at http://reformedtheology.org/SiteFiles/PublicLectures/Moore-KeishPL.html.

CHAPTER 8

THE PUBLIC SERVICE AS A "CELESTIAL THEATER" OF GRACE

"When I first arrived in this church there was almost nothing. They were preaching and that's all. They were good at seeking out idols and burning them, but there was no Reformation. Everything was in turmoil."[1]

Calvin's recollection of Geneva upon his arrival is well supported by secondary sources. It is also similar to Luther's description of Wittenberg while he was hidden away in the Wartburg Castle and Andreas Karlstadt was in charge. Ironically, many evangelicals were just as committed to religious externals as before—only now they lodged their piety in their *non*observance of Roman externals. Luther complained,

> We try to prove ourselves evangelical by receiving the sacrament in both
> kinds and in our own hands, by pulling down images, by devouring meat,
> by abstaining from prayer and fasting, and that sort of thing. But nobody
> will lay hold of faith and love, which alone are essential, and in which
> alone there is any power.[2]

---

[1] Calvin, quoted in Scott M. Manetsch, *Calvin's Company of Pastors: Pastoral Care and the Emerging Reformed Church, 1536–1609* (New York: Oxford University Press, 2012), 18.
[2] Martin Luther, *Word and Sacrament II*, in *Luther's Works*, American Edition, 55 vols., ed. Jaroslav Pelikan and Helmut T. Lehmann (Philadelphia: Fortress; St. Louis: Concordia, 1955–1986), 36:262.

It is relatively easy to dismantle; the difficult task is to build up, and it was that concern that drove Calvin's reforming passion throughout his tumultuous ministry. The ultimate goal of our salvation is the glory of God. As W. Robert Godfrey reminds us, the reformation of doctrine went hand in hand with the reformation of worship.[3]

The medieval Mass was a theatrical event, and worshipers were more spectators than participants. It is little wonder that the people had to be commanded to attend once a year. Returning to Geneva in 1541, Calvin was eager to implement what he had learned in Strasbourg with respect to the public worship.[4]

Like Luther and Bucer, Calvin sees the public gathering as God's service to us, like Jesus washing the feet of his disciples: "The Son of Man came not to be served but to serve, and to give his life as a ransom for many" (Matt. 20:28). The Christian life is a constant fleeing to the "asylum of forgiveness," and this is how Calvin thinks of the liturgy. Because we cannot ascend to God, he descends to us, Calvin says.[5] The ladders of glory we are told to climb to behold the "naked God" are now marked, "Danger: No Entry." Just as we would not have expected to find God in a feeding trough of a barn in an obscure village, much less hanging, bloody, on a Roman cross, we do not expect to find him delivering his gifts in such humble places and in such humble ways as human speech, a bath, and a meal. Think *cross*, not *glory*.

Come, See God in Action!

Calvin agreed that the divine service is a theater, to be sure. With the early fathers he called it a "celestial theater."[6] Here, heaven and earth embrace. The choir of heavenly hosts singing "Holy, Holy, Holy" is joined

---

[3] Calvin, "On the Necessity of Reforming the Church," in *Selected Works of John Calvin: Tracts and Letters*, ed. Henry Beveridge and Jules Bonnet, 7 vols. (Grand Rapids: Baker, 1983), 1:126. W. Robert Godfrey helpfully explains this dual concern in his *John Calvin: Pilgrim and Pastor* (Wheaton, IL: Crossway, 2009), 77–86.

[4] Luther reformed the mass in an evangelical direction. Zwingli adopted the medieval *prône* liturgy: basically, a service of prayers with a sermon. Although he went further in some of his reforms, Bucer followed Luther's approach: a service of Word and sacrament. Bucer reports the following order: confession and absolution, singing of Psalms and hymns, reading of Scripture, singing the Ten Commandments (sometimes sung before the confession), and the prayer for rulers and the whole church. Then there is the prayer for illumination, the sermon, and the congregational response of singing the Apostles' Creed. Finally, the Supper is celebrated and the benediction is given. Martin Bucer, "The Reign of Christ," in *Melanchthon and Bucer*, ed. Wilhelm Pauck (Philadelphia: Westminster, 1969), 182, 236–59.

[5] Herman J. Selderhuis, *Calvin's Theology of the Psalms* (Grand Rapids: Baker Academic, 2007), 203, on Pss. 42:2 and 24:7.

[6] Ibid., 204, on Ps. 138:1.

by the redeemed choir on earth. "He who wants to 'see' God then must come to church, to the sanctuary of God, where he is 'seen' in the word and sacraments."[7] "On this account," notes Selderhuis, "Calvin rejects the mystical approach. We cannot ascend to God, and indeed we have no need to do so, for in the church service he descends to us and we can see him. . . . It is the Holy Spirit, he insists, who elevates us to heaven *by means of* these external aids."[8] Justified and renewed and strengthened in our faith, we cannot remain silent or passive. We publicly confess our sins and our faith in God's promise, respond in prayer—said and sung—and give of our treasure.[9] The service becomes a covenantal conversation, where the church militant joins its voice with the church triumphant. God gives everything to us; we receive; then we exchange gifts with each other and take our gifts out into the world.

In this public event—this "celestial theater"—the triune God is present and active. "Calvin articulated a new conceptualization of 'liturgy' itself," according to Lee Palmer Wandel.

> For him, certainly, the Supper was a drama, but the source of that drama was God. No human movement could add to that meaning in any way, no crafted object could draw greater attention to those earthly elements. Perhaps most important of all, however, was Calvin's insistence on frequency. Most evangelicals condemned the medieval requirement of annual communion as nonscriptural. . . . But no other evangelical so explicitly situated the Eucharist within a dialogic process not simply of deepening faith, but of the increasing capacity to read the signs of the Supper itself, and by extension, of God, in the world.[10]

"The Supper, for Calvin," she adds, "was not 'external'—a ceremony . . . nor even 'worship' in the sense that other evangelicals, such as Zwingli and Luther, used: a mode of honoring God." Rather, it is a means of binding us together more and more with Christ in an ongoing relationship in which "Christ 'is made completely one with us and we with him.'"[11]

Surely the brightest flower of Reformed liturgies in English is the 1552 Book of Common Prayer, in which Bucer and Vermigli played a large

---

[7] Ibid., 205, on Ps. 27:8.
[8] Ibid., 205, on Pss. 96:6 and 132:7.
[9] Ibid., 207, on Ps. 105:44.
[10] Lee Palmer Wandel, *The Eucharist in the Reformation: Incarnation and Liturgy* (Cambridge: Cambridge University Press, 2006), 171.
[11] Ibid.

role.[12] As in Strasbourg and Geneva, besides the *Te Deum* and the Apostles' or Nicene Creed, the metrical Psalms (set in English by Sternhold and Hopkins) formed the core of praise. The public reading of Scripture went through the whole Bible each year, and the New Testament three times. The people came forward, standing rather than kneeling, to receive Christ's body and blood by faith. Families sat together in pews, instead of men and women being separated as in medieval services. All of this would have been familiar to those in other churches of the Reformation on the continent. Antoine Cathelan, a Franciscan visiting from Paris, wrote a satire of Geneva's service: people are seated "without any distinction of personal rank," he complained. "Everyone sings together while seated, men, women, girls, and infants."[13]

The Arts in Public Worship

Many readers will doubtless assume that in a study of Calvin's approach to the Christian life this topic would be the briefest. After all, Calvin imbued the very interiors as well as the liturgy of Reformed churches with an austere, plain, and even Spartan spirituality. According to some critics, he was possessed by a Platonist suspicion of the senses. Given the obsession with musical and visual media today in "high" and "low" churches alike, it's not surprising that Calvin's more "puritan" approach meets with an almost visceral reaction even among scholars who cannot hide their distaste for such an ostensibly limited vision of the beauty of holiness.

A few brief responses will have to suffice. First, Calvin never appeals to an argument that could be identified as Platonist. If historical precedents are considered, the direct influence would be the Hebrew prophets rather than Plato. It is true that Calvin encourages us to fix our hearts on the heavenly kingdom rather than on earthly temples and sacrifices, but this is based entirely on the New Testament teaching that the shadows of the law have given way to the reality in Christ. "We see the extraordinary insolence that is displayed by men as to the form and manner of worshiping God; for they are perpetually contriving new modes of worship."[14] Else-

---

[12] Diarmaid MacCulloch, *Thomas Cranmer* (New Haven, CT: Yale University Press, 1996), 414–17. At Cranmer's suggestion, Bucer wrote a full revision, titled *Censura*, with twenty-eight chapters of critique and analysis.

[13] Manetsch, *Calvin's Company of Pastors*, 32.

[14] Calvin on Matt. 15:1, in *Calvin's Commentaries*, vol. 16, trans. William Pringle (Grand Rapids: Baker, 1996), 245.

where he says, "They had such an itch for novelty that hardly any space was left for edification."[15]

It is a historical fact that in the earliest centuries Christians sang only songs from Scripture (the Psalms and a few other biblical songs), without instrumental accompaniment, and that representations of God (including the incarnate Son) were forbidden. No pictures, icons, or statues were allowed. Not only Calvin's conclusions but even his arguments are the same as those offered by the ancient fathers.

Visual Representations

In the second century, Irenaeus complained that the Gnostics made painted images of Christ, in violation of Scripture.[16] Justin Martyr rejected visual images in favor of instruction from God's Word.[17] Lactantius concluded in the third century, "There is no [true] religion wherever there is a statue or image."[18] "It is sinful to set up an image of God in a Christian temple," wrote Augustine.[19] Calvin also cites the fourth-century Council of Elvira: "It is decreed that there shall be no pictures in churches, that what is reverenced or adored be not depicted on the walls."[20]

Gregory the Great, the sixth-century bishop of Rome, began to allow for representations of God merely for instruction. Where earlier bishops would have cheered the bishop of Marseilles for destroying pictures and images of Christ that he discovered in a church, Gregory upbraided him for his "inconsiderate zeal." "And indeed in that you forbade them to be adored, we altogether praise thee; but we blame you for having broken them." "For to adore a picture is one thing," he said, "but to learn through the story of a picture what is to be adored is another."[21] Only with the Second Council of Nicaea (787) was the earlier ban overturned in the East, although only

---

[15] Calvin on Titus 2:15, in *Calvin's Commentaries*, vol. 21, trans. William Pringle (Grand Rapids: Baker, 1996), 323.

[16] Irenaeus, "Against Heresies," in *Irenaeus of Lyons*, ed. Robert Grant, The Early Church Fathers (New York: Routledge, 1997), 94 (1.25.6), 109 (2.13.3, 4, 8).

[17] Justin Martyr, in *Saint Justin Martyr*, ed. Thomas B. Falls, The Fathers of the Church (Washington, DC: The Catholic University of America Press/Consortium Books, 1948), 9–10, 41–43.

[18] Lactantius, in *The Divine Institutes*, trans. Mary F. McDonald, OP, The Fathers of the Church (Washington, DC: The Catholic University of America Press, 1964), 98–101 (1.2), 161–62 (2.18).

[19] In note 13 of Calvin, *Institutes of the Christian Religion*, ed. John T. McNeill, trans. Ford Lewis Battles (Philadelphia: Westminster, 1960), 1.11.6, Battles refers to Augustine, *Faith and the Creed*, 7.14 (J. P. Migne, *Patrologiae cursus completus, series Latina*, 40.188; tr. Library of Christian Classics 6.360); cf. *De diversis quaestionibus*, q. 78 (J. P. Migne, *Patrologiae cursus completus, series Latina*, 40.90).

[20] Calvin, *Institutes* 1.11.6.

[21] Gregory the Great, in *A Select Library of the Nicene and Post-Nicene Fathers of the Christian Church*, series 2, vol. 13, *Gregory the Great*, part 2, *Selected Epistles* (Oxford: James Parker; New York: The Christian Literature Company, 1898), 297–98.

icons were allowed (as is the case to this day). Eventually the West even accepted statues.

Even if they could not understand the liturgy or the sermons, the average medieval Christian could learn something of the biblical story from the sanctuary walls and stained glass. Martin Luther said he hoped and expected that images would fade away. His problem was with "heavenly prophets" like his erstwhile colleague Andreas Karlstadt, who ransacked the churches while Luther was hidden away in the Wartburg Castle. Just preach the Word. Take away the poison and the snake is harmless, Luther said. Karlstadt "blames me for protecting images contrary to God's Word, though he knows that I seek to tear them out of the hearts of all and want them despised and destroyed. It is only that I do not approve of his wanton violence and impetuosity."[22] Karlstadt was motivated by a legalistic spirit, Luther argued. "On the destruction of images I approached the task of destroying images by first tearing them out of the heart through God's Word and making them worthless and despised."[23] Luther did think that some representations could be allowed, but merely as "books for the unlearned."

Zwingli did not see images as an indifferent matter. The biblical proscription is not merely against adoring images, but also against making them.[24] Rome distinguished between worship (*latreia*) and veneration (*dulia* for the saints and *hyperdulia* for Mary). Devotion is offered not to the image but to the one represented, and only the triune God receives worship in the proper sense. Luther rejected this distinction, but thought that images could be retained for educational use as long as they were not honored. Yet Zwingli countered, "If one is not honoring them, then what are they doing on the altar?"[25] "At the same time," he added, contrary to Karlstadt's frenzied efforts, "one is to proceed carefully so that evil does not result. For until Christian people are instructed rightly, that one should not pay the images any honor, one may still have patience until the weak are also able to follow—so that the matter may be brought to a conclusion with unanimity."[26]

We must not imagine that Calvin's opposition to images was separate from his defense of the gospel. What had originally been intended to

---

[22] Martin Luther, "Against the Heavenly Prophets," in *Luther's Works*, American Edition, 55 vols., ed. Jaroslav Pelikan and Helmut T. Lehmann (Philadelphia: Fortress; St. Louis: Concordia, 1955–1986), 40:85.
[23] Ibid., 84–85.
[24] Ulrich Zwingli in *Huldrych Zwingli, Writings*, vol. 2, *In Search of True Religion: Reformation, Pastoral and Eucharistic Writings*, trans. H. Wayne Pipkin (Allison Park, PA: Pickwick, 1984), 69.
[25] Ibid., 68–70.
[26] Ibid.

boost interest in Christ—the intercession of saints, the images of saints, veneration of saints' relics—had become competitors to Christ. So there is a close connection between Calvin's passionate defense of the sufficiency of Christ's mediation and his rejection of ecclesiastical paraphernalia that distract our eyes from the Word of the gospel as it is preached and sealed before our eyes in the sacraments. Calvin has no interest in austerity, lack of imagination, and empty spaces. Indeed, Reformed churches have included ingenious representations of biblical scenes in wood carvings and glass along with decorative embellishments from nature.

What then are Calvin's own stated arguments against visual representations of God? First, he argues that God has already accommodated his revelation to our "rude and stupid wit" by communicating his Word "in the manner of the common folk."[27] It is ingratitude to invent our own representations in the conceit that we can make God more familiar to people than he has already done by his Word.

Second, God's majesty is always corrupted by human ingenuity in worship. No matter how helpful we seek to be in this matter, we have to bear an honest appraisal of our tendency even as Christians to misrepresent God and to turn helps into idols.[28] "I know that it is pretty much an old saw that images are the books of the uneducated," Calvin acknowledges. "Gregory said this; yet the Spirit of God declares far otherwise." After reviewing examples from the prophets, Calvin concludes that they "totally condemn the notion, taken as axiomatic by the papists, that images stand in the place of books."[29] "Indeed," Calvin adds, "those in authority in the church turned over to idols the office of teaching for no other reason than that they themselves were mute. Paul testifies that by the true preaching of the gospel 'Christ is depicted before our eyes as crucified' [Gal. 3:1]." From a smattering of passages testifying to Christ's saving work "they could have learned more than from a thousand crosses of wood or stone."[30]

History proves our idolatrous tendency. First, images were for instruction, but not for veneration; then for veneration, but not for adoration. As Calvin recounted his own youth and the average disposition of worshipers in his day, he saw that distinction as laughable. Hardly anyone entered a church without bowing and offering incense and payments to various idols

---

[27] Calvin, *Institutes* 1.11.1.
[28] Ibid.
[29] Ibid., 1.11.5.
[30] Ibid., 1.11.7.

in the various cubicles or chapels dedicated to them. Instead, pastors must preach and teach the faith. Believers must be taught to read the Scriptures in their own languages. The precipitous rise in literacy attests to the success of this instinct to raise the people out of ignorance and idolatry.

Third, Calvin says that the point of the original prohibition was to exclude all human representations of the Godhead in preparation for the revelation of Christ. "Therefore the Jews were absolutely forbidden so to abuse this pretext as to set up for themselves a symbol of deity in human form."[31] Yes, but now the Word has been made flesh! To be sure, Calvin replies, but not even the apostles gave us a description of Jesus's features—since it was precisely by his words and deeds that he secured redemption, and he has willed for us to know him by his Word. Beyond this, Jesus Christ is *God*. To argue that a painter or sculptor is representing only Jesus's humanity and not his Godhead is a Nestorian separation of the two natures.[32]

Fourth, the ancient church knew nothing of such representations. Calvin reminds readers that the early fathers all wrote against them. How could representations of God (including Christ) have been so essential even for the unlearned, Calvin asks, if for its first five centuries the church flourished so remarkably without them?[33]

Fifth, Calvin points out that God has sanctified his own visual media: "I mean baptism and the Lord's Supper, together with other rites by which our eyes must be too intensely gripped and too sharply affected to seek other images forged by human ingenuity."[34] Religions envelop worshipers in a sea of idols. The recurring taunt of Yahweh in the prophets is that idols cannot speak. More specifically, they cannot make promises that they actually fulfill in real history. The church's principal officers are not monks, artisans, and a retinue of priests whose calling is to serve images they've made, but heralds, announcing God's mighty acts in history. Zwingli's antipathy toward visible things as means of grace is categorical: the visible versus the invisible. However, the opposition that Calvin sees in Scripture is between *images we have made by our own imagination* and *images that God has made and commanded* so that we may be "intensely gripped" and "sharply affected" by his own Word and sacraments.

God knows what he is doing when he invents his means of grace. He

[31] Ibid., 1.11.3.
[32] Ibid., 1.11.3–4.
[33] Ibid., 1.11.13.
[34] Ibid.

knows how to reach us in our sin and misery. "God's service is corrupted if any strange invention be mingled with it. . . . Let us . . . learn not to intrude our own imaginations or inventions in God's service."[35]

"And yet," the Reformer adds, "I am not gripped by the superstition of thinking absolutely no images permissible." On the contrary, "sculpture and painting are gifts of God." Like all good gifts, though, they must be used properly. It is actually Calvin's critics who seem more likely pupils of Plato. They show little interest in this world of nature and history, wanting to soar to the clouds and imagine the realms of glory that they have never seen. For them, this world is merely a shadowy appearance of the real world above. However, for Calvin "only those things are to be sculpted or painted which the eyes are capable of seeing." Under this class "are histories and events" as well as "images and forms of bodies." Both are acceptable, but the former alone "have some use in teaching or admonishing."[36]

Thus, Calvin is not opposed to visual representations in a general way, and is willing to allow scenes from biblical history.[37] In fact, as Howard L. Rice observes, "Because he rejected body-mind dualism, Calvin could celebrate the glory of nature as God's gift to human beings."[38] This is precisely where Reformed artists went, as we'll see in chapter 13. The evidence of God's existence and attributes is everywhere, but we find him in saving peace only where he has promised to meet us in his unique wisdom and gracious condescension.

Where we see "emptiness" in a Reformed sanctuary, Calvin sees the beauty of Christ unobscured by silly distractions. The pulpit, font, and table are quite enough to direct us to the place where the triune God meets us in safety rather than dread. It is the theology of the cross over against theologies of glory that drives Calvin's reforming zeal.

Music

"As for public prayers, there are two kinds," Calvin says: "The ones with the word alone: the others with singing."[39] There is a time and place for different kinds of music. Citing Augustine, he says that singing in the church must

---

[35] Calvin, *Commentary on the Four Last Books of Moses*, vol. 2, trans. Charles William Bingham (Edinburgh: Calvin Translation Society, 1853), 329–30.
[36] Calvin, *Institutes* 1.11.12.
[37] Christopher Richard Joby, *Calvinism and the Arts: A Re-Assessment* (Leuven: Peeters, 2007), 51–88. Joby draws interesting parallels between Calvin's interest in metrical psalmody (celebrating biblical history) and his views on the visual arts.
[38] Howard L. Rice, *Reformed Spirituality* (Louisville: Westminster John Knox, 1991), 59.
[39] Calvin, quoted in Godfrey, *John Calvin*, 73.

"have weight and majesty," since "there is a great difference between music one makes to entertain men at table and in their houses, and the Psalms which are sung in the Church in the presence of God and his angels."[40]

Luther and Zwingli were accomplished musicians, but while much of the service was sung in Lutheran churches, Zwingli removed music entirely from the service. As on other issues, Calvin charted a middle course. He believed that singing is indispensable to public worship. Nevertheless, he followed the ancient church in excluding instrumental accompaniment as belonging to the shadows of worship under the law. Just as our brothers and sisters are God's visual images, their voice in confession and praise is his delight. Calvin thought that instruments obscure the words and voices of the congregation and tend to turn prayer and praise into entertainment. He harbored no general antipathy toward musical instruments. They are fine for singing songs and hymns at home or in other public places.

Furthermore, Calvin followed the ancient church practice of singing inspired texts—especially the Psalms, but also various other songs in the Old and New Testaments. He did include the public reciting of the Apostles' Creed (said and sung) and the *Te Deum*. However, his conviction was that God not only speaks his Word to us, but also gives us the proper words to say and sing back to him.

Calvin's argument is far from novel. It was the ancient practice in the East and the West. (The use of organs in public worship was debated even at the Council of Trent.) To this day singing in the churches of the East is *a cappella*. Even in the thirteenth century, Thomas Aquinas observed of the fourth-century father:

> Jerome does not condemn singing absolutely, but he corrects those who sing theatrically, or who sing not in order to arouse devotion but to show off or to provoke pleasure. Hence Augustine says, *When it happens that I am more moved by the voice than the words sung, I confess to have sinned, and then I would rather not hear the singer.* Arousing men to devotion through preaching and teaching is a more excellent way than through singing.

Aquinas adds, "Musical instruments usually move the soul to pleasure rather than create a good disposition in it. . . . The soul is distracted from the meaning of a song when it is sung merely to arouse pleasure."[41]

[40] Calvin, quoted in ibid., 76.
[41] Thomas Aquinas in *Summa theologiae*, vol. 39, *"Religion and Worship" (2a2æ, 80–91)*, ed. Kevin O'Rourke, OP (London: Blackfriars, 1964), 245, 247, 249, 251.

Even if we're not convinced by the exegetical argument, this distinguished line of argument from weighty writers should at least give us pause, especially when organs and choirs or praise bands often take center stage even in many Reformed and Presbyterian churches. Calvin is no more radical, reminding us that in worship, music must always serve the ministry of the Word rather than distract from it (Col. 3:16). In fact, where Augustine, Aquinas, and Zwingli warn against the emotion-arousing character of music, Calvin refers frequently to this as a benefit, as long as it is guided by truth. Although it can be abused like other good gifts, "singing has great power and vigor to move and inflame men's hearts to call upon and praise God with a more vehement and burning zeal."[42] Music should never aim to arouse the emotions directly, but should facilitate the delightful penetration of God's Word into our hearts and to help us to meditate on its truth.

It is not only what they teach us, but also what they enable us to interpret in our lives and to communicate with our Father that make the Psalms such a treasured repository of genuine piety. Thus for Calvin and the Reformed tradition generally, the Psalms became the song book that was carried to church and sung in the home and in the fields—even to the gallows and pyres. What better songs can we sing than the words that our Lord himself inspired and places on our lips? Calvin complained that the pope had deprived the faithful of this song book, but we must admit that in our own day Psalm singing has fallen on hard times even in Reformed circles.

First encountering Psalm singing during his Strasbourg sojourn, Calvin dedicated himself to the production of a complete song book in French.[43] John D. Witvliet explains, "The Genevan Psalter of 1562 was the object of what has been called 'the most gigantic enterprise ever undertaken in publishing until then.'"[44]

> For Calvin, the entire liturgical act, including psalm singing, was viewed as an activity of God among his people. . . . For Calvin, this divine action was construed in Trinitarian terms, where Christ is "the chief conductor of our hymns," the one who "hallows our lips . . . to sing the praises of God," while the Holy Spirit is the prompter who urges the people to sing.[45]

---

[42] Calvin, quoted in John D. Witvliet, "The Spirituality of the Psalter," in *Calvin Studies Society Papers, 1995, 1997: Calvin and Spirituality; Calvin and His Contemporaries*, ed. David Foxgrover (Grand Rapids: CRC Product Services, 1998), 102.

[43] Ibid., 95.

[44] Ibid., 94, citing Lucien Febvre and Henri-Jean Martin, *The Coming of the Book: The Impact of Printing, 1450–1800*, trans. David Gerard (London: NLB, 1976), 318.

[45] Witvliet, "The Spirituality of the Psalter," 101–2.

To this cause Calvin recruited two remarkable artists. The librettist was Clément Marot, a celebrated Renaissance poet and member of the royal household who embraced the Reformed cause despite imprisonment and exile. The music was composed by the Parisian songwriter Louis Bourgeois, celebrated especially for his ballads. The style of both the meter and the music conform to each Psalm, from sorrowful lament to exuberant praise. Two years before his death, Calvin saw the completion of a metrical Psalter with all 150 Psalms. It went through sixty-two reprints in its first two years and was translated into twenty-four languages.

Encountering Calvinists in France, Michel de Montaigne, one of the great leaders of the French Renaissance and a forerunner of modern skepticism, complained that they were irreverently singing the Scriptures in their daily tasks. "It is not right to allow the shop-boy, among his empty and frivolous thoughts, to entertain and amuse himself with them," he grumbled. "Nor surely is it right to see the holy book of the sacred mysteries of our faith tossed about in the hall and the kitchen. They were formerly mysteries; now they serve for recreation and pastime."[46]

Witvliet adds, "The matter of allowing women to sing in worship was common in Catholic critiques."[47] One Protestant in France reported, "I was led to knowledge of the Gospel by . . . my neighbor, who had a Bible printed at Lyon and who taught me the Psalms by heart. . . . The two of us used to go walking in the fields Sundays and feast days, conversing about the Scriptures and the abuses of the priests."[48] Anne du Bourg, a leading law professor and counselor to the Parliament of Paris, was arrested by King Henri II. Though "confined in a cage" in the Bastille, he "rejoiced always and glorified God, now taking up his lute to sing his psalms, now praising him with his voice."[49] "My friends," he said in his last words on the gallows, "I am not here as a thief or a martyr, but for the evangelium." Witvliet concludes, "Indeed, if the poor Genevan citizen had any book, it was just as likely to be a psalter as a Bible or catechism."[50]

What we're beginning to see more clearly is the extent to which, for Calvin, the public service shaped the daily life of the covenant community. Our relationship with Christ is personal, but never private. This is evident even in the intimacy of prayer, as we'll see in the next chapter.

---

[46] Michel de Montaigne, *"Of Prayers," The Essays of Michel de Montaigne*, trans. George B. Ives (New York: Heritage, 1946), 426, quoted in ibid., 110.
[47] Witvliet, "The Spirituality of the Psalter," 110n78.
[48] Quoted in ibid., 111.
[49] Ibid.
[50] Ibid., 115.

CHAPTER 9

BOLD ACCESS: PRAYER AS "THE CHIEF EXERCISE OF FAITH"

So far we have spent a lot of time on doctrine, focusing especially on the gospel, as well as the church and its public ministry. If this strikes us as odd for a book on the Christian life, perhaps it owes more to our own distance from the type of piety that Calvin commends. When we think of "spending time with the Lord," it's usually private practices we have in mind. Meditation on Scripture and praying in private are indeed important in Calvin's view of the Christian life. Nevertheless, the public ministry shapes private devotion, not vice versa.

This is true even with prayer. There is no lonely pilgrim making his way to the Celestial City, but rather a communion of saints traveling together, cheered on by a "cloud of witnesses" in heaven. Indeed, Calvin states, "whoever refused to pray in the holy assembly of the godly knows not what it is to pray individually, or in a secret spot, or at home."[1] Elsie Anne McKee explains, "Although Calvin provided guidelines for private prayers, he was primarily interested in defining public prayers, the liturgy, because he understood all personal or individual devotional acts as an extension of the

---

[1] Calvin, *Institutes of the Christian Religion*, ed. John T. McNeill, trans. Ford Lewis Battles (Philadelphia: Westminster, 1960), 3.20.29.

corporate worship of the body of Christ."[2] We have to resist the false choice between public and private, formal and informal, planned and spontaneous.[3] A rich life of prayer in the family and in private will flourish in the fertile soil that has been tilled and tended by "the apostles' teaching and fellowship, . . . the breaking of bread and the prayers" (Acts 2:42). Especially those reared in synagogue worship would have understood "*the* prayers" as public communion with God.

The Newborn's Cry

In Calvin's view, prayer not only is the first fruit of faith, but remains the most important response to God's gracious word and work throughout one's life. Through the gospel, God gives us our voice back, so that we answer his powerful Word with "Amen!" instead of Walt Whitman's "Song of Myself." No longer dead in sins, unresponsive to God, we are alive in Christ. No longer simply acted upon, we are active in piety.

In addition to the Lord's Day service, Calvin initiated the Wednesday prayer service. Shops were closed, and two services in the various parishes were held to accommodate everyone. Discussions of prayer are suffused throughout Calvin's writings. A direct treatment occupies one of the longest discussions of the *Institutes* (3.20.1–3.25.12). As David Calhoun notes, "Book 3 is about faith—'the way in which we receive the grace of Christ'— and prayer is the chief exercise of faith.' God, writes Calvin, 'has laid down this order: just as faith is born from the gospel, so through it our hearts are trained to call upon God's name' (3.20.1)."[4] So prayer is not a means of grace alongside the word and the sacraments, but "the first part of piety."[5] As the newborn's cry, the first sign of spiritual life is that we call upon the name of the Lord in prayer. In fact, the act of faith is itself prayer: the invocation of

---

[2] Elsie Anne McKee, "Context, Contours, Contents: Towards a Description of Calvin's Understanding of Worship," in *Calvin Studies Society Papers, 1995, 1997: Calvin and Spirituality; Calvin and His Contemporaries*, ed. David Foxgrover (Grand Rapids: CRC Product Services, 1998), 78.

[3] Ibid., 79–80: McKee puts it well: "Calvin, like most clerical reformers, gives more attention to liturgy than to devotional acts. It is significant that the two marks by which he identifies the true church, the pure preaching and hearing of the Word and the right administration of the sacraments, are both central to the liturgy. On the other hand, many lay reformers seem to give particular stress to the devotional life. . . . Although it has long been popular to assume that Reformed Christians were fiercely opposed to written liturgies, this common notion is in fact false for the sixteenth century and even for many later Reformed communities. (A primary reason for the misinterpretation is owed to the effect of revivalism on parts of the Reformed tradition.)" One should add that even the Puritan's antipathy toward the Book of Common Prayer lay principally in its being imposed by the monarch as *necessary* for worship.

[4] David C. Calhoun, "Prayer: 'The Chief Exercise of Faith,'" in *A Theological Guide to Calvin's Institutes: Essays and Analysis*, ed. David W. Hall and Peter A. Lillback (Phillipsburg, NJ: P&R, 2008), 349.

[5] Herman J. Selderhuis, *Calvin's Theology of the Psalms* (Grand Rapids: Baker Academic, 2007), 224. "Thus, prayer is not a '*medium salutis*,' but it is a '*medium honoris*.'"

the name of the Great King to rescue us. That name became flesh, and Jesus has been given "the name above every name" to call on for salvation.[6] If prayer is "the first part of piety," then the first part of prayer is invocation.[7] All other prayers spring from this invocation of God for deliverance from the condemnation and corruption of sin.

The cry for help and praise for deliverance is effective not because of the eloquence or earnestness of the one who calls, but because of the loving power and faithfulness of the One who hears. True worship consists not in outward rites but in casting ourselves on the Father's gracious care in Christ and by his Spirit. To be sure, the attitude of our heart is reflected in our outward demeanor. For example, Calvin encouraged kneeling in public and private prayer. "But we are to notice that [the psalmist] particularly condescends upon one point: the paternal favor of God, evidenced in his exclusive adoption of the posterity of Abraham unto the hope of eternal life."[8]

From the Heart

All things being equal, God prefers both sincere *and* disciplined prayers. Calvin explains, "We exhort people to worship God neither in a frigid nor a careless manner."[9] He never places reverence in opposition to emotions. "For the principle which the Stoics assume, that all the passions are perturbations and like diseases, is false, and has its origin in ignorance; for either to grieve, or to fear, or to rejoice, or to hope, is by no means repugnant to reason." It is reasonable to mourn over loss and to rejoice over blessings. Emotion, no less than reason, is a gift of God and essential to our nature. We cannot seek to eliminate emotions "without insulting God himself."[10] I expect that Calvin would evaluate our worship today not as too emotional, but as too narrow in its emotional repertoire.

This is why he was so enamored of the Psalms. There is praise and worship in the Psalter. Yet there are also songs of lament, songs of confession, and even cries of discouragement that verge on what we might otherwise consider irreverent. We deprive the saints of tremendous relief when we

---

[6] Calvin on Phil. 2:9–11, in *Calvin's Commentaries*, vol. 21, trans. John Pringle (Grand Rapids: Baker, 1996), 58–64.
[7] Calvin, *Institutes* 3.20.1.
[8] Calvin on Ps. 95:5, in *Calvin's Commentaries*, vol. 6, trans. James Anderson (Grand Rapids: Baker, 1996), 34–35.
[9] Calvin, quoted by McKee, "Context, Contours, Contents," 71.
[10] Calvin on Ex. 32:19, in *Calvin's Commentaries*, vol. 3, trans. Charles William Bingham (Grand Rapids: Baker, 1996), 346–47.

give them only upbeat words and tempos to sing and pray. That simply is not true to life. There is a theology of the cross as well as the resurrection in the Psalms. That theology makes room for the blues, as the heart cries out for a deliverance that seems at least to our experience beyond reach. Luther wrote, "In the Psalms we have a view of the inner heart of the faithful."[11] It was in the Psalms that Calvin found his own heart. In the Psalms, we discover "an anatomy of all feelings of the soul."[12] "The varied and resplendent riches which are contained in this treasury it is no easy matter to express in words," he says.[13] There is something for every occasion and "there is not an emotion of which any one can be conscious that is not here represented as in a mirror." We find here "all the griefs, sorrows, fears, doubts, hopes, cares, perplexities, in short, all the distracting emotions with which the minds of men are wont to be agitated." In other parts of Scripture God's servants bring God's word to us, but in the Psalms they give us God's words to bring to him. "It is certainly a rare and singular advantage, when all lurking places are discovered, and the heart is brought into the light, purged from that most baneful infection, hypocrisy."[14]

Calvin encourages the use of "the public prayers of the church," such as the *Form of Prayers*, which he drafted for public and private worship. However, such forms should not be used in a legalistic fashion that does not recognize, for instance, special and immediate needs in a given region.[15] Written forms discourage "wordiness," but formalism becomes mere "words."[16] Like a trellis, formal prayers can guide our hearts to articulate our honest feelings in the light of God's own Word. A trellis will not make a vine grow, but without one, the vine may not grow in the right direction. "Teach us to pray," the disciples asked Jesus, and he gave them—and us— the Lord's Prayer. Even when we use our own words, this prayer provides the structure.[17] Calvin unpacks this prayer over sixteen sections of the final *Institutes* (3.20.34–49). He encourages family and private prayers before work, at meals, and at bedtime. "But this must not be any superstitious observance of hours, whereby, as if paying our debt to God, we imagine

---

[11] Martin Luther, quoted in Selderhuis, *Calvin's Theology of the Psalms*, 21.
[12] Selderhuis, *Calvin's Theology of the Psalms*, 23.
[13] Calvin, preface to *Commentary on the Psalms*, in *Calvin's Commentaries*, vol. 4, trans. James Anderson (Grand Rapids: Baker, 1996), xxxvi.
[14] Ibid., xxxvii.
[15] Calvin, *Institutes* 3.20.29.
[16] Ibid.
[17] Ibid., 3.20.34–47.

ourselves paid up for the remaining hours. Rather, it must be a tutelage for our weakness."[18]

Like any other piece of piety, we need to learn how to pray well. Yet God is more eager to hear a sincere prayer—even an honest lament or a complaint hastily composed without due consideration—than one that is formally correct but perfunctory. Because he is our King, we should frame our prayers with reverent intentionality. However, because he is also our Father, we should not be too anxious about the quality of our prayers. In fact, "The prayers that God grants are not always pleasing to him."[19] So great is his fatherly indulgence.

Confiding in Our Father

More than anything else, God wishes to be treated as our Father, since he lavishes us with paternal liberality. "Men will allow themselves to be strangled by numerous severe laws, to be obliged to numerous laborious observances, to wear a severe and heavy yoke; in short, there is no annoyance to which they will not submit provided there is no mention of the heart."[20] Even the pagans pray, but without effect. "For they neither rely upon the promise, nor perceive the force of what is meant by having a Mediator through whom they will assuredly obtain what they ask." Christians should expect no greater access without this knowledge. Like the Prodigal Son, we often come to the Father with awareness of our offenses against him—content to be slaves in his house rather than sons. We turn prayer into a means of pacifying a Judge instead of pouring out our hearts to a Father. However, genuine prayer cannot be founded on anxiety and doubt about one's standing with the Father; we must come with confidence, not in ourselves but in Christ and his promise.[21] We are not trying to win his favor, but are seeking to rest in it, to bask in it, to delight in it. "Till we have a persuasion of being saved through the grace of God there can be no sincere prayer."[22]

Repeatedly, Calvin exults in the *privilege* of such familiar access to God in prayer. Even the untrained newborn's cry is music to the Father's ears.

---

[18] Ibid., 3.20.50.
[19] Ibid., 3.20.15.
[20] Calvin, "The Necessity of Reforming the Church," in *Selected Works of John Calvin: Tracts and Letters*, ed. Henry Beveridge and Jules Bonnet, 7 vols. (Grand Rapids: Baker, 1983), 1:154.
[21] Ibid., 157.
[22] Calvin on Ps. 140:6, in *Calvin's Commentaries*, 6:229.

Much of Calvin's treatment of prayer echoes the mysticism of writers like Bernard: prayer flows from the "sweetness of love." Even when we do not feel love toward God, we can be drawn by the awareness of his love for us.[23] Thus, we are called "to unburden our cares into God's bosom."[24]

Why Pray If God Is Sovereign?

Only a misunderstanding of Calvin's theology could prompt the question Why pray if God is sovereign? The Reformer himself might turn the question back on us: Why pray if God *isn't* sovereign? Calvin was not a fatalist. Although all things are comprehended in God's plan, Calvin emphasizes that God has ordained the means as well as the ends. Among the means through which God brings his plans to pass is prayer. Calhoun points to Calvin's comments on Elijah's prayer in James 5:17:

> It was a notable event for God to put heaven, in some sense, under the control of Elijah's prayers, to be obedient to his requests. By his prayers, Elijah kept heaven shut for two years and a half. Then he opened it, and made it suddenly pour with a great rain, from which we may see the miraculous power of prayer.[25]

It is part of God's accommodation to us that he uses our prayers to accomplish his purposes, as when Moses interceded for the people and God restrained his wrath: "so that whereas diverse time he would destroy all, he is as it were changed, if we come and humble ourselves before him."[26] Our prayers do not change God's decree, but are included in God's decree as the means through which he brings things about. Just as Christ himself in Gethsemane did not "turn His eyes to the divine plan but rested His desire that burned within Him upon His Father's knees," we too "in pouring out prayers do not always rise to speculate upon the secret things of God."[27] Instead of trying to decode God's hidden purposes, our prayers should focus on the good that he has published concerning us. "So true it is that we dig up by prayer the treasures that were pointed out by the Lord's gospel, and which our faith has gazed upon."[28]

---

[23] Calvin, *Institutes* 3.20.28.
[24] Ibid., 3.20.5.
[25] Calhoun, "Prayer," 351.
[26] Cited in ibid.
[27] Cited in ibid., 353.
[28] Calvin, *Institutes* 3.20.2.

We should be as bold in our prayers as the biblical examples repeatedly encourage. Once more the fatherly image dominates: "We shall be permitted to pour into [God's] bosom the difficulties which torment us, in order that he may loosen the knots that we cannot untie."[29] Prayer is not magic. We must beware of superstition and "not be confident in our ability to wrest something from God by beating upon his ears with a garrulous flow of talk."[30] At the same time, we should be persistent; God often answers our third, fifth, or twentieth petition as a way of drawing us close to him in sole reliance on his Word.[31] In summary, "Genuine and earnest prayer proceeds first from a sense of our need, and next, from faith in the promises of God," so that "even when in the midst of doubts, fears, and apprehensions, let us put forth our efforts in prayer, until we experience some consolation which may calm and bring contentment to our minds."[32]

"To the Father, in the Son, by the Spirit"

Across Calvin's writings, one of the recurring terms for God's lavish gift-giving disposition is "liberality"—often "fatherly liberality." God is not stingy. As we see in nature, God has provided for us far beyond our needs, to delight us with the diversity of pleasures that ought to lead us to gratitude for his bounty.[33] Nevertheless, we pray not only when all is well and we have a vivid sense of God's presence and goodwill. Indeed, an even better time to pray is when God seems remote and his care is less than evident to us in view of our circumstances.[34] In some expressions of Calvinism, a stoic resolve has been confused with reverence. One should suffer difficulties in quiet. In any case, one should never give vent, especially in public, to any frustration with God and his ways. No, Calvin replies; in this covenantal relationship, God even gives believers "license" to complain. He can handle it.[35]

If prayer is directed to the Father, it is always in the Son. "For as soon as God's dread majesty comes to mind, we cannot but tremble and be driven

---

[29] Calvin on Gen. 18:25, in *Calvin's Commentaries*, vol. 1, trans. Charles William Bingham (Grand Rapids: Baker, 1996), 489.
[30] Calvin, *Institutes* 3.20.29.
[31] Ibid., 3.20.51.
[32] Calvin, preface to *Commentary on the Psalms*, xxxvii–xxxviii.
[33] Calvin, *Institutes* 3.10.2–3.
[34] Selderhuis, *Calvin's Theology of the Psalms*, 223, on Ps. 116:1.
[35] Ibid., 221, on Ps. 102:3.

far away by the recognition of our own unworthiness, until Christ comes forward as intermediary, to change the throne of dreadful glory into the throne of grace."[36] The medieval church had made Christ the first among many intercessors. "There is scarcely any subject on which the Holy Spirit more carefully prescribes than on the proper method of prayer; but there is not a syllable which teaches us to have recourse to the assistance of dead saints."[37] Calvin appeals to the Council of Carthage (AD 397), which condemned all prayers through the mediation of anyone but Christ.[38] There can be no lawful participation in prayer in a venue where Christ is not invoked or other mediators are added.[39]

When we come to a Judge instead of a Father and in our own righteousness, any exhortation to pray more, much less to pray better, is counterproductive. God does not "reject those prayers in which he finds neither perfect faith nor repentance, together with a warmth of zeal and petitions rightly conceived."[40] "Even in our best formed prayers, we have always need of pardon," but because we are in Christ, the Father indulgently overlooks the infirmities of our prayers.[41] "No one has ever carried this out with the uprightness that was due; for, not to mention the rank and file, how many complaints of David savor of intemperance!" This is not a license, but God would rather have us cast our cares—even frustrations—on him than avoid prayer out of false humility or fear of his majesty.[42] In truth, "there is no prayer which in justice God would not loathe if he did not overlook the spots with which all are sprinkled."[43] With such a faithful High Priest, we should come boldly with our halfhearted and half-witted prayers rather than be put off by fear. "Our prayers are acceptable to God only insofar as Christ sprinkles and sanctifies them with the perfume of his own sacrifice."[44] We can never take the gospel for granted. Repentance "terrifies us while [faith] gladdens us," but both are as necessary in prayer as in conversion.[45] "The one true aim of prayer consists in the fact that the promises of God should have their way with us."[46] As the gospel is the soil of faith, faith—this "firm

---

[36] Calvin, *Institutes* 3.10.17.
[37] Calvin, "The Necessity of Reforming the Church," 156.
[38] Calvin, *Institutes* 3.20.22.
[39] Ibid., 3.20.15.
[40] Ibid., 3.20.16.
[41] Ibid.
[42] Ibid.
[43] Ibid., 3.10.16.
[44] Calvin on Ps. 20:3, in *Calvin's Commentaries*, 4:336.
[45] Calvin, *Institutes* 3.20.11.
[46] Calvin, quoted in Wilhelm Niesel, *The Theology of John Calvin*, trans. Harold Knight (Philadelphia: Westminster, 1956), 157.

assurance of mind that God is favorable and benevolent to them"—is the root of sincere prayer.[47]

Once again, public prayers shape our private prayers. In a sermon Calvin says:

> As often as the goodness of God is witnessed by us and His grace promised (although we are wretched sinners), as oft also as we hear that our sins were forgiven by the death and suffering of our Lord Jesus Christ, and that atonement was made for our transgressions and the obligations which were against us, and that God is at peace with us, the way is opened for us to pray to Him and implore His blessings.[48]

As on other topics, Calvin's treatment of prayer exhibits the point that all good gifts come from the Father, in the Son, by the Spirit. Although all riches *from* the Father are stored up *in* the Son, "no particle of grace from God may come to us except *through* the Holy Spirit."[49] The Spirit stirs us to pray and directs us to remain within the bounds of his Word in our prayers.[50] The indwelling Spirit not only gives us faith, uniting us to Christ, but also gives its fruit, whose first flower is prayer.[51] Calvin emphasizes that the whole Trinity is involved in our prayers. We are never alone in prayer, but are met by the Son and the Spirit who conspire to make our prayers acceptable.

Prayer in the Covenant

We have access to the Father, in the Son, by the Spirit. The context of this familiar and secure relationship is the covenant of grace. From a misreading of James 5:16, we often assume that God hears—or at least answers—our prayers only if at that moment we are sufficiently pious. Selderhuis points up Calvin's objection: "In the first place," Calvin argues, Scripture "points to the fact that the covenant finds its origin exclusively in the initiative of God; thus God has committed himself unconditionally and voluntarily." Accordingly, "the certainty of God's promises does not hang upon human obedience."[52]

---

[47] Calvin, *Institutes* 3.20.12.
[48] Calvin, "The Privilege of Prayer," in *The Mystery of Godliness and Other Sermons* (Grand Rapids: Eerdmans, 1950), 184.
[49] Calvin, "1539 Institutes," in *John Calvin: Selections from His Writings*, ed. John Dillenberger (Atlanta: Scholars Press, 1975), 294, emphasis added.
[50] Calvin, *Institutes* 3.20.5.
[51] Ibid.
[52] Selderhuis, *Calvin's Theology of the Psalms*, 214, on Ps. 132:12.

Even in the exile, God kept his promise without relaxing his demands, but he shows "in the coming of King Jesus that he has not broken his covenant and that he fulfills his promise."[53]

Believers actually have a "right" to protection from God on the basis of his own promises; this is the nature of a covenant.[54] In short, the God who is not bound nevertheless binds himself freely to his Word. He *cannot* go back on his promises, and he even delights in our appealing to his covenant pledge and its signs and seals as we bring our case before him. Our cries for help even in a sense compel God to come to our aid.[55] Selderhuis observes:

> Just like Luther, Calvin points out that we should remind God of his own promises since this is the only way to receive God's favor. . . . At the same time, though, Calvin relates this to the hardships entailed in the *theologia crucis* [theology of the cross], which affirms that "there is no place for the promises of God in shadow and peace but only in the fiercest struggle."[56]

For Calvin, Selderhuis adds, "meditation on God's promises through the covenant only makes sense when it results in prayer," where we call on God with familiarity, as "my God" and "our Father."[57]

Indeed, this last point—"*our* Father"—captures Calvin's emphasis on covenantal solidarity. We do not think of ourselves apart from concern for God's glory, the good of the whole church, and the needs of the world.[58] The public liturgy includes prayers for rulers and for the whole church everywhere, especially under persecution. Even alone, when we pray with Christ, we are praying with and for his church. "He would not have each one to remain by himself, but would have us unite in peace and concord"— as when Jesus teaches us to pray not only "my Father," but "our Father."[59] In fact, he goes so far as to say:

> Let the Christian, then, conform his prayers to this rule in order that they may be in common and embrace all who are his brothers in Christ, not only those whom he at present sees and recognizes as such but all men who dwell on earth. For what God has determined concerning them is beyond our knowing except that it is no less godly than humane to wish

---

[53] Ibid., on Ps. 132:12.
[54] Ibid., 215, on Ps. 68:35.
[55] Ibid., 225, on Ps. 27:7.
[56] Ibid., 217, on Ps. 37:14.
[57] Ibid., 219.
[58] Ibid., 222.
[59] Calvin, "The Privilege of Prayer," 190.

and hope the best for them. Yet we ought to be drawn with a special affection to those, above others, of the household of faith.[60]

Along these lines, Jesus calls us to seek forgiveness "as we forgive our debtors" (Matt. 6:12). When we kneel in prayer while plotting evil or retribution against our neighbors for their offenses against us, we are in effect asking God to treat us as we treat them. However, this clause "is not added because by the forgiveness we grant to others we deserve his forgiveness, as if this indicated the cause of it. Rather, by this word the Lord intended partly to comfort the weakness of our faith." It is a comparison that Jesus draws. The forgiveness we grant to others is an imperfect fruit and reminder of God's forgiveness toward us.[61] The central petition throughout the Christian life is "forgive us our debts," with confidence in his covenanted mercy.[62]

Praying *with* Christ

As union with Christ is deeper than mere imitation, believers should recognize that they are actually praying with Christ and not simply imitating his example of devotion. In fact, as T. H. L. Parker remarks, "it is not . . . simply a matter of praying through Christ, but rather with Christ, of our prayers being united with his intercession for us."[63] According to Calvin, Wilhelm Niesel adds, "the possibility of prayer does not really lie within our grasp." However, "the priestly office of Christ which renders possible our prayer to God is fulfilled without intermission."[64] On this basis, Christ joins us in prayer here and now. "Our own praying is nothing other than our uniting ourselves with the prayer of Christ; we have no hope of being heard unless He precedes us with His prayer."[65] We are not Christ, but we are one with him—even on our knees.

The Psalms are more than a quarry from which to take our own prayers; through them and in them we find Christ praying with us. These inspired songs not only spoke of Christ, but also were in his heart and on his lips throughout his life. Properly speaking, Christ alone is the "blessed one" who perfectly keeps God's law, the King greater than David who has kept

[60] Calvin, *Institutes* 3.20.38.
[61] Ibid., 3.20.46.
[62] Ibid., 3.20.16.
[63] T. H. L. Parker, *John Calvin* (Tring, UK: Lion, 1975), 110.
[64] Niesel, *The Theology of John Calvin*, 154, referring to *Institutes* 3.20.17.
[65] Niesel, *The Theology of John Calvin*, 154.

his hands from bloodshed, and the "King of Glory" for whom the gates of heaven rightfully opened in welcoming exultation. Nevertheless, we are in Christ and can therefore pray even these Psalms with him. Not only are we clothed in his righteousness; we are also so united to him that we can no longer say that we are still "dead in trespasses and sins" and "a child of wrath" like the Gentiles, under the dominion of sin and death. We are his people and the sheep of his pasture, so we can claim what is properly and perfectly true of the Shepherd as a valid though imperfect description of us as well.

Nobody felt the pains, anxieties, and sorrows of the songs of lament more than Jesus. And no one felt greater joy in the Father's love and will expressed in the songs of praise. It is a remarkable privilege to join our Savior in all of these prayers. Not only does God descend far beneath his majesty to speak "baby talk" in communicating with us; he also follows the same pattern in helping us communicate with him. "When God descends to us he, in a certain sense, abases himself and *stammers with us*, so he allows us to *stammer with him*."[66]

When we are drawn out of our self-enclosed cocoon and join in prayer with our fellow saints, we find Christ himself praying with us as our elder Brother, bone of our bone and flesh of our flesh. And therefore we find ourselves able to bear the cross that our Father places on our shoulders throughout the ups and downs of life.[67]

---

[66] Calvin on Gen. 35:7, in *Calvin's Commentaries*, 1:238, emphasis added.
[67] Calvin, preface to *Commentary on the Psalms*, xxxix.

CHAPTER 10

LAW AND LIBERTY IN THE CHRISTIAN LIFE

Calvin and his spiritual heirs may be unique in the extent to which they are charged simultaneously with legalism and license. What did Calvin think about the role of the law in the Christian life? And how did he negotiate the interests of Christian freedom and love in the body of Christ?

Law and Gospel

Augustine's treatise *The Letter and the Spirit* underscored the different ways in which God worked judgment and grace through his Word as "law" and "gospel." For later interpreters, however, the gospel meant the New Testament, or "the new law." They often spoke of "the law of the gospel" and, therefore, of Christ's commands as easier than the Old Testament laws.

Like Luther, Calvin found this confusion of law and gospel fundamental to the errors of medieval faith and practice. "Those who did not comprehend these teachings," he says, "fancied Christ another Moses, the giver of the law of the gospel, which supplied what was lacking in the Mosaic law"—" in many respects a most pernicious opinion!"[1] Although believers seek to love God and neighbor, "they do nothing with the required perfection." "If they look upon the law, whatever work they attempt or intend they see to be accursed." Their best works are imperfect and, as

---

[1] Calvin, *Institutes of the Christian Religion*, ed. John T. McNeill, trans. Ford Lewis Battles (Philadelphia: Westminster, 1960), 2.8.7.

such, are judged "to be a transgression of the law" if considered before God's righteous bar.[2]

Calvin also appropriated Melanchthon's threefold use of the law: (1) to arraign us before God's judgment and prove the world guilty; (2) to remind all people, even non-Christians, of their obligations to the moral law written on their consciences, and (3) to guide believers in the way of gratitude.[3]

In its first use, the law's purpose is "to shut us up deprived of all confidence in our own righteousness, so that we may learn to embrace [God's] Covenant of Grace, and flee to Christ, who is the end of the law."[4] The law is good, true, and right, but we are not. So when it comes to assuring the conscience of God's good favor, the law is completely opposed to the gospel. "For the words of Paul always hold true, that the difference between the Law and the Gospel lies in this: that the latter does not like the former promise life under the condition of works, but from faith. *What can be clearer than the antithesis . . .* ?"[5] If we have in mind the Law as the first five books of the Bible, then of course it contains the gospel. However, if we're thinking about "that part only which was peculiar to [Moses's] ministration, which consisted of precepts, rewards, and punishments," then it is completely distinct from the gospel. The goal of Moses's ministry was to lead the people of God

> to despair as to their own righteousness, that they might flee to the haven of divine goodness, and so to Christ himself. This was the end or design of the Mosaic dispensation. . . .
>
> And whenever the word law is thus strictly taken, Moses is by implication opposed to Christ: and then we must consider what the law contains, as separate from the gospel.[6]

As firmly as did Luther, Calvin emphasizes the importance of distinguishing law and gospel in reading, preaching, and interpreting Scripture. In Romans 10:3–7, Paul's object is once again "to show how great is the difference between the righteousness of the law and that of the gospel."[7]

---

[2] Ibid., 3.19.4.

[3] The Formula of Concord, art. 6; Calvin, *Institutes* 2.7.6, 10, 12.

[4] Calvin, preface to *Commentaries on the Four Last Books of Moses*, in *Calvin's Commentaries*, vol. 2, trans. Charles William Bingham (Grand Rapids: Baker, 1996), xviii.

[5] Calvin, "Antidote to the Council of Trent," in *Selected Works of John Calvin: Tracts and Letters*, ed. Henry Beveridge and Jules Bonnet, 7 vols. (Grand Rapids: Baker, 1983), 3:156, 250.

[6] Calvin on Rom. 10:5, in *Calvin's Commentaries*, vol. 19, trans. John Owen (Grand Rapids: Baker, 1996), 386–87.

[7] Ibid., 390–91. See also Calvin, *Selected Works of John Calvin*, 3:251.

"Sufficient then for pacifying minds, and for rendering certain our salvation, is the word of the gospel," Calvin says. "The contrast between Law and Gospel is to be understood, and from this distinction we deduce that, just as the Law demands work, the Gospel requires only that men should bring faith in order to receive the grace of God."[8] The law is a mirror to show us our sin and send us to Christ.[9] The law tells us simply "what we owe" God, "according us no hope of life unless we fulfill every part of it, and, on the contrary, annexing a curse if we are guilty of the smallest transgression."[10] Because of our sinfulness, "The life of the Law is man's death."[11] "The peculiar office of the Law [is] to summon consciences to the judgment-seat of God."[12] The law's purpose is not to incline our hearts to godliness, but to reveal our misery so that we would flee to Christ.

Calvin even echoes Luther's famous maxim "The law always accuses." For example, in a sermon on Isaiah 53:11 he says:

> The Law only begets death; it increases our condemnation and inflames the wrath of God. . . . The Law of God speaks, but it does not reform our hearts. . . . For in the Gospel God does not say, "You must do this or that," but "believe that my only Son is your Redeemer; embrace his death and passion as the remedy for your ills; plunge yourself beneath his blood and it will be your cleansing."[13]

Calvin also anticipates the emerging Reformed distinction between law and gospel in terms of "two covenants," which he identifies as "Legal and Evangelical." "The two covenants, then, are the mothers, of whom children unlike one another are born; for the legal covenant makes slaves, and the evangelical covenant makes freemen."[14] In this sense, the law "can do nothing but condemn."[15] In Galatians 3, Paul offers "an argument from contradictions, for the same fountain cannot yield both hot and cold."

[8] Calvin on Rom. 10:8, in *Calvin's Commentaries*, 19:390–91.

[9] Ibid., 386–87.

[10] Calvin, *Institutes* 2.9.4.

[11] Calvin, *Calvin's Commentaries*, 2:316.

[12] Calvin on John 16:10, in *Calvin's Commentaries*, vol. 18, trans. William Pringle (Grand Rapids: Baker, 1996), 140.

[13] Calvin, *Sermons on Isaiah's Prophecy and the Death and Passion of Christ*, trans. T. H. L. Parker (London: James Clarke, 2002), on Isa. 53:11.

[14] Calvin on Gal. 4:24, in *Calvin's Commentaries*, vol. 21, trans. William Pringle (Grand Rapids: Baker, 1996), 137–38. He makes the same point in his Romans commentary (cited above), 298.

[15] Calvin on 2 Cor. 3:7, in *Calvin's Commentaries*, vol. 20, trans. John Pringle (Grand Rapids: Baker, 1996), 178.

"The Law holds all men under its curse. From the Law, therefore, it is useless to seek a blessing."[16]

The gospel is "the instrument of regeneration and offers to us a free
reconciliation with God."[17] "The gospel promises are free and dependent
solely upon God's mercy, while the promises of the law depend upon the
condition of works."[18] Even as believers, "we need to hear this for our whole
life." We must be vigilant in distinguishing the law and gospel, or we will
fall back into reliance on works, and our consciences will be forever perplexed.[19] Not even the justified and renewed believer can appeal to the law
as the basis for assurance of God's favor.[20]

The Third Use: God's Wisdom for Living

After laying out the three uses of the law, Calvin explores its third use as a
moral guide. "Now, the law has power to exhort believers," he says. "This
is not a power to bind consciences with a curse, but one to shake off their
sluggishness, by repeatedly urging them, and to pinch them awake in their
imperfection." He adds, "Not that the law no longer enjoins believers to do
what is right, but only that it is not for them what it formerly was: it may
no longer condemn and destroy their consciences by frightening and con-
founding them."[21] Calvin holds that assurance is synonymous with faith:
to believe the gospel is to be assured. While some of his later followers emphasized strict self-examination to find signs of election, "Calvin, by contrast, had always pointed believers toward scripture and the sacraments to
reassure them that Christ had died for them."[22]

Yet immediately after warning against giving any place to the law in
assuring the conscience, Calvin adds, "Nor can any man rightly infer from
this that the law is superfluous for believers, since it does not stop teaching and exhorting and urging them to do good, even though before God's
judgment seat it has no place *in their conscience*."[23] The law is good, but it
has a specific job description. It tells us what God's holiness demands, but
gives us no power to fulfill those demands. It reveals God's righteousness,

---

[16] Calvin on Gal. 3:10, in *Calvin's Commentaries*, 21:88.
[17] Calvin, *Institutes* 3.11.17.
[18] Ibid.
[19] Calvin, *Calvin's Commentaries*, 19:136.
[20] Calvin, *Institutes* 2.7.4.
[21] Ibid., 2.7.14.
[22] Irena Backus and Philip Benedict, introduction to *Calvin and His Influence, 1509–2009*, ed. Irena Backus and Philip Benedict (New York: Oxford University Press, 2011), 14.
[23] Calvin, *Institutes* 3.11.2, emphasis added.

but it cannot justify or sanctify; it cannot assure our conscience that God is favorable toward us, since we always falls short of its perfection. The call to follow Christ, imitating his example, is law rather than gospel. As a command to those who are already justified by Christ's imputed righteousness, it is good and wise. Used as a way of becoming right before God, it is pure condemnation. If my salvation depends on conforming to it, nothing is more hopeless to me than Christ's example. The gospel remains the wellspring of Christian security throughout one's life, in assurance and sanctification as well as in faith and justification.

However, this is precisely why for Calvin the third use of the law—that is, as the moral guide for our lives—is "the principal use."[24] We are no longer "under the law" in the judicial sense—that is, as a covenant of law.[25] "For the law is not now acting toward us as a rigorous enforcement officer who is not satisfied unless the requirements are met," but is pointing out "the goal toward which throughout life we are to strive."[26] Calvin would sharply oppose any preaching that exhorts believers to greater faithfulness as if it were a condition for their assurance of God's good favor. The believer "lays hold not only of the precepts," says Calvin,

> but the accompanying promise of grace, which alone sweetens what is bitter. For what would be less lovable than the law if, with importuning and threatening alone, it troubled souls through fear, and distressed them through fright? David especially shows that in the law he apprehended the Mediator, without whom there is no delight or sweetness.[27]

Here again we discern the "distinction without separation" maxim at work. The law and the gospel must never be confused, but they are also never to be separated.

Finding God's Will

In this third sense, then, the law "is the best instrument" for learning God's will for our lives and it also exhorts and arouses us to obedience.[28] Even its threats remind us of the gravity of our sin, so that we will flee to Christ and, holding fast to him alone, be reminded of our duty. Only because the

---

[24] Ibid., 2.17.12.
[25] Ibid., 2.7.15.
[26] Ibid., 2.7.12–13.
[27] Ibid., 2.7.12.
[28] Ibid., 2.7.15.

law itself is not the source of our peace with God can it now serve as the constant guide for grace-filled gratitude. The same God who commands us and calls us to obedience is the one who has justified us, removing the law's terrors. For those who find their justification in Christ alone, the law is now a friend rather than an enemy. God speaks his law to us now not from Mount Sinai, with its ominous threats attended by lightning, but from Mount Zion, where the throne of judgment has been turned into a hearth of peace.

Although there are different emphases and nuances, we should beware of pitting Luther against Calvin even on this point. Luther's *Against the Antinomians* affirmed the law and argued that separating justification and sanctification was just as heretical as Rome's confusion of justification with sanctification. It was Melanchthon who first introduced the "three uses of the law," and the Book of Concord takes more space to affirm directly the third use than Reformed confessions and catechisms.[29] Hesselink's conclusion suffices: "Here Calvin does not differ significantly from Luther, except in emphasis and discretion."[30]

In its first use, the law thunders forth from heaven as the word of the Judge. In its third use, it directs, reproves, and exhorts us as the Father's loving hand on our shoulder. Consequently, God's discipline is never a sign of his wrath. Whatever trials he sends our way are not payback for sins, but his fatherly training. "For God does not consider, in chastening the faithful, what they deserve; but what will be useful to them in the future; and fulfills the office of a physician rather than of a judge."[31]

The problem with Roman Catholic piety is that it does not truly know this transition from law to grace, from Judge to Father. Jesus becomes another Moses—or even another Aristotle, who gives us an unparalleled philosophy of life. After disclosing the riches of God's grace in Christ for eleven chapters of Romans, Paul turns to the "reasonable service" that follows "in view of God's mercies." "And this is the main difference between the gospel and philosophy," says Calvin. This point was also made by Luther, targeting especially Aristotle's basic premise that good habits make the person good.

---

[29] In fact, both Melanchthon and Calvin referred to the "two-fold use" of the law—pedagogical (theological) and civil (Calvin combined the civil and moral use until the 1559 *Institutes*, although there is a reference to the "three-fold use" in the 1539 edition)—still after Melanchthon's identification of the three uses in the 1535 *Loci communes*. See Timothy Wengert, *Law and Gospel: Philip Melanchthon's Debate with John Agricola of Eisleben over* Poenitentia (Grand Rapids: Baker, 1997), especially p. 195.

[30] I. John Hesselink, *Calvin's Concept of the Law* (Allison Park, PA: Pickwick, 1992), 158.

[31] Calvin on Gen. 3:19, in *Calvin's Commentaries*, vol. 1, trans. Charles William Bingham (Grand Rapids: Baker, 1996), 178.

phers teach ethics without any adequate foundation. "Not very
is the mode of teaching under the Papacy: for though they mention, by the way, faith in Christ and the grace of the Holy Spirit, it yet appears quite evident that they approach heathen philosophers far nearer
than Christ and his Apostles."[32]

We have to ground obedience in the gospel, Calvin insists.

> It is enough for the Papists if they can extort by terror some sort of forced
> obedience, I know not what. But Paul, that he might bind us to God, not
> by servile fear, but by the voluntary and cheerful love of righteousness,
> allures us by the sweetness of that favor by which our salvation is ef-
> fected; and at the same time he reproaches us with ingratitude unless we,
> after having found a Father so kind and bountiful, do strive in our turn to
> dedicate ourselves wholly to him.[33]

Children want to please their parents not to win their favor but because
they already enjoy it. They want to learn what their parents approve and
disapprove. Natural law provides enough revelation to build reasonably
just societies. "But man is so shrouded in the darkness of errors that he
hardly begins to grasp through this natural law what worship is acceptable
to God." Therefore, "the Lord has provided us with a written law to give us a
clearer witness of what was too obscure in the natural law."[34] It is foolish—
and selfish—to imagine that we know better than God what is pleasing to
him. So, Calvin reminds us, "it is not fitting for us to measure God's glory
according to our ability; for whatever we may be, he remains always like
himself: the friend of righteousness, the foe of iniquity."[35]

With these bearings, Calvin launches into his exposition of the Ten
Commandments. Here, in summary, God tells us what true piety and reverence require.

House Rules: The Ten Commandments as the Pattern for Grateful Living

Beginning with the preface in Exodus 20, Calvin observes, "[God] holds out
the promise of grace to draw [the Israelites] by its sweetness to a zeal for
holiness." The motive is gratitude for his kind and merciful deliverance.[36]

---

[32] Calvin on Rom. 12:1, in *Calvin's Commentaries*, 19:449.
[33] Ibid., 450.
[34] Calvin, *Institutes* 2.8.1.
[35] Ibid., 2.8.2.
[36] Ibid., 2.8.13.

"I am Yahweh your God," not only *a* god or even the supreme being, but the God who identifies himself with his chosen ones. We are therefore to be holy because God is holy, and Calvin also appeals to Malachi 1:6: "If I am a father, where is your love?"[37] "The recital of his benefit follows." This God, "your God," has delivered his people from Egypt, the house of bondage.[38]

Calvin observes that the scholastics (he cites Aquinas) followed Aristotle in teaching that one is virtuous by abstaining from vice. However, Calvin emphasizes that, especially in light of the Sermon on the Mount, "virtue goes beyond this to contrary duties and deeds." For example, "You shall not kill" not only means refraining from malicious violence, but also is "the requirement that we give our neighbor's life all the help we can."[39] This emphasis on the positive aspect of each commandment is found in Luther's catechisms, as well as in the Heidelberg and Westminster Catechisms.

Calvin also emphasizes that the second table (love and service toward neighbor) is grounded in the first (love and worship of God). "What kind of righteousness will you call it not to harass men with theft and plundering, if through impious sacrilege you at the same time deprive God's majesty of its glory? Or that you do not defile your body with fornication, if with your blasphemies you profane God's most holy name?" False worship "is as unreasonable as to display a mutilated, decapitated body as something beautiful."[40]

Loving God: The First Table

On this basis, Calvin says, God commands "no other gods." As Luther explains in his Small Catechism, this first commandment means "we should fear, love, and trust in God above all things." The root of all sin is a refusal to trust in the one true God, as he has revealed himself in his Word. Similarly, Calvin breaks the commandment down into four parts: adoration, trust, invocation, and thanksgiving. To adore God is to reverence him, submitting our conscience to his will and refusing to surrender it to anyone or anything else. To trust God is to find our only saving consolation in his mercy and goodness. To invoke God is to call on no other name, including Mary and the saints, but to embrace him in Christ the Mediator. Finally, just

---

[37] Ibid., 2.8.14.
[38] Ibid.
[39] Ibid., 2.8.9.
[40] Ibid., 2.8.11.

as the essence of human sin is identified with being "no longer thankful" (Rom. 1:21), the essence of obedience is gratitude.[41]

If the first commandment summons us to worship the correct God, the second commands us to worship this God correctly. Luther had collapsed the second into the first, which is of no small consequence in the differences between Lutheran and Reformed interpretations of what is allowable in public worship.[42]

"You shall not take the name of the LORD your God in vain," according to the third commandment. Luther explains in the Small Catechism, "We should fear and love God that we may not curse, swear, use witchcraft, lie, or deceive by His name, but call upon it in every trouble, pray, praise, and give thanks." Calvin's explanation in his own catechism is similar, but he expands on it in the *Institutes*. We see once again the priority of the positive thrust of the command: "First, whatever our mind conceives of God, whatever our tongue utters, should savor of his excellence, match the loftiness of his sacred name, and lastly, serve to glorify his greatness." This encompasses a reverent use of "his Holy Word and worshipful mysteries" and "praise of his wisdom, righteousness, and goodness. That is what it means to hallow God's name."[43] Calvin recognizes that this commandment in its original context referred especially to oaths taken in court. We must see these oaths as confessions that we make to God, not simply to other people.[44] At the same time, Calvin challenges the Anabaptist interpretation of the Sermon on the Mount as forbidding such oaths in court.[45]

His interpretation of the fourth commandment has received considerable attention. Like Luther, Zwingli, Bucer, and most of the other Reformers, Calvin reacted sharply against the "superstitious" attachment to days, which he identified with Rome and the Anabaptists. First, he says, "The purpose of this commandment is that, being dead to our own inclinations and works, we should meditate on the Kingdom of God, and that we should practice the meditation in the ways established by him." He adds, "The early fathers customarily called this commandment a foreshadowing because it contains the outward keeping of a day which, upon Christ's coming, was abolished with the other figures."[46] Third, Calvin sharply rejects

---

[41] Ibid., 2.8.16.
[42] Ibid., 2.8.21.
[43] Ibid., 2.8.22.
[44] Ibid., 2.8.23.
[45] Ibid., 2.8.26.
[46] Ibid., 2.8.28.

the medieval distinction between the ceremonial and moral aspect of this commandment, which left the Sabbath command intact only after changing the day to Sunday.

> Thus vanish the trifles of the false prophets, who in former centuries inflicted the people with a Jewish opinion. They asserted that nothing but the ceremonial part of this commandment has been abrogated (in their phraseology the "appointing" of the seventh day), but the moral part remains—namely, the fixing of one day in seven. Yet this is merely changing the day as a reproach to the Jews, while keeping in mind the same sanctity of the day. . . . For those of them who cling to their constitutions surpass the Jews three times over in crass and Sabbatarian superstition.

In short, the part of this command that remains for us is that "we should diligently frequent the sacred meetings and make use of those external aids which can promote the worship of God."[47] Calvin argues here that "this foreshadowing of spiritual rest occupied the chief place in the Sabbath."[48] "But there is no doubt that by the Lord Christ's coming the ceremonial part of this commandment was abolished. For he himself is the truth, with whose presence all figures vanish; he is the body, at whose appearance all the shadows are left behind. He is, I say, the true fulfillment of the Sabbath." Therefore, the true meaning of the command "is not confined within a single day but extends through the whole course of our life, until, completely dead to ourselves, we are filled with the life of God. Christians ought therefore to shun completely the superstitious observance of days."[49]

This does not mean that we are forbidden to be called by the elders to assemble on certain days. Central importance was given to the weekly Lord's Day, and Christ's nativity, crucifixion, resurrection, ascension, and Pentecost were also celebrated on the Sunday nearest to each.[50] "Although the Sabbath has been abrogated," Calvin says, "there is still occasion for us: (1) to assemble on stated days for the hearing of the Word, the breaking of the mystical bread, and for public prayers [Acts 2:42]; (2) to give surcease

---

[47] Ibid., 2.8.34.
[48] Ibid., 2.8.29.
[49] Ibid., 2.8.31.
[50] There is some difference between Continental and British developments on this point. The Church Order of Dort, for example, requires special services for Christmas, Good Friday, Easter, Ascension, and Pentecost. The Puritans eliminated these days from the church calendar, but encouraged Parliament to call special days of fasting and thanksgiving.

from labor to servants and workmen." He adds, "Meetings of the church are enjoined upon us by God's Word," and the church is given authority to regulate the times and places of their regular assembly. We should assemble daily! "But if the weakness of many made it impossible for daily meetings to be held, and the rule of love does not allow more to be required of them, why should we not obey the order we see laid upon us by God's will?"[51]

The Lord's Day is to be set aside therefore not because it is the Sabbath, Calvin says, but because "we are using it as a remedy needed to keep order in the church."[52]

> However, the ancients did not substitute the Lord's Day (as we call it) for the Sabbath without careful discrimination. The purpose and fulfillment of that true rest, represented by the ancient Sabbath, lies in the Lord's resurrection. Hence, by the very day that brought the shadows to an end, Christians are warned not to cling to the shadow rite. Nor do I cling to the number "seven" so as to bind the church in subjection to it. And I shall not condemn churches that have other solemn days for their meetings, provided there be no superstition.[53]

Loving the Neighbor: The Second Table

Calvin points to the wider scope of the fifth commandment. Under the honoring of parents, he includes (by appeals to New Testament passages) respect for and obedience to all whom God places in authority.[54] At the same time, "if they spur us to transgress the law, we have a perfect right to regard them not as parents, but as strangers who are trying to lead us away from obedience to our true Father."[55]

The sixth commandment not only forbids killing but also requires the inner intent and outer action to enhance our neighbor's welfare.

> We are accordingly commanded, if we find anything of use to us in saving our neighbors' lives, faithfully to employ it; if there is anything that makes for their peace, to see to it; if anything harmful, to ward it off; if they are in danger, to lend a helping hand.

---

[51] Calvin, *Institutes* 2.8.32.
[52] Ibid., 2.8.33.
[53] Ibid., 2.8.34.
[54] Ibid., 2.8.35.
[55] Ibid., 2.8.38.

It summons the heart, not just the hands, for "hatred is nothing but sustained anger" toward our neighbor.[56]

It was just such an understanding of this commandment's breadth and depth that many Protestants appealed to in Germany, the Netherlands, and France as they hid Jews during the Nazi occupation.

> Scripture notes that this commandment rests upon a twofold basis: man is both the image of God, and our flesh. Now, if we do not wish to violate the image of God, we ought to hold our neighbor sacred. And if we do not wish to renounce all humanity, we ought to cherish his as our own flesh. We shall elsewhere discuss how this exhortation is to be derived from the redemption and grace of Christ.[57]

Servants are not slaves. "Every expression of disdain arising from the pride of masters is included in the single word threatening," Calvin says in commenting on Ephesians 6:9. "They are charged not to assume a lordly air or a superior attitude," he warns. "Threatenings and every kind of barbarity originate in this, that masters look upon their servants as if they had been born for their sake alone, and treat them as if they were of no more value than cattle."[58]

The seventh commandment requires sexual purity, but not celibacy. Some are given the gift of celibacy. However, those who struggle with sexual temptation but do not marry "depart from their calling."[59] In short, "let every man abstain from marriage only so long as he is fit to observe celibacy."[60] Among others, Emory University's John Witte Jr. argues that Calvin transformed the Western view of marriage. Like Luther and the other Reformers, he denied the superiority of celibacy over marriage. Beyond this, though, he offered a new vision of courtship and marriage based on love rather than merely on social standing (i.e., arranged marriages). In addition, he encouraged the remarriage of widows and brought attention to the problem of abused wives. All of these problems, though severe, were largely overlooked in medieval piety. However, Calvin addressed them head-on, as did the church consistory.[61] In an age in which women were

---

[56] Ibid., 2.8.39.
[57] Ibid.
[58] Calvin on Eph. 6:9, in *Calvin's Commentaries*, , 21:332.
[59] Calvin, *Institutes* 2.8.42.
[60] Ibid., 2.8.43.
[61] See John Witte Jr. and Robert M. Kingdon, *Sex, Marriage, and Family in Calvin's Geneva*, vol. 1, *Courtship, Engagement, and Marriage* (Grand Rapids: Eerdmans, 2005).

only a little higher than servants, Calvin warned, "Therefore, the man who does not love his wife is a monster."[62]

The eighth commandment not only forbids the crime of theft, but also prohibits us "to pant after the possessions of others" and, positively, calls us "to help every man to keep his own possessions." Calvin ultimately grounds this not in the right of private property, but in God's providence: "We must consider what every man possesses has not come to him by mere chance but by the distribution of the supreme Lord of all."[63] Thus, the God-centered rather than human-centered orientation once again appears. The rule is not merely "do no harm," as if not violating our neighbor's rights were the ultimate aim. Rather, it is to respect our neighbor and his or her possessions because we are answerable *to God*. Sometimes our neighbor's goods are stolen "by seemingly legal means." God knows this. "He sees the hard and inhuman laws with which the more powerful oppresses and crushes the weaker person." We are obligated to oppose "such injustice."[64] The command also obliges us to "share the needs of those whom we see pressed by the difficulty of affairs, assisting them in their need with our abundance."[65]

The ninth commandment forbids perjuring oneself in court. Positively, Calvin says, it enjoins us to protect the good reputation of our neighbor. Luther offers a similar interpretation in his Small Catechism when he says that this command calls us to think well of our neighbor and "put the best construction on everything." When we jump to conclusions, Calvin says, it is usually to censure our neighbor. We should be more disposed to covering our neighbor's blemishes than to publicize them. "And yet," he observes, "it is amazing with what thoughtless unconcern we sin in this respect time and again! Those who do not markedly suffer from this disease are rare indeed." Gossip is one of those sins that we easily tolerate even in the church, but Calvin is strict in his rebuke: "Indeed, this precept even extends to forbidding us to affect a fawning politeness barbed with bitter taunts under the guise of joking." Many bring shame to others and "sometimes grievously wound their brothers with this sort of impudence."[66]

With the prohibition of coveting in the tenth commandment, Calvin points out that love must be the rule of our lives. Love is indeed the sum-

---

[62] Calvin on Eph. 5:28, in *Calvin's Commentaries*, 21:322.
[63] Calvin, *Institutes* 2.8.45.
[64] Ibid.
[65] Ibid., 2.8.46.
[66] Ibid., 2.8.48.

mary of the law. This commandment reminds us that what God requires in all of these rules is not just outward conformity but inward righteousness.[67]

In conclusion, Calvin notes that there is no difference in substance between these commands in the moral law and those exhortations that we find in the New Testament. God's character has not changed. Today, as always, God summons us to a life of love that reflects that divine love that is the fountain of our very existence.[68] "Faith, then, is the root of true piety," Calvin says.[69] The gospel creates faith, and faith bears the fruit of love and good works.

Like the Decalogue itself, Calvin emphasizes the duties that we have toward God and others. Compare this with the usual lists of spiritual disciplines and virtue-enhancing strategies that keep us focused on ourselves. Calvin knew well the Rule of Saint Benedict. It offers a ladder with "twelve steps of humility" leading to perfect love and to heaven itself.

The first is "keeping in mind that all who despise God will burn in hell for their sins, and all who reverence God have everlasting life awaiting them."[70] Our thoughts and bodily desires "are in God's sight and are reported by angels at every hour."[71] "The second step of humility is that we love not our own will nor take pleasure in the satisfaction of our desires."[72] The third step is to "submit to the prioress or abbot in all obedience for the love of God."[73] Fourth, "our hearts quietly embrace suffering and endure it without weakening or seeking escape."[74] Fifth, confession is made regularly of all sins to the abbot or prioress.[75] Sixth and seventh, "we are content with the lowest and most menial treatment" and acknowledge "in our hearts that we are inferior to all and of less value"—even "a worm."[76] The eighth step requires strict adherence only to the common rule of the monastery, while the ninth requires silence unless spoken to, and the tenth and eleventh warn against laughter.[77] The twelfth step of humility calls monks and nuns to bear constantly in their mind their guilt before God on

---

[67] Ibid., 2.8.50.
[68] Ibid., 2.8.51.
[69] Calvin on Ps. 78:21, in *Calvin's Commentaries*, vol. 5, trans. James Anderson (Grand Rapids: Baker, 1996), 245.
[70] Joan Chittister, OSB, *The Rule of Benedict: A Spirituality for the Twenty-First Century* (New York: Cross-road, 2010), 79.
[71] Ibid.
[72] Ibid., 83.
[73] Ibid., 84.
[74] Ibid., 85.
[75] Ibid., 88.
[76] Ibid., 91.
[77] Ibid., 92–95.

account of their sins.[78] "Now, therefore, after ascending all these steps of humility, we will quickly arrive at the 'perfect love' of God 'which casts out fear' (1 John 4:18)."[79]

These and the many other prescriptions of the rule focus mainly on the individual. This makes sense, since the life it seeks to regulate is one of withdrawal from the world. Indeed, it is even withdrawal from the church, since everything happens within the walls of the monastery.

In sharp contrast, Calvin argues, God's commands make sense only in a social context where we are engaging in ordinary life together with God and each other: spouse, children, parents, employers, coworkers, employees, fellow citizens, and brothers and sisters in the church.

The piety that Calvin enjoins guards against legalism and antinomianism, and this is summarized well in the Reformed confessions: "In this life even the holiest have only a small beginning of this obedience. Nevertheless, with all seriousness of purpose, they do begin to live according to all, not only some, of God's commands."[80] "Therefore it is so far from being true that this justifying faith makes men remiss in a pious and holy life, that on the contrary without it they would never do anything out of love to God, but only out of self-love or fear of damnation."[81]

This releases us finally for a life of considering others and their needs rather than obsessing over ourselves and our standing before God. It is not a question of whether we are called to live in a way that is pleasing to God, but of whether we are trying to please God as our Judge who weighs our works in court or as our Father who already accepts us as coheirs with Christ.

> But if, freed from this severe requirement of the law, or rather from the entire rigor of the law, they hear themselves called with fatherly gentleness by God, they will cheerfully and with great eagerness answer, and follow his leading. To sum up: Those bound by the yoke of the law are like servants assigned certain tasks for each day by their masters. . . . But sons, who are more generously and candidly treated by their fathers, do not hesitate to offer them incomplete and half-done and even defective works, trusting that their obedience and readiness will be approved by

---

[78] Ibid., 97–98.
[79] Ibid., 98.
[80] The Heidelberg Catechism, Lord's Day, q. 113, in *The Psalter Hymnal: Doctrinal Standards and Liturgy of the Christian Reformed Church* (Grand Rapids: Board of Publications for the CRC, 1976), 56.
[81] The Belgic Confession, art. 24, in *The Psalter Hymnal*, 80.

our most merciful Father, however small, rude, and imperfect these may be. . . . But how can this be done amidst all this dread, where one doubts whether God is offended or honored by our works?[82]

Law and Liberty in the Christian Life

In *The Freedom of a Christian* (1520), Luther explores the paradox of the believer as simultaneously, in Christ, the lord of all and servant of none and the servant of all and lord of none. Precisely because in Christ we are free from the law's regency, "we must not think it strange that we submit ourselves to our neighbors, for God created us with that condition in view."[83] To be a free heir of God is to be a servant of our neighbor. The law still tells us what it means to love and summons us to that calling, though no longer out of fear but out of free submission to each other.

For Calvin, Christian liberty is not a secondary matter that we can take or leave. He calls it "an appendage [or appendix] to justification," and it follows on the heels of his treatment of that doctrine.

> We must now discuss Christian freedom. He who proposes to summarize gospel teaching ought by no means to omit an explanation of this topic. For it is a thing of prime necessity, and apart from a knowledge of it consciences dare undertake almost nothing without doubting; they hesitate and recoil from many things; they constantly waver and are afraid. But freedom is especially an appendage of justification and is of no little avail in understanding its power.[84]

Of what use is a doctrine of justification if we do not actually experience God's liberality toward us in our daily lives?

What about the Weaker Brother?

At this point, Calvin observes, critics often raise the question of the "weaker brother" in Romans 14. Perhaps recalling the practice in Zurich of holding meat dinners on Friday and public sausage barbeques on Ash Wednesday, Calvin rebukes those who parade their newfound liberty. Here once again, the thing itself is indifferent, but is corrupted by a spiritual arrogance that is as offensive to God as that occasioned by

---

[82] Calvin, *Institutes* 3.19.5.
[83] Calvin, *Sermons on the Epistle to the Ephesians* (Edinburgh: Banner of Truth, 1973), 564.
[84] Calvin, *Institutes* 3.19.1.

its prohibition. It is a sort of reverse legalism that vaunts superiority by waving the flag of Christian freedom. You shouldn't encourage someone to eat meat on Friday or to drink wine if at that moment they believe it is contrary to God's will. Teach them first so that their conscience will be free before God.

Yet too often legalism takes shelter under the "weaker brother" argument, Calvin argues. In this case, an act that is not committed "by ill will or malicious intent" is nevertheless "wrenched into an occasion for offense . . . to persons of bitter disposition and pharisaical pride." "Accordingly," Calvin concludes, "we shall call the one the offense of the weak, the other that of the Pharisees. Thus we shall so temper the use of our freedom as to allow for the ignorance of our weak brothers, but for the rigor of the Pharisees, not at all!"[85]

Paul encourages Timothy to be circumcised so as not to cause offense to Jews who do not yet understand the gospel, but vehemently opposes those Jewish Christians who required it.[86] Similarly, the pope and his monks

> are not to be listened to who, after making themselves leaders in a thousand sorts of wickedness, pretend that they must act so as not to cause offense to their neighbors; as if they were not in the meantime building up their neighbors' consciences into evil, especially when they ever stick fast in the same mud without hope of getting out. And suave fellows are they who, whether their neighbor is to be instructed in doctrine or in example of life, say he must be fed with milk while they steep him in the worst and deadliest opinions.[87]

Restricting the church's authority in doctrine, worship, and life to that which God has clearly commanded in his Word, Calvin is the enemy of legalism. He calls it "this irreligious affectation of religion" to "delight in contriving some way of acquiring righteousness apart from God's Word." "Hence, among what are commonly considered good works the commandments of the law are accorded too narrow a place, while that innumerable throng of human precepts occupies almost the whole space."[88] As if he had Benedict's Rule in mind, the Reformer adds, "And we have never been forbidden to laugh, or to be filled, or to join new possessions to old or ancestral

---

[85] Ibid., 3.19.11.
[86] Ibid., 3.19.12.
[87] Ibid., 3.19.13.
[88] Ibid., 2.8.5.

ones, or to delight in musical harmony, or to drink wine." These are good gifts that we dare neither despise nor corrupt by avarice, gluttony, and intoxication.[89]

Christ purchased our liberty. "And the knowledge of this freedom is very necessary for us," Calvin says, "for if it is lacking, our consciences will have no repose and there will be no end to superstitions." It is no small matter when the believer's conscience is bound by human regulations. "For when consciences once ensnare themselves, they enter a long and inextricable maze, not easy to get out of." One begins to doubt whether he really needs to use "linen sheets, shirts, handkerchiefs, and napkins" and soon "afterward [will] be uncertain also about hemp; finally, doubt will even arise over tow."

> For he will turn over in his mind whether he can sup without napkins, or go without a handkerchief. . . . If he boggles at sweet wine, he will not with clear conscience drink even flat wine, and finally he will not dare touch water if sweeter and cleaner than other water. To sum up, he will come to the point of considering it wrong to step upon a straw across his path, as the saying goes.[90]

It is possible even for those who affirm the doctrine of justification to live like a scrupulous monk, worrying over the enjoyment of things that serve one's delight rather than strict necessity. This sad state creates confusion for some and provokes unbridled license for others, says Calvin. In other words, such legalism is the fuel for antinomianism.[91] Isn't this obvious in history and in our own experience in the church? Wherever extrabiblical expectations reign, there is bound to be a rebellion.

The proper course is to remember that "we should use God's gifts for the purpose for which he gave them to us, with no scruple of conscience, no trouble of mind. With such confidence our minds will be at peace with him, and will recognize his liberality toward us."[92] Our Father's "liberality" is so generous that he gives us not only what we need, but also what brings us delight and pleasure. This is the importance of Christian liberty. "Its whole force consists in quieting frightened consciences before God—that are perhaps disturbed and troubled over forgiveness of sins, or anxious

---

[89] Ibid., 3.19.9.
[90] Ibid., 3.19.7.
[91] Ibid.
[92] Ibid., 3.19.8.

whether unfinished works, corrupted by the faults of the flesh, are pleasing to God, or tormented about the use of things indifferent."[93]

Equally repugnant to Calvin were luxurious indulgence and that ascetic deprivation that he saw as especially encouraged by monastic and Anabaptist rigor. According to Calvin, Richard Gamble summarizes,

> the beauty and scent of the flower demonstrates that God does not want Christians to live only with the bare necessities of life. The Bible teaches that "wine makes the heart glad." In light of the goodness of creation, Christian consciences cannot be bound to obey laws regarding earthly goods that go beyond Scripture. However, Calvin was firmly convinced that the Scripture gives the Christian community certain guidelines for using and enjoying the earth's goods.[94]

"Sanctification and church membership are inseparable."[95] We are fellow pilgrims and must grow up into one body, walk together, and bear each other's burdens.

Given this purpose, how can Christian liberty be understood (by legalists and antinomians alike) as opening the floodgate to license? Even the believer still feels the desire "to outstrip his neighbors in all sorts of elegance," and may seek to justify it "under the pretext of Christian freedom." Indeed, it is indifferent, Calvin says, "provided they are used indifferently." "But when they are coveted too greedily, when they are proudly boasted of, when they are lavishly squandered, things that were of themselves otherwise lawful are certainly defiled by these vices."[96]

Faith Is the Root, Love Is the Rule

Calvin finally arrives at the heart of the argument, again following Paul. With faith as its root, *love* is the rule of Christian fellowship. Can't we see that everything contained in the gospel serves the end of creating a community of love in a world of selfishness and pride? The Pharisee *and* the anti-Pharisee are acting out of self-righteousness rather than out of love. But we cannot be forced to choose between faith's freedom and love's law.

---

[93] Ibid., 3.19.9.
[94] Richard Gamble, "Calvin and Sixteenth-Century Spirituality: Comparison with the Anabaptists," in *Calvin Studies Society Papers, 1995, 1997: Calvin and Spirituality; Calvin and His Contemporaries*, ed. David Foxgrover (Grand Rapids: CRC Product Services, 1998), 35–36.
[95] Ibid., 38.
[96] Calvin, *Institutes* 3.19.9.

"For as our freedom must be subordinated to love, so in turn ought love itself to abide under purity of faith."[97]

In short, because the Christian faithful "should not be entangled with any snares of observances in those matters in which the Lord has willed them to be free, we conclude that they are released from the power of all men."

> For Christ does not deserve to forfeit our gratitude for his great generosity—nor consciences their profit. And we should not put a light value upon something that we see cost Christ so dear, since he valued it not with gold and silver but with his own blood [1 Pet. 1:18–19]. Paul does not hesitate to say that Christ's death is nullified if we put our souls under men's subjection [cf. Gal. 2:21]. For in certain chapters of the letter to the Galatians, Paul is solely trying to show how to us Christ is obscured, or rather extinguished, unless our consciences stand firm in their freedom.[98]

The easy solution is either to make a rule or break a rule. The more difficult course is to uphold this liberty that Christ has purchased for us, with wisdom and love for each other. Calvin's description of the reaction to this subject remains as relevant and contemporary as ever: "For, as soon as Christian freedom is mentioned," he says, some, "on the pretext of this freedom, shake off all obedience toward God and break out into unbridled license." In reaction, "others disdain it, thinking that it takes away all moderation, order, and choice of things."

> What should we do here, hedged about with such perplexities? Shall we say good-by to Christian freedom, thus cutting off occasion for such dangers? But, as we have said, unless this freedom be comprehended, neither Christ nor gospel truth, nor inner peace of soul, can be rightly known. Rather, we must take care that so necessary a part of doctrine be not suppressed, yet at the same time that those absurd objections which are wont to arise be met.[99]

Calvin shares Luther's emphasis on the importance of the conscience.[100] The weak, with their scruples about certain matters, must not have their consciences bruised by the strong. Nor may the "Pharisees" bind

---

[97] Ibid., 3.19.13.
[98] Ibid., 3.19.14.
[99] Ibid., 3.19.1.
[100] Ibid., 3.19.2.

the consciences of others by their own laws. "Let love be the rule," Calvin counsels, "and all will be well."[101] "The mortification of the flesh is the effect of the cross of Christ."[102] The Spirit produces faith through the Word; this faith bears the fruit of love, shown in good works as defined by God's law. As justification is the chief part of the gospel for Calvin, "love forms the chief part of Christian perfection [sanctification]."[103]

Yet even as believers, we find that this love is mixed with selfishness, Calvin observes. "Though the gospel is at this day purely preached among us, when we consider how little progress we make in brotherly love, we ought justly to be ashamed of our indolence."[104]

Inevitably, our life together in Christ's body encounters negotiations when it comes to the practical questions of daily life. There are "Pharisees" and there are "Libertines."[105] As different as they appear at first, both are driven by pride rather than the love that comes from faith in the gospel.

Calvin's argument thus follows Luther's in *The Freedom of a Christian*. Precisely because the believer has been raised in Christ above all legal bondage, he or she can be the servant of everyone in freedom and love. Here we need wisdom, which simply making a rule or breaking a rule short-circuits. We do not live in a world of scarcity, but sit at a table of abundance—together with our brothers and sisters. We already possess everything together in Christ, so our life together in the body should be like Christmas, exchanging gifts in thanksgiving. We can accept each other because, in Christ, the Father accepts us all. "And we need this assurance in no slight degree, for without it we attempt everything in vain."[106]

---

[101] Ibid., 3.19.13.
[102] Calvin on Gal. 5:24, in *Calvin's Commentaries*, 21:169.
[103] Calvin on Gal. 5:14, in *Calvin's Commentaries*, 21:159.
[104] Calvin on Mic. 4:3, in *Calvin's Commentaries*, vol. 14, trans. John Owen (Grand Rapids: Baker, 1996), 264.
[105] "The sectarian movements in France were not so much Anabaptist as they were Libertine and mystic. There were some rebaptizers in Orléans and in Bourges during Calvin's youth. This term, however, described all kinds of German mystics, Italian rationalists, heterodox anarchists, and the so-called *libertins spirituels*, or Quintinites." Willem Balke, *Calvin and the Anabaptist Radicals*, trans. William J. Heynen (Grand Rapids: Eerdmans, 1981), 21.
[106] Calvin, *Institutes* 3.19.5.

CHAPTER II

GOD'S NEW SOCIETY

If the public service is God's "celestial theater" of grace, then the church is not only the place where the drama is performed, but the fruit of its performance. "Although the whole world is 'the theater of God's kindness, wisdom, justice and power,' Calvin mentions that in this theater the church is actually the part which illustrates it best—like an orchestra."[1] "The church is thus elected by God to be 'the theater of his fatherly care.'"[2] Calvin would not have comprehended the contrast between "getting saved" and "joining a church." In his understanding, the church is not only the spiritual body of true believers, but also a visible institution—indeed, "the mother of the faithful." "And the ministry of the Church, and it alone, is undoubtedly the means by which we are born again to a heavenly life."[3]

How to Find a Church

But then the question arises: How do you know where there is a true church, especially given so many deviations, corruptions, and divisions? The answer was easy, according to Rome and the Anabaptists. In different ways, both reduced the marks of the church to one: discipline. According to Rome, the right *ministers* guarantee the right *ministry*. Wherever there is a congregation that submits to the discipline of the pope, it is part of the true

---

[1] Herman J. Selderhuis, *Calvin's Theology of the Psalms* (Grand Rapids: Baker Academic, 2007), 228, on Ps. 135:13.
[2] Ibid., on Ps. 68:8.
[3] Calvin on Ps. 87:5, in *Calvin's Commentaries*, vol. 5, trans. James Anderson (Grand Rapids: Baker, 1996), 402.

visible church. The right doctrine and sacramental ministry will be present wherever the right government is observed. Obviously, radical Protestants did not acknowledge the pope. However, they identified the true church with the visible holiness of the members. There was a clean and obvious separation between the godly and the ungodly.

For the magisterial Reformers, these answers identify the wrong source of the church's existence. The church cannot give birth to itself. The source of the church's existence is not the pope or the holiness of its members, but the gospel that comes to the church outside of itself. The marks are to be found not in the majesty of an outward form of organization or in the faith and piety of the members, the Reformers argued, but in the presence of the triune God where he has promised to meet us in saving blessing: "namely, the pure preaching of God's Word and the lawful administration of the sacraments."[4] "Wherever we find the word of God purely preached and heard, and the sacraments administered according to the institution of Christ, there . . . is a Church of God."[5]

The appeal to "right discipline" as *the* distinguishing mark of the true church assumes an over-realized eschatology—in other words, expecting perfection before Christ returns. We want to be able to point to the one true church, with no questions, reservations, or uncertainties. We don't want to wait for Christ's return to separate the wheat from the weeds, the sheep from the goats. It must all be visible and unambiguous now.

An important Roman Catholic theologian summarized the view some years ago. In criticizing Augustine's "mixed assembly" view of the church, he wrote, "Certainly, the Church is full of sinners, but *inasmuch* as they are sinners, they cannot be counted in with the Church. They can only be in her as 'improper,' 'so-called,' 'seeming,' 'reckoned,' 'pretended' members, but cannot *qua* sinners, express membership in the one body of love."[6] According to Vatican I, "the Church itself, with its marvelous extension, its eminent holiness, and its inexhaustible fruitfulness in every good thing, with its Catholic unity and its invincible stability, is a great and perpetual motive of credibility and an irrefutable witness of its own divine mission."[7]

Of course, there are many Protestant sects that make such claims,

---

[4] Calvin, *Institutes of the Christian Religion*, ed. John T. McNeill, trans. Ford Lewis Battles (Philadelphia: Westminster, 1960), prefatory address to King Francis I, 25.
[5] Ibid., 4.1.9.
[6] Hans Urs von Balthasar, *Church and World*, trans. A. V. Littledale with Alexander Dru (Montreal: Palm, 1967), 145–46.
[7] Quoted by Avery Dulles, SJ, *Models of the Church* (Garden City, NY: Doubleday, 1974), 123.

appealing to charismatic leaders, miracles, obvious piety, and visible impact. Obviously, this movement, that leader, or our particular brand must be the true church: just look at the visible fruit and that is enough to persuade you that it has God's seal of approval. Many of us were raised hearing mature believers identify the false churches in town by the lack of intensity of their piety. Unlike us, they were not truly born again. They didn't have a *personal* relationship with Jesus.

No, Calvin says. You can't trust your eye, but only your ear on this one. We hear the promise that even though the church is still sinful, it is justified and is being renewed by the powerful energies of the Word and Spirit. We hear and believe in the promise of what the church will one day be. We hear the gospel here and now, ratified in baptism and the Supper. The unity, holiness, catholicity, and apostolicity of the church depend entirely on what it hears and tells. The marks of the church lie not within the church itself, but in the ministry that gives birth to it and continually feeds, grows, and expands it to the ends of the earth. And if you can only handle a perfect garden, then—as Jesus said—you will end up pulling up wheat with the weeds, Calvin warns.[8]

The right *ministry* determines the right *ministers*, not vice versa, in Calvin's view. As Paul warned, anyone who preaches a different gospel is anathema—condemned—even if he were an apostle or an angel from heaven (Gal. 1:8). The pope is hardly exempt from that threat, Calvin reminds us.[9] "It is by the preaching of the grace of God alone that the Church is kept from perishing," Calvin is convinced, and the sacraments ratify this gospel to each of us personally.[10] Therefore, the only legitimate reason for breaking fellowship with a church is its abandonment of this message and ministry. "For the Lord esteems the communion of his church so highly," Calvin warns, "that he counts as a traitor and apostate from Christianity anyone who arrogantly leaves any Christian society, provided it cherishes the true ministry of Word and sacraments."[11]

Demanding a perfect church ensures that bruised reeds will be broken off and faintly burning candles will be extinguished. Or conceited souls

---

[8] Calvin, *Institutes* 4.1.13.
[9] Calvin on Gal. 1:2–10, in *Calvin's Commentaries*, vol. 21, trans. William Pringle (Grand Rapids: Baker, 1996), 25–35.
[10] Calvin on Ps. 22:31, in *Calvin's Commentaries*, vol. 4, trans. James Anderson (Grand Rapids: Baker, 1996), 389.
[11] Calvin, *Institutes* 4.1.10.

will never be able to settle for long in a church that they regard as beneath their own remarkable spiritual attainments.

> In bearing with imperfections of life we ought to be far more consider-ate. For here the descent is very slippery and Satan ambushes us with no ordinary devices. For there have always been those who, imbued with a false conviction of their own perfect sanctity, as if they had already become a sort of airy spirits, spurned association with all men in whom they discern any remnant of human nature.
>
> The Cathari of old were of this sort, as well as the Donatists, who approached them in foolishness. Such today are some of the Anabaptists who wish to appear advanced beyond other men. There are others who sin more out of ill-advised zeal for righteousness than out of that insane pride. When they do not see a quality of life corresponding to the doctrine of the gospel among those to whom it is announced, they immediately judge that no church exists in that place. . . . For where the Lord requires kindness, they neglect it and give themselves over completely to immod-erate severity. Indeed, because they think no church exists where there are not perfect purity and integrity of life, they depart out of hatred of wickedness from the lawful church, while they fancy themselves turn-ing aside from the faction of the wicked. . . . But if the Lord declares that the church is to labor under this evil—to be weighed down with the mix-ture of the wicked—until the Day of Judgment, they are vainly seeking a church besmirched with no blemish.[12]

Paul, too, warned Timothy that some in the church would teach mis-erable errors and lead many astray. "But God's firm foundation stands, bearing this seal: 'The Lord knows those who are his,' and, 'Let everyone who names the name of the Lord depart from iniquity'" (2 Tim. 2:18–19). Commenting on this verse, Calvin reminds us not to take to ourselves the presumption of separating the elect from the nonelect.[13]

Just as an individual believer is simultaneously justified and sinful, a congregation does not lose its claim to be called a church simply because of a spate of bad sermons or imperfections in doctrine and ceremonies. "The purest churches have their blemishes; and some are marked, not by a few spots, but by general deformity."[14] In Calvin's appraisal, Rome had indeed

---

[12] Calvin, *Institutes* 4.1.13.
[13] Calvin on 2 Tim. 2:19, in *Calvin's Commentaries*, 21:228.
[14] Calvin on Gal. 1:2, in *Calvin's Commentaries*, 21:25.

fallen into such a "general deformity." In fact, it had lost its status as a legitimate church, although "we do not for this reason impugn the existence
of [true] churches among them," subjected to the tyranny of the pope.[15]

No doubt drawing on personal experience, Calvin acknowledges, "The
Church . . . has had no enemies more inveterate than the members of the
Church."[16] Nevertheless, "as long as the doctrine and the liturgy remain
pure, the unity of the church may not be broken due to sins committed by
members of the church."[17]

Making Disciples: A Family Affair

The sentiment expressed in Billy Joel's line "Go ahead with your own life—
leave me alone!" was not unfamiliar to Calvin, and he saw this as the nadir
of pride. Precisely because the sacrifice for guilt has been offered once and
for all, we can offer our lives as a sacrifice of thanksgiving. There is no sacrifice of thanks more pleasing to God, Calvin says, than cultivating "brotherly good-will."[18]

Bucer held that discipline was a third mark of the church, and this
became the standard view in the Reformed confessions. Even Luther included it as a mark in his treatise *On Councils and the Church*, although
the Augsburg Confession includes only the first two. The high esteem in
which Calvin held church discipline for the *well-being* of the church is in-
disputable, but he did not consider it a mark of the very *being* of the church
itself. Rather than regarding it a third mark, Calvin considered discipline
to be part of the proper application of the Word and administration of the
sacraments.[19]

We hear a lot about spiritual disciplines, where we are in control of
the situation, but especially in our modern Western context, church discipline is viewed widely as a threat to personal autonomy. After all, it is

[15] Calvin, *Institutes* 4.2.12.
[16] Calvin on John 13:18, in *Calvin's Commentaries*, vol. 18, trans. William Pringle (Grand Rapids: Baker, 1996), 66.
[17] Selderhuis, *Calvin's Theology of the Psalms*, 232, quoting Calvin on Ps. 15:1.
[18] Calvin on Ps. 16:3, in *Calvin's Commentaries*, 4:219.
[19] We should beware of overstating Calvin's difference from the Reformed confessions at this point. To some extent, it is semantic: what do we mean by "discipline"? For Calvin's opponents, it was a rigorous practice that admitted no church mixed with apostasy, sin, and error among its members. Our confessions understand it simply as having sufficient order and appropriate offices in the church to oversee its members, correcting faults in doctrine and life, and caring for their spiritual and temporal needs. Although Calvin properly observed that the Church of Corinth was still a church in spite of its disorder, it is nevertheless true that Paul was calling the leadership to exercise a discipline that he had already put in place.

my personal relationship with Jesus. We join or don't join churches, as we please. We also leave as we please, even for trivial reasons and without feeling obliged to meet with the elders to discuss the reasons or transfer membership. It is ironic that we are among the most likely to lament the demise of marital fidelity in our culture when we seem at such liberty to come and go as we please in a covenant with even greater oaths and bonds. Some groups do not even have church membership, even as they decry the popularity of living together outside the formal bonds of marriage. In spite of their differences, all of the sixteenth-century disputants at least took the church more seriously than is usually the case today.

Invoking a dictum from the church father Cyprian, Luther referred to the church as our mother in his Large Catechism: "Outside the Christian Church, that is, where the Gospel is not, there is no forgiveness, and hence no holiness. . . . The church is the mother that begets and bears every Christian through the word of God." Calvin, too, described the church as the mother "into whose bosom God is pleased to gather his children, not only that they may be nourished by her help and ministry so long as they are infants and children, but also that they may be guided by her motherly care until they mature and at last reach to the goal of faith."

> For what God has joined together, it is not lawful to put asunder, so that, for those to whom he is Father the Church may also be Mother. . . . Furthermore, away from her bosom one cannot hope for any forgiveness of sins or any salvation, as Isaiah [37:32] and Joel [2:32] testify. . . .
>
> By these words God's fatherly favor and the especial witness of spiritual life are limited to his flock, so that it is always disastrous to leave the church.[20]

In fact, "certainly he who refuses to be a son of the Church in vain desires to have God as his Father; for it is only through the instrumentality of the Church that we are 'born of God' [1 John 3:9] and brought up through the various stages."[21] We are always weak and we never outgrow the church, any more than sheep outgrow their Shepherd.

To our ears today, "church discipline" conjures the idea of being called on the carpet. However, in the New Testament it simply means being a "disciple," someone who is under the yoke of Christ, who teaches and guides

---

[20]Calvin, *Institutes* 4.1.1, 4.
[21]Calvin on Gal. 4:26, in *Calvin's Commentaries*, 21:140–41.

his sheep through undershepherds. Regular discipline is precisely what reduces the need for such emergency measures as censures and excommunication. The Greek verb meaning "to discipline" was commonly used to refer to training, like attending regularly to a vine. You attach the vine to a trellis and prune, water, and feed it so that it flourishes and grows in the right direction. Or the term could be used of the soldier who, by submitting to the instruction, example, and drills of superiors, is prepared for battle. It's amazing that many things we regard as essential to the Christian life cannot be found in Scripture, even as we ignore or regard as trivial its clear commands. Ironically, many who think that the New Testament provides a blueprint for social, economic, and foreign policy seem to think that it is virtually silent about the church's government and worship.

Calvin did not imagine that the New Testament gave us a precise liturgy or church order, but he was convinced that it gives us clear guidelines. From his study of the New Testament Calvin suggested that there are four offices: doctor, pastor-teacher, elder, and deacon. However, the emphasis falls on the latter three.

Pastors: Feeding the Flock

Pastors are trained, examined, and ordained to preach, teach, and administer the sacraments. They give their full time to the ministry of the Word and prayer. Over against Rome, the Reformers taught that baptism, not ordination, makes a priest. In their *person*, officers share with all the saints "one Lord, one faith, one baptism." In their *office*, though, they are not mere facilitators or team leaders. Rather, they are Christ's ambassadors through whom he builds and extends his own kingdom. As Calvin reminds us, Christ told the apostles "that the ministers of the Gospel are porters, so to speak, of the kingdom of heaven, because they carry its keys; and, secondly, he adds that they are invested with a power of binding and losing, which is ratified in heaven."[22] Ministers exercise this ministerial authority "by the doctrine of the gospel" in preaching and absolution and the sacraments.[23]

"Among us, should some ministers be found of no great learning, still none is admitted who is not at least tolerably apt to teach."[24] No pastor

---

[22] Calvin on Mark 8:19, in *Calvin's Commentaries*, vol. 16, trans. William Pringle (Grand Rapids: Baker, 1996), 292.
[23] Ibid., 293.
[24] Calvin, "The Necessity of Reforming the Church," in *Selected Works of John Calvin: Tracts and Letters*, ed. Henry Beveridge and Jules Bonnet, 7 vols. (Grand Rapids: Baker, 1983), 1:170.

holds an office without actually executing that office in that church, Calvin argues, over against the common practice of buying and selling church positions. It was normal for noblemen to purchase a bishopric for their adolescent children. Not only parish priests but even upper clergy, even archbishops and cardinals, did not have to submit to any formal education and examination for their calling.

Calvin wonders how they can boast of apostolic succession when they do not even follow the explicit prescriptions for the offices and the quali-fications for holding them as set forth in the New Testament.[25] "The an-cient canons require that he who is to be admitted to the office of bishop or presbyter shall previously undergo a strict examination both as to life and doctrine," he says. Furthermore, the acclamation of the whole congregation was required for ordination. All bishops taught; they did not govern secular affairs.[26] "In the ordination of a presbyter, each bishop admitted a council of his own presbyters." Are we really to believe that these are successors of the apostles, Calvin asks, regardless of how far they bury the doctrine and government laid down in the apostolic writings?[27]

As Scott Manetsch points out, key to Calvin's ecclesiology was "a com-mitment to a plurality of church ministries." "For Calvin, church gover-nance was never intended to be the prerogative of one person nor even the responsibility of pastors alone."[28] "Hence, Calvin and his colleagues rejected any notion of preeminence or hierarchy of authority within the pastoral company." Each, including Calvin, would submit to the decision of the majority.[29]

The pastor is not a lord, and the congregation is not his fiefdom. He rules in his office, not in his person, and a good pastor attaches the sheep to the Great Shepherd, not to himself. Calvin took up his regular place in the rotation not only for preaching but also for teaching the catechism to the youth during the week. "Christ does not call his ministers to the teaching office that they may subdue the Church and dominate it," Calvin declares, "but that he may make use of their faithful labors to unite it to himself." "It is a great and splendid thing for men to be put in authority over the Church to represent the person of the Son of God," he continues. "They are like

---

[25] Ibid., 170–71.
[26] Ibid., 171.
[27] Ibid., 172.
[28] Scott M. Manetsch, *Calvin's Company of Pastors: Pastoral Care and the Emerging Reformed Church, 1536–1609* (New York: Oxford University Press, 2012), 62.
[29] Ibid.

the friends attached to the bridegroom to celebrate the wedding with him, though they must observe the difference between themselves and what belongs to the bridegroom." They "should not stand in the way of Christ alone having the dominion in his Church or ruling it alone by his Word. . . . Those who win the Church over to themselves rather than to Christ faithlessly violate the marriage which they ought to honor."[30]

Elders: Governing the Flock

Besides preaching, teaching, and administering the sacraments, the ministers serve with the elders in caring for the spiritual needs of their flock.[31] Taken from the laity, elders are the spiritual governors. Pastors are not CEOs, but serve with the elders as Christ's undershepherds. Only as a body do the pastors and elders rule. Not even the church's officers can determine who is truly elect and regenerate, but they can only approve credible professions of faith that in some cases may in the end prove to be false. We know that some of those who seemed far advanced beyond us in the faith turn aside from the Way, while many who seemed weak and immature in their faith and obedience nevertheless persevered to the end, Calvin observes.[32]

Only as one body do elders bind and loose in church discipline. Properly speaking, their ministry is to *loose* or *open* the door. The calling to *bind* or *shut* the door "does not belong to the nature of the Gospel, but is accidental," when manifest unbelievers are excluded from the church.[33] Believers should take great comfort that when they hear themselves absolved from the lips of a fellow sinner ordained to that office, they are dealing with Christ and not merely with men. Conversely, the rebellious should be struck by the fact that the heavenly judgment is being rendered on earth against their impenitence.[34] As with preaching and the sacraments, this action is *ministerial*; Christ ordinarily speaks through his ambassadors, but only on the basis of his Word; the King reserves to himself the sole right to final clemency.[35]

A good parent not only feeds and bathes his or her children, but also teaches, trains, and disciplines them. However, Calvin discerned in both Roman Catholic and Anabaptist discipline a rigor that was opposed to the

---

[30] Calvin on John 3:29, in *Calvin's Commentaries*, 4:80.
[31] Calvin, *Institutes* 4.3.2–8.
[32] Ibid., 3.24.7–9.
[33] Calvin on Mark 8:19, in *Calvin's Commentaries*, 16:293.
[34] Ibid., 294.
[35] Ibid., 296–97.

gospel. Roman Catholic scholar Killian McDonnell notes, "Calvin would rather, however, demand too little than too much in the way of moral disposition, and wants above all to avoid the tortured, harassed, and pitiable conscience he seems to find in Roman Catholicism and also among the Anabaptists."[36]

Observing that the Anabaptists seek a pure church, Luther once commented, "But I neither can nor may as yet set up such a congregation; for I do not as yet have the people for it. If however the time comes that I must do it, so that I cannot with a good conscience refrain from it, then I am ready to do my part."[37] Calvin agreed with this and with Luther's conviction that personal admonitions and correction of vices must take place, but directly with offenders, not in the public service (except in the cases of excommunication and readmission).[38] While Rome lost its title of a true church, Calvin saw the Anabaptists as heirs of the Gnostic and Donatist sects.[39]

Calvin regarded discipline as crucial for the proper administration of the Supper. Yet he was opposed to treating Communion as a reward for the faultless. In his 1536 edition of the *Institutes*, he warns against placing the emphasis in Communion on eating worthily rather than on the words "given for you." "Certain ones, when they would prepare men to eat worthily, have tortured and harassed pitiable consciences in dire ways," as if to "eat worthily" meant "to be purged of all sin." "Such a dogma would debar all the men who ever were or are on earth from the use of this Sacrament. For if it is a question of our seeking our worthiness by ourselves, we are undone; only ruin and confusion remain in us." Anabaptists do not regard the sacrament as God's objective pledge to weak and sinful believers. According to them, "we either know . . . or do not know that God's word preceding the sacrament is His true will. If we know it, we learn nothing new from the sacrament, which follows. If we do not know it, the sacrament (whose whole force and energy rests in the word) also will not teach it."[40]

Whereas Anabaptists were interested in church discipline as a means

---

[36] Killian McDonnell, *John Calvin, the Church, and the Eucharist* (Princeton: Princeton University Press, 1967), 276.

[37] Martin Luther, quoted in Leonard Verduin, *The Reformers and Their Stepchildren* (Grand Rapids: Eerdmans, 1964), 127.

[38] Ibid., 128.

[39] Calvin, *Institutes* 4.1.23. Verduin does not deny this connection. "The Donatists were the original Anabaptists" (*The Reformers and Their Stepchildren*, 192). After quoting numerous sources from various Gnostic groups in the Middle Ages, he adds, "The time is coming, if it is not already here, when people will be proud to acknowledge that they stand in a tradition that leads back to the medieval 'heretic'" (159).

[40] McDonnell, *John Calvin, the Church, and the Eucharist*, 151, quoting Calvin's summary in his 1536 *Institutes* (ed. Battles).

primarily of creating a pure church, Calvin was more concerned with the honor of God and care of Christ's sheep.[41] It is not for us to separate the sheep from the goats, and Calvin constantly warned against rushing to judgment.[42] We cannot say that where "excommunication be not in use," as important as it is, there is no church if nevertheless "she retaineth that doctrine upon which the church is founded."[43] Anabaptists, he says, make much of "sinning willingly." "Among ten, hardly shall we find one that after he knew God hath not sinned willingly."[44]

At the same time, Calvin is convinced that correction and reproof as well as encouragement and instruction belong to the New Testament job description for pastors and elders. The goal of church discipline, Calvin often emphasizes, is restoration of the wayward and good counsel to pilgrims. "The pastor ought to have two voices," Calvin advises: "one for gathering the sheep and another for warding off and driving away wolves and thieves."[45] Only when long-suffering admonitions are rebuffed by unrepentant and unbelieving hearts does discipline become exclusionary. Even then, Calvin insists, the door is always left open with pleas for the prodigal's welcome return.

Elements and Circumstances

Whether in worship or in government and discipline, the unity of the church consists not in circumstances, but in elements. *Elements* are those things that are commanded by Scripture directly or as a necessary conclusion drawn from various biblical passages. It is clear enough that there must be preaching, prayer, and the sacraments in the public service. *Circumstances*—that is, precise details concerning how, when, and in what order to do them—are left to the discretion of the elders. When we turn free circumstances into required elements, we are in danger of legalism; when we turn required elements into free circumstances, we are in danger of antinomianism.

For example, Calvin says that in the celebration of the Supper, "as for the outward details of the action," such as manner of distribution or

[41] Willem Balke, *Calvin and the Anabaptist Radicals*, trans. William J. Heynen (Grand Rapids: Eerdmans, 1981), 223.
[42] Selderhuis, *Calvin's Theology of the Psalms*, 230.
[43] Calvin, quoted by Balke, *Calvin and the Anabaptist Radicals*, 225.
[44] Calvin, quoted in ibid., 226.
[45] Calvin on Titus 1:9, in *Calvin's Commentaries*, 21:296.

"whether the bread should be leavened or unleavened, whether red or white wine should be used—all this is of no importance." On these matters, "we can decide freely."[46] Indeed, he argues, the circumstances will vary, depending on different times and places.[47] He adds:

> It would be extraordinary indeed if in those matters in which the Lord has granted us freedom, in order that we may have greater scope for the edification of the church, we were to strive to attain a slavish uniformity without really caring about the true ordering of church life. For when we appear before the judgment seat of God in order to give account of our deeds we shall not be asked about ceremonies. . . . The right use [of our freedom] will be that one which has contributed most to the edification of the church.[48]

Whether by imposing specific forms or by excluding them, too many people make uniformity in such matters part of the essence of the church. However, "the Christian faith does not consist in such matters."[49]

Another important contribution of Calvin and his heirs is an emphasis on particular circumstances in conduct. Care must be taken to examine each situation and to apply general scriptural principles and godly common sense in concrete cases that might admit different solutions in other cases. This requires circumspection—which means, literally, "looking around." Some of the leading Puritan ministers in England wrote "cases of conscience." In these often lengthy tomes, they laid out in detail particular pastoral issues and how they resolved them—with no expectation that every other pastor or consistory would have followed exactly the same course. The underlying assumption was that while the elements of God's commands were to be observed, the circumstances were a matter of godly liberty.

The same was true in church government. In fact, on some matters that Calvin considered an element, he was remarkably tolerant of different views—more so than some of his followers, in fact. Though convinced that the New Testament prescribed a Presbyterian model, he did not regard it as a determinative mark of the true church. Reformed churches in

---

[46] Calvin, *Institutes* 4.17.43.
[47] Andrew Pettegree, "The Spread of Calvin's Thought," in *The Cambridge Companion to John Calvin*, ed. Donald K. McKim (Cambridge: Cambridge University Press, 2004), 207–8.
[48] Calvin, quoted by Wilhelm Niesel, *The Theology of John Calvin*, trans. Harold Knight (Philadelphia: Westminster, 1956), 207.
[49] Ibid.

England, Hungary, and Poland had bishops. He told Archbishop Cranmer that he would be willing to "cross ten seas" to assist in the unification of Reformed churches—even those with bishops—although if he had made the trip, we can be relatively sure that he would have made a case for a more Presbyterian polity.[50] Thus, the Reformer could see even among elements a ranking order, prizing unity above polity. Here we see a man of principle, to be sure, but among the principles was love. While wanting to obey everything that Christ commanded, he realized that not everything was equally clear or equally important.

Deacons: Extending God's Hospitality

In addition to the offices of minister and elder, the diaconal office was established for the temporal relief of the saints.[51] We have seen that besides a "celestial theater" of God's grace, the church is compared to the site of a lavish banquet where we are served by a generous Father and a selfless Host, in bonds that only the Spirit can produce. What can salvation be likened to better than such divine hospitality?

Yet we are not merely souls, but bodies too, and Christ looks after us in every respect. It is not only the case that the poor need the generosity of the wealthier believers.[52] The hospitality that God showers on us overflows into a cycle of gift giving among the saints. In Strasbourg and Geneva, Calvin and Idelette embraced this calling—even when it was especially difficult in Geneva, given the often fierce inhospitality of the citizens to the sea of foreigners. Calvin oversaw personally the disbursement of funds for children who had sought refuge in Geneva and the establishment of diaconal funds for poor exiles. It is not surprising that he saw the Christian life in terms of pilgrimage, exile, and fleeing to the asylum of forgiveness.

In her book *Making Room: Recovering Hospitality as a Christian Tradition*, Christine E. Pohl draws attention to Calvin's example.[53] "No duty can be more pleasing or acceptable to God" than hospitality, Calvin said—especially to refugees.[54] In contrast with the example of the ancient church,

---

[50] Calvin, "Letter to Cranmer," in *Selected Works of John Calvin*, 5:345.

[51] Calvin, *Institutes* 4.3.8–9.

[52] Among many close studies of this topic, see Jeannine E. Olson, *Calvin and Social Welfare: Deacons and the Bourse Française* (Selinsgrove, PA: Susquehanna University Press, 1989).

[53] Christine E. Pohl, *Making Room: Recovering Hospitality as a Christian Tradition* (Grand Rapids: Eerdmans, 1999).

[54] Calvin on Isa. 16:4, in *Calvin's Commentaries*, vol. 7, trans. William Pringle (Grand Rapids: Baker, 1996), 484.

especially Chrysostom, Calvin complained that hospitality has "nearly ceased to be properly observed among men; for the ancient hospitality celebrated in histories, is unknown to us, and inns now supply the place of accommodation for strangers."[55] He adds, in the *Institutes*:

> Therefore, whatever man you meet who needs your aid, you have no reason to refuse to help him. Say, "He is a stranger"; but the Lord has given him a mark that ought to be familiar to you, by virtue of the fact that he forbids you to despise your own flesh (Is. 58.7). Say, "He is contemptible and worthless"; but the Lord shows him to be one to whom he has deigned to give the beauty of his image. Say that you owe nothing for any service of his; but God, as it were, has put him in his own place in order that you may recognize toward him the many and great benefits with which God has bound you to himself. Say that he does not deserve even the least effort for his sake; but the image of God, which recommends him to you, is worthy of your giving yourself and all your possessions.[56]

This generous hospitality is grounded not only in redemption, calling us to fellowship with other believers, but in creation as well, calling us to friendship with all of our neighbors.

> [God] has impressed his image in us and has given us a common nature, which should incite us to providing one for the other. The man who wishes to exempt himself from providing for his neighbors should deface himself and declare that he no longer wishes to be a man, for as long as we are human creatures we must contemplate as in a mirror our face in those who are poor, despised, exhausted, who groan under their burdens. . . . If there come some Moor or barbarian, since he is a man, he brings a mirror in which we are able to contemplate that he is our neighbor.[57]

When we encounter less fortunate neighbors, we have no basis for a patronizing or condescending attitude. Rather, we should think:

> Now I have been in that condition and certainly wanted to be helped. . . . When we are comfortable, it is not a matter of our remembering our human poverty; rather we imagine that we are exempt from that and that

---

[55] Calvin on Heb. 13:2, in *Calvin's Commentaries*, vol. 22, trans. John Owen (Grand Rapids: Baker, 1996), 340.

[56] Calvin, *Institutes* 3.7.6.

[57] Calvin, *Corpus Reformatorum: Johannis Calvini opera quae supersunt omnia*, 51.105.

we are no longer part of the common class. And that is the reason why we forget, and no longer have any compassion for our neighbors or for all that they endure.[58]

While hospitality is enjoined upon all Christians, Calvin sought to restore the diaconal office that had been moribund through the Middle Ages. The *Ecclesiastical Ordinances* that Calvin drafted provided for two types of deacons: administrators and those who cared for the poor, sick, and elderly. There was a close connection between Communion and the fellowship and care of the saints. The offering was not a perfunctory moment in the church service. As André Biéler comments, "In imitation of the primitive church, Calvin had money re-enter the circuit of spiritual life."[59] A general hospital was established, along with accommodations for refugees, as deacons and deaconesses (some of them former nuns) assisted in finding long-term housing and work. It was a somewhat complicated cooperative venture. However, nowhere was Calvin's view of the church and state as "distinct but inseparable" institutions more apparent than in the operation of the diaconate.

Reformed churches in France followed the model. In fact, ex-nuns formed the Order of the Sisters of Charity, though it did not impose any lifelong vow. It is perhaps not surprising that the Red Cross was founded in Geneva as part of a revival of Calvinism.[60] Who could be more remote from most of us than a refugee, an undocumented worker, and a foreigner without proper papers? The Reformer observes that we too shrug off the Lord's parable of the good Samaritan with the volley, "Who is my neighbor?" "Christ has shown us in the parable of the Samaritan that the term 'neighbor' includes even the most remote person (Luke 10.36), [and therefore] we are not expected to limit the precept of love to those in close relationships."[61] Of course, we must be wise. However, Calvin warns, "let us beware that we seek not cover for our stinginess under the shadow of prudence." Though it is appropriate to discern honest need, our inquiries should not be "too exacting," but must be done with a "humane heart, inclined to pity and compassion."[62]

Once again we see the movement in Calvin's thinking from public to

---

[58] Calvin, *John Calvin's Sermons on the Ten Commandments*, trans. Benjamin W. Farley (Grand Rapids: Baker, 1980), 127.

[59] André Biéler, *The Social Humanism of Calvin*, trans. Paul T. Fuhrmann (Richmond, VA: John Knox, 1961), 38.

[60] John B. Roney and Martin I. Klauber, eds., *The Identity of Geneva: The Christian Commonwealth, 1564–1864* (Westport, CT: Greenwood, 1998), 2, 14, 179, 186.

[61] Calvin, *Institutes* 2.8.54.

[62] Calvin, *Sermons from Job* (Edinburgh: Banner of Truth, 1993), 202.

private, from the formal to the informal, from being served by God through his ministry, to serving each other in the body and our neighbors in the world. There is an important place for the service of each member in the body. Whereas 1 Corinthians 12 and Romans 12 provide an extended list of spiritual gifts, Ephesians 4 singles out the ministers of the Word because it is through this special office that the general office of the saints can flourish. Richly served by the special offices of pastor, elder, and deacon, the rest of the body is ready to fulfill the general office entrusted to all believers in less official ways each day. One may not be a pastor and yet may be engaged in "speaking the truth in love" to fellow believers and those who don't yet know Christ. Even if one is not an elder, we all encourage and admonish each other in faith and good works. One need not be a deacon in order to have the gift of hospitality. We should see these formal offices instituted by Christ not as dead ends, but rather as fountains that spill over into the whole body and, through each person's gifts, flow out into the world.

Our Unity Together

Where is the only place where true redemption is to be found? In Christ alone, revealed in the gospel. Therefore, it is only in the gospel that we find the source of "one holy, catholic, and apostolic church." The church is one or catholic not because we share the same political views or cultural affinities, age demographics, or pastimes, but because with all of our diversity we share in "one Lord, one faith, one baptism."

The unity of the church is no small matter to Calvin. Nor does he hide behind the idea of an invisible church to justify divisions in the visible church. Calvin counsels, "Even when the church lies in ruins, we still love the heap of ruins."[63] "Unity is something invaluably good," he exhorts, something more than a means to an end.[64] When we look at division, "we not only shed a few tears in our eyes, but a whole river."[65]

Whether one views the Reformation as a tragic division or as a glorious healing of Christ's body depends on how seriously one takes the issues at stake. From the Reformers' point of view, it was the pope who had corrupted the ancient faith, contradicted the gospel, and torn the body of Christ into competing factions. It was the pope who excommunicated the Reformers

---

[63] Selderhuis, *Calvin's Theology of the Psalms*, 235, quoting Calvin on Ps. 102:15.
[64] Ibid., quoting Calvin on Ps. 133:1.
[65] Ibid., 237, quoting Calvin on Ps. 119:136.

and their followers and set armies in motion to exterminate evangelicals. The Reformation sought to bring greater genuine unity to the visible body, a unity determined not by emperor, pope, or common culture and laws, but by Christ and his gospel—with a government that was spiritual and bound by mutuality rather than tyranny. Many bishops and priests embraced the reform explicitly; others, including archbishops and cardinals, showed sympathy with its teachings, even on justification. Often at the risk of their own lives, the Reformers themselves attended every major conference to which they were invited. Nevertheless, when the final "anathemas" of the Council of Trent came down in the 1560s, all who believed that they were justified by grace alone, in Christ alone, through faith alone were placed under Rome's condemnation.

By his teaching, warnings, and personal example, Calvin constantly displayed disdain for trivial contentions. In his speech to the emperor, Calvin acknowledged that "the Church always has been and always will be liable to some defects which the pious are indeed bound to disapprove, but which are to be borne rather than be made a cause of fierce contention." However, the complete corruption of the gospel and pollution of worship are not merely "some defects."[66] How can the Reformers be saddled with dividing the church, Calvin asks, when Rome has separated the body from its Head?[67]

> Your Imperial Majesty is aware how wide a field of discussion here opens upon me. But to conclude this point in a few words: I deny that See to be Apostolic wherein nothing is seen but a shocking apostasy—I deny him to be the vicar of Christ who, in furiously persecuting the gospel, demonstrated by his conduct that he is Antichrist—I deny him to be the successor of Peter who is doing his utmost to demolish every edifice that Peter built—and I deny him to be the head of the Church who by his tyranny lacerates and dismembers the Church, after dissevering her from Christ, her true and only Head.[68]

How can those who seek to restore the connection between the body and its ascended Head be accused of schism? After all, it was not the Reformers who were employing the civil powers with ferocious hatred against fellow Christians.

---

[66] Calvin, "The Necessity of Reforming the Church," 186.
[67] Ibid., 213.
[68] Ibid., 219–20.

While he was still living in Strasbourg, Geneva's senate asked Calvin in 1539 to compose a response to Cardinal Sadoleto's plea for the city's return to the papal fold. The Reformer wrote,

> We indeed, Sadoleto, deny not that those over which you preside are Churches of Christ, but we maintain that the Roman Pontiff, with his whole herd of pseudo-bishops, who have seized upon the pastoral office, are ravening wolves whose only study has hitherto been to scatter and trample upon the kingdom of Christ, filling it with ruin and devastation.

"Nor are we the first to make the complaint," he adds, returning to the historical record—this time the fourteenth-century Cistercian reformer Bernard of Clairvaux: "With what vehemence does Bernard thunder against Eugenius and all the bishops of his own age? Yet how much more tolerable was its condition then than now?"[69]

Sure, there was greater quiet before the Reformers arrived, Calvin acknowledges. Everyone was ignorant of the gospel. "You cannot, therefore, take credit for a tranquil kingdom when there was tranquility for no other reason than because Christ was silent."[70] Are there many sects now? Yes, as the Christian faith has always been assailed by sects even in its finest days.[71] Having spoken so freely from his heart, Calvin concludes with a gracious and fervent plea:

> The Lord grant, Sadoleto, that you and all your party may at length perceive that the only true bond of ecclesiastical unity would exist if Christ the Lord, who hath reconciled us to God the Father, were to gather us out of our present dispersion into the fellowship of his body, that so, through his one Word and Spirit, we might join together with one heart and one soul.[72]

Although the Reformers longed for an ecumenical council to settle the matters, the Council of Trent, called in 1547, "was of a very different description" from earlier councils.[73] It was called an "ecumenical council, . . . as if it were said that all the bishops throughout the habitable globe had

---

[69] Calvin, "Reply by John Calvin to Cardinal Sadoleto's Letter," in *Selected Works of John Calvin: Tracts and Letters*, ed. Henry Beveridge and Jules Bonnet, 7 vols. (Grand Rapids: Baker, 1983), 1:50.
[70] Ibid., 67.
[71] Ibid., 68.
[72] Ibid.
[73] Calvin, "Acts of the Council of Trent," in *Selected Works of John Calvin*, 3:31.

flocked to Trent. Even if it had been only a Provincial Council they should still have been ashamed of the fewness of its members."[74] Of course, there were no representatives from the Eastern church (since the East and the West had excommunicated each other), and no one was allowed who favored the evangelical views of the Reformers. "Perhaps forty Bishops or so are present," and none of them among the distinguished pastors of the church.[75] The Holy Spirit, speaking in his Word, is the ultimate authority to which popes and councils are subject, yet, Calvin reports, there has thus far been no genuine discussion between both parties on the teaching of Scripture.[76] Only two bishops were sent from France, "both equally dull and unlearned."[77] None of this matters in any case. "For nothing is determined there save at the nod of the Roman Pontiff."[78] In short, Calvin charges that it should be obvious to everyone that the Council of Trent is a kangaroo court.[79]

Commenting point by point on each session as the council met, Calvin marshals historical evidence to measure Rome's departure from apostolic practice. He cites the third-century bishop of Carthage Cyprian, who denied any universal primacy but Christ's, and Gregory the Great, bishop of Rome, who said that any man who claimed such primacy was "a forerunner of Antichrist." Calvin appeals to Jerome's detailed account of equality among bishops until, "at the instigation of the devil," bishops began to jockey for priority. "But though with one assent the Roman See were raised to the third heaven, how ridiculous is it to make a primate of bishops of one who is no more like a bishop than a wolf is like a lamb!"[80] Lacking any grounding in Scripture or the ancient church, the Roman church simply appeals to power. "Accordingly, we see that they take the usual course of tyrants. When unable any longer to support their domination by moderate measures, they have recourse to truculence and barbarian ferocity."[81]

When all hopes of reconciliation with Rome seemed futile, Calvin did not give up. In fact, his successor, Theodore Beza, continued to attend such conferences despite personal dangers and diminishing hopes. Turn-

---

[74] Ibid., 57.
[75] Ibid., 33.
[76] Ibid.
[77] Ibid.
[78] Ibid., 35.
[79] Ibid., 36–37.
[80] Ibid., 49.
[81] Calvin, "Articles Agreed Upon by the Faculty of Sacred Theology of Paris, with Antidote (1542)," in *Selected Works of John Calvin*, 1:120.

ing to the Lutherans, Calvin argued for a view of the Supper that he and Melanchthon hoped would reconcile the evangelical churches.[82] However, Melanchthon was losing credibility as Luther's theologian-in-chief among many Lutherans, such as the polemicist Joachim Westphal, who claimed victories at the cost of completely misrepresenting Calvin's stated views. On the other side, Zurichers were overly sensitive to any criticism of Zwingli and wondered why Calvin seemed so obsessed with reconciling with the Lutherans, which he indeed attempted especially in his *Small Treatise on the Lord's Supper*.[83]

Calvin went directly to Zurich itself and forged a consensus statement with Heinrich Bullinger that brought greater unity to the Swiss churches.[84] In spite of being treated unfairly by Bullinger on some occasions, he was always the initiator of renewed friendship: "What ought we, my dear Bullinger, to correspond about at this time rather than the preserving and confirming, by every means in our power, brotherly kindness among ourselves?"[85] After determined effort, he was able in 1549 to reach a general agreement with Bullinger on a non-Zwinglian understanding of the Supper.[86] By the time Bullinger wrote the Second Helvetic Confession, even he had moved somewhat from his mentor's view, toward Calvin and the other Reformed leaders.

Even if all parties had possessed the goodwill for it, political circumstances did not allow any greater unity of the visible church than the pope sanctioned and the Protestant state churches, princes, and city councils could negotiate. Especially when Archbishop Cranmer's plan for an ecumenical synod came to nothing, Calvin lamented that Christ's body was left "bleeding, its members severed."[87] Like many of his goals, the visible unity of Christ's body was something for which the Reformer strove unceasingly, with disappointments often outweighing successes.

Especially when compared to our own age, the Reformed churches in

---

[82] Calvin, *Institutes* 4.14.17.
[83] T. H. L. Parker, *John Calvin* (Tring, UK: Lion, 1975), 162. Parker relates: "Luther is reported to have said to a friend as he read it: 'This is certainly a learned and godly man, and I might well have entrusted this controversy to him from the beginning. If my opponents had done the same we should soon have been reconciled.' But even before this, Luther had read the *Institutes*, probably the 1539 edition, and had sent friendly greetings through Bucer: 'Salute for me respectfully Sturm and Calvin whose books I have read with special delight.' And Calvin himself reported, 'Luther and Pomeranus have asked that Calvin should be greeted. Calvin has acquired great favor in their eyes.'"
[84] Theodore Beza, "Life of Calvin," in *Selected Works of John Calvin*, 1:liv.
[85] Calvin, quoted in Parker, *John Calvin*, 164.
[86] François Wendel, *Calvin: Origins and Development of His Religious Thought*, trans. Philip Mairet (New York and London: Harper & Row, 1963), 101.
[87] Calvin, quoted in Parker, *John Calvin*, 165.

the late sixteenth century represented the closest thing to a united Protestantism. Even after the sometimes bitter polemics from Lutheran quarters, Reformed and Puritan writers continued to cite important Lutheran theologians as "our theologians." Beza included the Augsburg Confession in his *Harmony of Reformed Confessions* (1581). The Church of England repeatedly sought further reform based on "the example of the best Reformed churches on the continent."

Tragically, circumstances—especially due to the politics of a state church—led to an unraveling of Reformed unity in England. At the moment when the Church of England saw itself as most Reformed, it was the most ecumenical. It was only with the rise of the Arminian and High Church Archbishop Laud under Charles I that the English Church became distinctly "Anglican" and veered increasingly from its own Articles of Religion. Calvin's ecumenical passion contrasts sharply with the complacency with which his spiritual heirs seem to accept the proliferation and continued existence of so many separate denominations with a common faith.

Our Mission Together

Ecumenism and mission were inseparable in Calvin's thinking. It is by the same gospel that creates the church that Christ's kingdom spreads throughout the world. Calvin was deeply impressed by the growth of the new covenant church from the vine of Israel. He speaks repeatedly of the Jews as having "the right of the first begotten," "always chief in the Church of God."[88] Israel is expanded with the arrival of foreigners, as the prophets foretold.

> Then the true religion, which had before been shut up within the narrow limits of Judea, was spread abroad through the whole world. Then God, who had been known only by one family, began to be called upon in the different languages of all nations. . . . Then all men, vying with each other, associated themselves in companies to the society of the Jews, whom they had before abhorred.[89]

Calvin adds, "We are considered as children of God in no other way than by being grafted into Abraham and his offspring."[90] In this way, "the heathen

---

[88] Calvin on Acts 13:45, in *Calvin's Commentaries*, vol. 18, trans. Henry Beveridge (Grand Rapids: Baker, 1996), 551.

[89] Calvin on Ps. 87:16, in *Calvin's Commentaries*, 5:395.

[90] Selderhuis, *Calvin's Theology of the Psalms*, 239, quoting Calvin on Pss. 47:10 and 110:2.

are subjected to Israel," Calvin observes in commenting on Psalm 47:4. "It is the delight of the Jews that they may be the fountain from which God waters the whole earth"—all the more reason they themselves must trust in Christ.[91]

In a Pentecost Sunday sermon, Calvin observes the remarkable change in the apostles at this history-altering feast. The Spirit descended with flaming tongues, first, "to show that by this means the doctrine of the Gospel was approved and sealed by God," to make his ambassadors witnesses for that gospel, and to raise hearers from spiritual death to embrace that gospel in their hearts.[92] While the Spirit descended in judgment to scatter the proud nations and divide their languages at Babel, at Pentecost he descended to unite them in one gospel, yet in various languages. Thus, God has turned a judgment into a blessing, with the gospel being proclaimed to the ends of the earth in a multitude of tongues, "that we might together be made partakers of this covenant of salvation which belonged only to the Jews until the wall was torn down."[93] Calvin adds, "This is also why this Holy Table is now prepared for us." Although the ascended Lord does not return bodily to earth, "let us know that what cannot be conceived of by men is accomplished nevertheless by the secret and invisible grace of the Holy Spirit; for this is how we are made partakers of the body and the blood of Jesus Christ."[94] Like that early community, the church today is a small and scattered remnant that is nevertheless gathered by the Spirit through his word, united to its Head, and preserved in spite of persecution in order to proclaim the gospel to the whole world.[95]

In Calvin's native France, the tiny bands of evangelical Christians who had escaped martyrdom swelled to over three million by 1562, and Calvin was in close and regular correspondence with the pastors and missionary-evangelists leading the efforts. Frank James III remarks, "Far from being disinterested in missions, history shows that Calvin was enraptured by it."[96] We preach not only to build up the saints but also "to persuade those who are strangers to the faith, and seem to be utterly deprived of the goodness of God, to accept salvation. Jesus Christ is not only a Savior of few,

---

[91] Ibid., 239, quoting Calvin on Ps. 47:4, 10.
[92] Calvin, "First Sermon on Pentecost," in *John Calvin: Selections from His Writings*, ed. John Dillenberger (Atlanta: Scholars Press, 1975), 560–73.
[93] Ibid., 564–65.
[94] Ibid., 571.
[95] Ibid., 572–73.
[96] Frank A. James III, cited in Keith Coleman, "Calvin and Missions," *WRS Journal* 16, no. 1 (February 2009): 29–30.

but he offers Himself to all." "God has at heart the salvation of all because he invites all to the acknowledgment of his truth. . . . God wishes that the gospel should be proclaimed to all without exception."[97] The same gospel that we take to the ends of the earth creates and sustains the church at home each week.

The Reformation itself was the most massive missionary movement since the days of the apostles. Millions across Europe considered themselves re-evangelized. As missions historian Ruth Tucker points out, it was extremely difficult for evangelicals to send missionaries. Nations loyal to the pope controlled the ports, while missionary monks attended Europe's conquerors across the seas.[98] "Calvin himself, however, was at least outwardly the most missionary-minded of all the Reformers," Tucker notes. "He not only sent dozens of evangelists back into his homeland of France, but also commissioned four missionaries, along with a number of French Huguenots, to establish a colony and evangelize the Indians in Brazil." In fact, these were the first Protestant missionaries to have set foot in the New World. The renegade leader of the company defected to the Portuguese "and left the few remaining defenseless survivors to be slain at the hands of the Jesuits."[99]

Calvin believed that missionaries should be as thoroughly prepared and trained as any minister at home. Aspiring missionaries came for training from every part of Europe, as well as Africa, the Middle East, and Ottoman lands. Geneva "was a dynamic centre of missionary concern and activity," the first major center for the training and sending of evangelical missionaries.[100] These churches provided leadership throughout the whole course of the modern missionary movement to the present day.[101]

Only Christ the Head can unite his members to himself in one body. Only through his gospel does the Spirit create, preserve, and expand this body to the ends of the earth. Getting the gospel right and getting the gospel out form an inextricable bond. Where the good news of God's saving grace in Christ is continually proclaimed, worldly divisions are overcome and a desert waste blossoms into a lavish field ripening into a glorious harvest.

[97] Calvin on 1 Tim. 2:4, in *Calvin's Commentaries*, 21:54–55.

[98] Ruth Tucker, *From Jerusalem to Irian Jaya: A Biographical History of Christian Missions* (Grand Rapids: Zondervan, 1983), 67. See also Fred Klooster, "Missions, the Heidelberg Catechism, and Calvin," *Calvin Theological Journal* 7, no. 2 (1972): 183.

[99] Tucker, *From Jerusalem to Irian Jaya*, 67–68.

[100] P. E. Hughes, ed., *The Register of the Company of Pastors of Geneva in the Time of Calvin* (Grand Rapids: Eerdmans, 1966), 25.

[101] See Michael Horton, *For Calvinism* (Grand Rapids: Zondervan, 2012), 151–69.

PART 4

LIVING IN THE WORLD

CHAPTER 12

CHRIST AND CAESAR

According to some, Calvin is the father of the modern world—everything that we either love or loathe. He is simultaneously the ayatollah of the Genevan theocracy and the revolutionary democrat who paved the way for religious and political liberties. Depending on one's agenda, he is the spirit behind free enterprise capitalism or state socialism. Yet André Biéler is exactly right: "The reality is that each of these movements has taken inspiration, in perfectly good faith, from that portion of Calvin's writings which justified its program and has left aside (of the immense and subtle work of the Reformer) that which was contrary to its platform."[1] More importantly, all of these appeals (or uses) are flawed by historical anachronism—projecting backward to a sixteenth-century French pastor distinctively modern motives, convictions, and visions that he would not even have understood. His goal was to preach the Word, in season and out of season, and leave the results to God. There is no evidence that he had any ambition to change the course of civilization.

On the one hand, as in H. Richard Niebuhr's famous typology, Augustine and Calvin are the progenitors of a "Christ Transforming Culture" approach.[2] On the other hand, Calvin specialist Richard Gamble is dumb-

---

[1] André Biéler, *The Social Humanism of Calvin*, trans. Paul T. Fuhrmann (Richmond, VA: John Knox, 1960), 27.

[2] H. Richard Niebuhr, *Christ and Culture* (New York: Harper, 1951). Niebuhr offers four types: Christ above culture (Roman Catholic), Christ of culture (liberal), Christ and culture in paradox (Lutheran), and Christ transformer of culture (Augustine/Calvin). This typecasting obscures more than it clarifies. There is little to distinguish Calvin's view of Christ and culture from Luther's, and Augustine can hardly be recruited as a "culture transformer," which is Neibuhr's own preferred type.

founded by such a thesis. "Can this notion of 'redeeming civilization or creation' be supported by primary texts in Calvin?" He cites John Leith for support of the point that although the Reformer has a brief section on the state, nowhere in the *Institutes* does he talk about a calling that Christians have to transform the world.[3]

In my view at least, Calvin's view of the relationship between Christ and culture cannot be easily categorized as "world-transforming." At the same time, to suggest that for Calvin "human life is primarily 'world-flight' rather than world-affirming" is an overcorrection.[4] As on other points, Calvin's outlook on this question is more complex and even para-doxical.

While the Reformation coincided with the rise of modern nation-states, Calvin could not have envisioned the extent to which culture and society would be reduced to politics. Nevertheless, it is on this topic—the relationship of church and state—that we may gain concrete insight into his broader understanding of Christ and culture.

Before dipping into some of Calvin's key writings on the subject, it might help to begin with an illustrative episode. The House of Guise took advantage of the minority of King Francis II to attempt an extermination of Reformed Christians. In 1560 a Reformed group of French nobility (including Louis de Bourbon, Prince of Condé) plotted to abduct the adolescent monarch and execute as tyrants Francis, Duke of Guise, and his brother, the Cardinal of Lorraine. Writing to a Reformed leader who was the admiral of the French navy, Calvin expressed his utter contempt for this conspiracy:

> I replied simply to such objections that if a single drop of blood were spilled, floods of it would deluge Europe; that thus it would be better we should perish a hundred times than expose Christianity and the gospel to such opprobrium. I admitted, it is true, that if the princes of the blood [those in direct line of succession] demanded to be maintained in their rights for the common good, and if the Parliament joined them in their quarrel, that it would then be lawful for all good subjects to lend them armed assistance. The man afterwards asked me if one of the princes of the blood, though not the first in rank, had decided upon taking such a

---

[3] Richard Gamble, "Calvin and Sixteenth-Century Spirituality: Comparison with the Anabaptists," in *Calvin Studies Society Papers, 1995, 1997: Calvin and Spirituality; Calvin and His Contemporaries*, ed. David Foxgrover (Grand Rapids: CRC Product Services, 1998), 50.
[4] Ibid., 49.

step, we were not then warranted to support him. I gave him an answer
in the negative with regard to that supposition.[5]

Note the two all-important qualifications. First, even a violent tyrant
ought not be overthrown by private citizens but only by proper authorities
invoking their secular rights, with the support of the parliament. Second,
their rights must be invoked "for the common good," not specifically to
protect the gospel, and certainly not for private gain. As it turned out,
Calvin's warning was prophetic. The Conspiracy of Amboise sparked the
Wars of Religion, although the Prince of Condé, moved especially by Calvin's disapproval, was successful in bringing about the short-lived Peace
of Amboise.

The Kingdom of Christ and the Kingdoms of This Age

Once again, "distinction without separation" was the rule for Calvin when
it came to relating Christ's kingdom and secular states. On the one hand,
he opposed the "contrived empire" of Christendom.[6] Crusades, holy wars,
and inquisitions were justified from Old Testament passages as if Europe
were theocratic Israel reborn, with the pope as high priest and the emperors and kings as the Lord's anointed to drive out the Canaanites. For Calvin,
Christ's kingdom is completely distinct from all kingdoms of this age. On
the other hand, he rejected the antithesis of Christ and culture that Anabaptists advocated.

We remember the Anabaptists as pacifists. Yet many leaders among
the first generation were actually revolutionaries who sought to usher in by
force what they considered the millennial kingdom of Christ. As Marx and
especially Engels saw, the radical Anabaptists were harbingers of the modern revolutionary spirit. Despite the rhetoric, utopian visions of liberation
are typically motivated less by a love of this world and of humanity than by
an impatient attitude that will sacrifice both on the altar of its perfectionistic ideology. Eric Voegelin put it well: "The saint is a Gnostic who will not

[5] Calvin, "To the Admiral de Coligny" (Geneva, April 16, 1561), in *Selected Works of John Calvin: Tracts and Letters*, ed. Henry Beveridge and Jules Bonnet, 7 vols. (Grand Rapids: Baker, 1983), 7:176–77.
[6] Oliver O'Donovan and Joan Lockwood O'Donovan, eds., *From Irenaeus to Grotius: A Sourcebook in Chris-tian Political Thought, 100–1625* (Grand Rapids: Eerdmans, 1999), 662; see also the research in this area by David VanDrunen, "The Context of Natural Law: John Calvin's Doctrine of the Two Kingdoms," *Journal of Church and State* 46 (Summer 2004): 503–25; VanDrunen, *Natural Law and the Two Kingdoms: A Study in the Development of Reformed Social Thought* (Grand Rapids: Eerdmans, 2009). For a positive statement of the relevance of this understanding in our context, see VanDrunen, *Living in God's Two Kingdoms: A Biblical Vision for Christianity and Culture* (Wheaton, IL: Crossway, 2010).

leave the transfiguration of the world to the grace of God beyond history but will do the work of God himself, right here and now, in history."[7]

In this phase, the movement shared the broader medieval confusion of Christ and empire. The crucial twist was that now the so-called Holy Roman Empire was cast as the "Canaanites." At first, Thomas Müntzer lobbied the princes to embrace his utopian vision for this so-called Age of the Spirit, but when they refused (partly through Luther's influence), Müntzer and John of Leyden entered cities with their peasant armies of the Lord, proclaiming themselves kings, torturing and slaughtering men, women, and children. Though short-lived, the regime that they instituted is described by Columbia University historian Eugene F. Rice as "violent, polygamous, and communist."[8] Ironically, they differed from medieval Christendom not as much in principle as in passion and the purity of vision: they wanted a fully realized kingdom of God here and now on the earth. Müntzer and other revolutionaries became historical icons in the lore of modern communism.

With such grand hopes of establishing Christ's millennial reign dashed, Anabaptists withdrew from society. Yet the underlying antithesis between an impure world and a pure society of saints remained the dominant rationale. In the Schleitheim Confession (1527), for example, the Manichean antithesis between holy believers and the godless world, light and darkness, is absolute and unambiguous.[9] Anabaptists seem to have dissented from medieval assumptions not so much in the ideal of a Christian society—with a fusion of church and state—as in the radical purity of their idealism. Like liberation theology's "base communities" in Central and South America, the church and society were even more radically identified than they were in Roman Catholic and Protestant lands.

At least in theory, the magisterial Reformers challenged the notion that Europe was the kingdom of Christ, much less a revival of the old covenant theocracy. However, unlike the Anabaptists, they also did not correlate the

---

[7] Eric Voegelin, The New Science of Politics (Chicago: University of Chicago Press, 1952), 147.

[8] Eugene F. Rice Jr. and Anthony Grafton, The Foundations of Early Modern Europe, 1460–1559 (New York: W. W. Norton, 1994), 138.

[9] The Schleitheim Confession, trans. and ed. John Howard Yoder (Scottdale, PA: Herald, 1977), 8–12. There is an absolute antithesis between the world (hence, the visible church) and the elect who have "separated from the world." Since those who have not joined Anabaptist communities "are a great abomination before God, therefore nothing else can or really will grow or spring forth from them but abominable things. Now there is nothing else in the world and all creation than good or evil, believing and unbelieving, darkness and light, the world and those who are [come] out of the world. . . . and none will have part with the other. . . . Furthermore, He admonishes us therefore to go out from Babylon and from the earthly Egypt that we may not be partakers of their torment and suffering, which the Lord will bring upon them" (art. 4).

church of their day with the exiles leaving Babylon to return to the Holy Land. Rather, the condition of the church in this age is more similar to that of the exiles in Babylon. Like Daniel, they refused pagan worship, but made use of its education, while praying for, participating in, and contributing to the good of the city.

Calvin stresses the point that Israel enjoyed a unique covenantal relationship with God when he identified his church with a particular nation. Now all nations are common. "Christ's spiritual kingdom and the civil jurisdiction are things completely distinct. . . . Yet this distinction does not lead us to consider the whole nature of government a thing polluted, which has nothing to do with Christian men." These two kingdoms are "distinct," yet "they are not at variance."[10] Even under the old covenant the king and the high priest were distinct, but not so in Christendom, where the pope and his clergy crave worldly power. In Matthew 20 Jesus sets out "to distinguish between the spiritual government of his Church and the empires of the world, that the apostles might not look for the favors of a court. . . . Christ appoints pastors of his Church, not to *rule*, but to *serve*." This refutes the pope *and* the Anabaptists, Calvin asserts.[11]

Augustine, especially his *City of God*, is an obvious influence on Calvin's thinking. The temporal kingdoms are important means of God's restraint of evil in the world, according to the bishop of Hippo, but they are not the kingdom of Christ.[12] If the church itself is a "mixed body" of elect and nonelect, argues Augustine, then surely we cannot identify the empire with Christ's kingdom. Consequently, each city has its own polity, serving distinct ends through distinct means. Augustine says that these two cities we find "interwoven, as it were, in this present transitory world, and mingled with one another."[13] The common goods we share are valuable, even if they are not ultimate, while the elect look for Christ's return, when "all injustice disappears and all human lordship and power is annihilated and God is all in all."[14] In spite of this distinction between the two cities, Augustine's practice seemed to contradict his theory when he encouraged the state to extirpate the Donatist sect.

---

[10] Calvin, *Institutes of the Christian Religion*, ed. John T. McNeill, trans. Ford Lewis Battles (Philadelphia: Westminster, 1960), 4.20.1–2.

[11] Calvin on Matt. 20:25, in *Calvin's Commentaries*, vol. 16, trans. William Pringle (Grand Rapids: Baker, 1996), 424.

[12] Augustine, *City of God*, ed. David Knowles, trans. Henry Bettenson (New York: Penguin, 1972), 527.

[13] Ibid., 430.

[14] Ibid., 875.

Like Augustine, Luther emphasizes the distinction between "things heavenly" and "things earthly," true righteousness before God and civil righteousness before fellow-humans. Luther puts forward his two kingdoms doctrine in detail in his important work *On Temporal Authority* (1523), comparing the relation of civil and spiritual realms to that between the body and the soul.[15] He complains:

> The devil never stops cooking and brewing these two kingdoms into each other. In the devil's name the secular leaders always want to be Christ's masters and teach Him how He should run His church and spiritual government. Similarly, the false clerics and schismatic spirits always want to be the masters, though not in God's name, and to teach people how to organize the secular government. Thus the devil is indeed very busy on both sides, and has much to do.[16]

In fact, Luther continues, "no ruler ought to prevent anyone from teaching or believing what he pleases, whether gospel or lies. It is enough if he prevents the teaching of sedition and rebellion."[17] "Suffering, suffering; cross, cross! This and nothing else, is the Christian law!"[18] Christians could take up arms to defend their country and property, but not to defend the gospel.[19] When Paul came to Athens, he did not destroy the idols by force but proclaimed the Word.

> For the Word created heaven and earth and all things; the Word must do this thing, and not we poor sinners. . . . In short, I will preach it, teach it, write it, but I will constrain no man by force, for faith must come freely without compulsion. Take myself as an example. I opposed indulgences and all the papists, but never with force. I simply taught, preached, and wrote God's Word; otherwise I did nothing. And while I slept, or drank Wittenberg beer with my friends Philip and Amsdorf, the Word so greatly weakened the papacy that no prince or emperor ever inflicted such losses upon it. I did nothing; the Word did everything.[20]

---

[15] See Bernhard Lohse, *Martin Luther's Theology: Its Historical and Systematic Development*, trans. Roy A. Harrisville (Minneapolis: Fortress, 1999), 151–59.
[16] Martin Luther, "Commentary on Psalm 101," in *Luther's Works*, American Edition, 55 vols., ed. Jaroslav Pelikan and Helmut T. Lehmann (Philadelphia: Fortress; St. Louis: Concordia, 1955–1986), 13:194–95.
[17] Martin Luther, "Friendly Admonition to Peace Concerning the Twelve Articles of the Swabian Peasants," in *The Protestant Reformation*, ed. Hans Hillerbrand (New York: Harper & Row, 1968), 71.
[18] Ibid., 76.
[19] Ibid., 78.
[20] Martin Luther, "On God's Sovereignty," in *Luther's Works*, 51:77.

Luther is not engaging in self-flattery when he adds, "Had I desired to foment trouble, I could have brought great bloodshed upon Germany; indeed, I could have started such a game that even the emperor would not have been safe. But what would it have been? Mere fool's play. I did nothing; I let the Word do its work."[21]

Nevertheless, he could say in 1530 that the prince had the authority to punish those who reject teachings "clearly grounded in Scripture and believed throughout the world by all Christendom."[22] Just as Augustine accommodated the punishment of the Donatists by the sword, Luther was far from our modern notion of religious liberty.

Calvin's expertise in Greco-Roman and medieval law also gave his reflections a depth and nuance that is often missing from radical social-religious agendas. He had a sober sense—historical as well as theological—of what cultural, political, and social engagement can and cannot achieve.

Biéler reminds us of the Reformer's roots in evangelical humanism, the influences of which are evident in the way he talks about our life both in the church and in the world. "Now, evangelical humanism, that is, the humanism of Calvin, is primarily a social humanism. . . . 'God has created man,' Calvin says, 'so that man may be a creature of fellowship.'"[23] In civil society, "this order does not consist in Christ's renewing man unto liberty but, on the contrary, in external constraint which maintains man in a relative morality."[24] It is a "transitory" order: neither ultimate nor unimportant. "While waiting for this final consummation, and in order to live, all societies need a provisory order, that is, a human system which is the political order."[25] "Of course, Calvin wished that magistrates be Christian. But in encouraging persecuted churches, Calvin has shown that the Christian's obedience to state officials in no way depends on the faith or un-faith of these authorities."[26] Biéler adds:

> A consequence of the political teaching of Calvin is that a Christian, except in altogether exceptional cases, cannot be a radical revolutionary seeking to uproot the social order in which he lives. On the other hand, the Christian cannot be completely conservative. . . . In summary, when

---

[21] Ibid.
[22] Martin Luther, "Psalm 82," in *Luther's Works*, 13:61.
[23] Biéler, *The Social Humanism of Calvin*, 17.
[24] Ibid., 23.
[25] Ibid.
[26] Ibid., 24.

Christians are aware of the responsibility flowing from their faith, they are under obligation to participate actively in political life.[27]

Although sojourners like John Knox laurelled the city with praise as "the most perfect school of Christ since the apostles," Calvin told Geneva's senators on his deathbed that they are trustees of a "perverse and unhappy nation."[28] He could conclude no more than this: "Matters, as you see, are tolerably settled"; and he added a final exhortation: "The more guilty, therefore, will you be before God if they go to wreck through your indolence."[29] It is hardly a victory speech. In Calvin's view, we all fall short of our duty before God, and civil kingdoms are never the city of God.

Calvin's discussion of the two kingdoms in the *Institutes* comes between his treatment of Christian freedom and his section "On Civil Government." One reason for treating Christian freedom prior to "On Civil Government" is the tension in Europe over radical Anabaptists like Müntzer and John of Leyden still fresh in everyone's memory—especially in that of the French king to whom Calvin dedicates the *Institutes*. In a letter to the Duke of Somerset, Calvin strongly encourages the Lord Protector to punish "frenzied spirits" who, under pretense of the gospel, seek to upset the whole commonwealth.[30]

So Calvin begins,

> Therefore, in order that none of us may stumble on that stone, let us first consider that there is a twofold government: one aspect is spiritual, whereby the conscience is instructed in piety and in reverencing God; the second is political, whereby man is educated for the duties of humanity and citizenship that must be maintained among men.[31]

Anyone who can distinguish (without separating) the body and the soul can understand this point. He adds, "The question . . . is not of itself very obscure or involved." It simply requires a distinction between outward conformity to the laws of society and the ultimate surrender of the conscience to God alone, assured of God's grace in Christ.[32]

---

[27] Ibid., 25.
[28] William Monter, *Calvin's Geneva* (New York: John Wiley and Sons, 1967), 120.
[29] Theodore Beza, "Life of Calvin," in *Selected Works of John Calvin*, 1:xciv.
[30] Calvin, "To the Protector Somerset" (Geneva, October 22, 1548), in *Selected Works of John Calvin*, 5:187. In this he anticipated the chaotic enthusiasm that reached its zenith during Cromwell's Protectorate.
[31] Calvin, *Institutes* 3.19.15–16.
[32] Ibid., 3.19.15.

On this basis, Calvin challenged the medieval view that the state (lower in rank) must take its cues from the church (higher in rank), as well as the Anabaptist rejection of the secular as such. With Luther, he spoke of two kingdoms or "a two-fold government." "Man contains, as it were, two worlds, capable of being governed by various rulers and various laws. This distinction will prevent what the gospel inculcates concerning spiritual liberty from being misapplied to political regulations."[33]

The New Testament therefore lacks anything like the civil legislation of Israel's theocracy, since the church now is no longer identified with a particular nation. "For [the apostles'] purpose is not to fashion a civil government, but to establish the spiritual Kingdom of Christ."[34] The glory of Jerusalem with its walls and towers was but a type of the greater glory of the spiritual gifts that adorn the new covenant church.[35]

The analogy of body and soul for the state and the church may have its own problems. What is interesting, though, is how Calvin views the relationship. The soul (papacy) is not over the body (empire), as in Rome's view. Nor is the state over the church, as in the view of fellow reformers, Lutheran and Reformed. And the two are not set in opposition, as in the Anabaptist view. For Calvin, they are side by side: distinct but not separate. Biéler explains, "As a Christian who strictly bases himself on the gospel, Calvin knows nothing about that pagan antagonism which opposes pretended spiritual values to material realities. Calvin repudiates that age-long struggle which, since ancient times, contrasts spiritualism and materialism."[36]

Common Grace

God's speech is not only a saving but also a sustaining Word, according to Calvin. John Murray has justifiably concluded concerning the doctrine of common grace, "On this question Calvin not only opened a new vista but also a new era in theological formulation."[37] In addition to these natural remnants of the image of God in every person, Calvin speaks of God's common grace: "not such grace as to cleanse it [nature], but to restrain it inwardly." This common grace is tied to providence, by which God holds

[33] Ibid.
[34] Ibid., 4.20.12.
[35] Herman J. Selderhuis, *Calvin's Theology of the Psalms* (Grand Rapids: Baker Academic, 2007), 130.
[36] Biéler, *The Social Humanism of Calvin*, 30.
[37] John Murray, *The Collected Writings of John Murray*, vol. 2, *Select Lectures in Systematic Theology* (Edinburgh: Banner of Truth, 1978), 94.

nature in check "but he does not purge it within."[38] Only the gospel can purge within. Thus, common grace is not saving grace, and natural law is not Scripture, but each has its proper function in God's twofold reign. The concepts are neither identical (as Rome assumes) nor opposed (as Anabaptists seem to teach); they are distinct but not contradictory.[39]

Therefore, Calvin does not have to subsume cultural activity under the category of *holy* and *redemptive* in order to affirm its importance.[40] Even the ungodly Roman emperors can be called God's "ministers" (Rom. 13:1–7). Christ is indeed therefore the Lord of all: the kingdoms of this age by his providence and common grace, and his holy kingdom by saving grace through the ministry of the church. Christians are called to be salt and light in the world, but Calvin never speaks of their "redeeming culture." Christ alone is the subject of redemptive grace, and he applies his redemption by the holy ministry of Word and sacrament, not by the sword.

With good reason, we naturally think of the Spirit's work in the lives of believers, Calvin says. Yet the Spirit is also at work in the lives of unbelievers, stirring the gifts that he has given them in his common grace. Radical Protestants assume that believers can learn nothing from non-Christians. "But if the Lord has willed that we be helped in physics, dialectic, mathematics, and other like disciplines by the work and ministry of the ungodly, let us use this assistance," Calvin counters. "For if we neglect God's gift freely offered in these arts, we ought to suffer just punishments for our sloths."[41] After offering examples from the arts, sciences, philosophy, and medicine, he concludes, "Let us, accordingly, learn by their example how many gifts the Lord left to human nature even after it was despoiled of its true good."[42] Even in its fallenness, the world—including humanity—reflects God's wisdom and goodness, truth and justice, beauty and love.

"For the spiritual leaders of the Anabaptists," Willem Balke relates,

> the "possession" of the Holy Spirit fully compensated for their lack of education. In Münster the books and manuscripts were taken out of the library and burned. All books, except the Bible, were forbidden. The Münster Anabaptists were proud that they were not guilty of having book

---

[38] Calvin, *Institutes* 4.20.8, 14.
[39] For precisely the same view, see Philip Melanchthon, *Loci communes* (1543), trans. J. A. O. Preus (St. Louis: Concordia, 1992), 70.
[40] Calvin, *Institutes* 2.2.15.
[41] Ibid., 2.2.16.
[42] Ibid., 2.2.15.

learning. For Calvin, on the other hand, "science" could not be valued highly enough as a gift of the Holy Spirit. He repeatedly and strongly opposed this Anabaptist tendency toward anti-intellectualism.[43]

Common Law

God secretly governs the nations just as he does his church, although he governs the former through natural law and common grace and the latter through his Word written and preached. Calvin considers it a "pernicious error" to expect a government to be framed according to "the political system of Moses," rather than by "common laws of nations."[44]

Following Paul's claim that the moral law revealed in Scripture is the natural law revealed in creation, Calvin strongly opposes the idea that a valid civil order must be based on the Bible.

> How malicious and hateful toward public welfare would a man be who is offended by such diversity, which is perfectly adapted to maintain the observance of God's law! For the statement of some, that the law of God given through Moses is dishonored when it is abrogated and new laws preferred to it, is utterly vain.[45]

After all, Calvin says, "it is a fact that the law of God which we call the moral law is nothing else than a testimony of natural law and of that conscience which God has engraved on the minds of men."[46]

Natural law—the law of God written upon the conscience of every person—allows for a marvelous diversity in constitutions, forms of government, and laws.[47] The Mosaic theocracy was limited to the old covenant and is no longer the blueprint for nation-states.[48] This natural law is not grounded in autonomous reason, as the radical Enlightenment continues to insist. Rather, it is God's original summons to his image bearers in creation that continues to render us accountable ultimately to him, but it does not save.[49] Calvin argues along the same lines as would the Westminster

---

[43] Willem Balke, *Calvin and the Anabaptist Radicals*, trans. William J. Heynen (Grand Rapids: Eerdmans, 1981), 237–38.

[44] Calvin, *Institutes* 4.20.14.

[45] Ibid., 4.20.8, 14. The basic ligaments of Calvin's political theology can be found in 4.20.1–32.

[46] Ibid., 4.20.16.

[47] Ibid.

[48] Ibid.

[49] See Francis Turretin, *Institutes of Elenctic Theology*, trans. John Musgrave Giger, ed. James T. Dennison, vol. 2 (Phillipsburg, NJ: P&R, 1994), 2.1.7. The seventeenth-century Genevan theologian Francis Turretin was already aware of those who were arguing that secular government arises from the autonomous power

Confession a century later: the judicial laws of Moses are "expired," "not obliging any other [nation] now, further than the general equity thereof may require."[50] Therefore, the one system that Calvin's exegesis strictly forbids is a theocracy. So all truth (and law) comes from God, but not necessarily from the Bible.

The political laws of Moses cannot be *abrogated* by secular nations, since they were never *given* to them in the first place, Calvin argues.[51] Natural law can be summarized by the word "equity," which generally meant a fairness in human relations that balances strict justice with charitable moderation. It requires careful discrimination of particular cases. Consequently, "equity alone must be the goal and rule and limit of all laws."[52] As a natural virtue common to all people, this equity is "the perpetual rule of love," fountain of all laws. "Surely every nation is left free to make such laws as it foresees to be profitable for itself. Yet these must be in conformity to that perpetual rule of love, so that they indeed vary in form but have the same purpose."[53] There is no biblically mandated form of government for our common life under God's common grace.

Even Luther defended the medieval prohibition against charging interest on loans (based on Ex. 22:25). However, Calvin says that the practice "is not now unlawful, except in so far as it contravenes equity and brotherly union."[54] Once again, Calvin thinks that the principle of general equity offers an adequate way of navigating this issue. "Heathen authors also saw this," he wrote, "although not with sufficient clearness, when they declared that, since all men are born for the sake of each other, human society is not properly maintained except by an interchange of good offices."[55] Of all the Reformers, Calvin had the greatest confidence in the common sense even of pagans enlightened by common grace.

The equity that the moral law enjoins may find expression in varied legal codes, just as the elements of worship and Christian living may be applied in a variety of ways, depending on specific circumstances. Even those who agree on the universal principle may reach different conclusions about

---

either of despots or of social contracts. "But the [Reformed] orthodox speak far differently," he says. "They affirm that there is a natural law, not arising from a voluntary contract or law of society, but from a divine obligation being impressed by God upon the conscience of man in his very creation."
[50] Westminster Confession of Faith, 19.4.
[51] Calvin, *Institutes* 4.20.16.
[52] Ibid., 4.20.15.
[53] Ibid.
[54] Calvin on Ex. 22:25, in *Calvin's Commentaries*, vol. 3, trans. Charles William Bingham (Grand Rapids: Baker, 1996), 132.
[55] Ibid., 126.

policies. Calvin does not flinch from proclaiming God's judgment against "the hard and inhuman laws with which the more powerful oppresses and crushes the weaker person."[56] "Authorities are thus the 'protectors' of the poor."[57] Fred Graham notes, "It was, for Calvin, the treatment of the weak in society that really determined the value of a political regime."[58] Yet he does not assume the mantle of the magistrate and offer specific policies or laws, but leaves the application of the rule to the wisdom of those to whom it is entrusted.

Calvin shows the same discretion even when it comes to the significant question of political constitutions.[59] In spite of his expertise in such matters (or perhaps because of it), he exercises remarkable circumspection. Pointing out the dangers of pure democracy and tyranny, he says he personally prefers "aristocracy or a mixture of aristocracy and democracy." He opposes both anarchy and tyranny in both church and state. In both spheres he encourages representative government, where power is shared. Nevertheless, he immediately adds that this is not a universal rule and that some cultures may be better suited by their historical character to other forms of government.[60]

Though he was conservative by nature and theological inclination, Calvin's thinking did have political implications. Owing to his training in Roman jurisprudence, Calvin's insights on natural rights and equality before the law have been influential for subsequent generations.[61] It is certainly true that many of his spiritual heirs developed—and in some ways went beyond—Calvin's thinking. These theological successors contributed major advances in constitutional theory, the right of resistance to tyrants, and religious liberty.[62] Furthermore, Calvin's interpretation of Scripture,

---

[56] Calvin, *Institutes* 2.8.45.

[57] Selderhuis, *Calvin's Theology of the Psalms*, 153, on Ps. 82:3.

[58] W. Fred Graham, *Constructive Revolutionary: John Calvin and His Socio-Economic Impact* (Richmond, VA: John Knox, 1971), 62.

[59] There are many studies of Calvin's political thinking. Key among them are Harro Höpfl, *The Christian Polity of John Calvin* (Cambridge: Cambridge University Press, 1982); Quentin Skinner, *The Foundations of Modern Political Thought: The Age of the Reformation*, vol. 2 (Cambridge: Cambridge University Press, 1978); Ronald Wallace, *Calvin, Geneva and the Reformation* (Eugene, OR: Wipf & Stock, 1998). A good essay surveying Calvin's political thought is David W. Hall, "Calvin on Human Government and the State," in *A Theological Guide to Calvin's Institutes*, ed. David W. Hall and Peter A. Lillback (Phillipsburg, NJ: P&R, 2008), 411–40.

[60] Calvin, *Institutes* 4.20.8. See again note 6 for VanDrunen's excellent work on this.

[61] John Witte Jr., *The Reformation of Rights: Law, Religion and Human Rights in Early Modern Calvinism* (Cambridge: Cambridge University Press, 2007), 2: "Calvin developed arresting new teachings on authority and liberty, duties and rights, and church and state that have had an enduring influence on Protestant lands."

[62] For example, Beza wrote one of the first modern treatises on resistance to tyrants, and most contemporaries who shared his view were also Reformed. The German Reformed political theorist Johannes Althusius brought the insights of federal theology to bear on his concept of a federal system of constitu-

specific doctrinal emphases, and the type of piety that they generate also had a significant social impact. This was no doubt due in part to the fact that many leading thinkers, artists, educators, lawyers, and political theorists were drawn to the Reformer's teaching of Scripture. The two kingdoms intersect in the life of every Christian, who is a citizen of both cities. With others, Calvin's insights and emphases offered a rich resource for understanding, negotiating, and wisely engaging these two callings.

Calvin never imagined any more than Luther did that these two kingdoms would be unrelated. By the standards of their own day, religious laws and their enforcement were more lenient in Protestant states. Yet by modern standards there was nothing like a separation of church and state.[63] Geneva's practice by comparison was fairly liberal. Nevertheless, as with Augustine, Luther, Zwingli, and others, a theoretical distinction between the two kingdoms did not keep Calvin from assuming still that kings, emperors, and city councils were entrusted with the protection of the true church. In his speech before Charles V, Calvin called upon the emperor to exercise his paternal stewardship of the church as did Constantine, Theodosius, and Charlemagne of old.

If Calvin diverged from fellow Reformers in this regard, it was to distinguish these two kingdoms more sharply by laboring for the independence of the church from political meddling—and vice versa. He even reproved the ancient custom in Augustine's day of involving bishops in secular matters "that were foreign to their office." These church officers "wronged God in making his authority and command a pretext for turning aside from their proper calling."[64] Yet if we are to appropriate Calvin's wisdom in these matters, it must be with discretion and sensitivity to widely different historical circumstances. Ironically, many of his greatest insights on Christ and culture are suited better to a post-Christendom reality that the Reformer himself could not even imagine, much less anticipate.

---

tional government. Yet Calvin was conservative, wary of chaos, and there is nothing in his writings to suggest that he would have approved of, much less pioneered, the liberal political and economic systems familiar to the modern world.

[63] Leonard Verduin, *The Reformers and Their Stepchildren* (Grand Rapids: Eerdmans, 1964), 202. He points out that the Imperial Diet of Speyer (1529) decreed, "Every Anabaptist or rebaptized person, of either sex, is to be put to death by fire or by the sword or by some other means." Yet even in Strasbourg unbaptized children were to be baptized if necessary "by the officers of the law."

[64] Calvin on 1 Cor. 6:5, in *Calvin's Commentaries*, vol. 20, trans. John Pringle (Grand Rapids: Baker, 1996), 203.

CHAPTER 13

VOCATION: WHERE GOOD WORKS GO

Deep within us all, there is a desire to appease God by following a way of life that we imagine is more spiritual and extraordinary than the common vocations we have become accustomed to think of merely as jobs or occupations. Often, upon joining a church, new members are encouraged to "find a ministry" there. After all, every believer is a minister. Being a doctor, baker, or homemaker may be good, but "full-time Christian service" is better. Somehow, we have to justify our everyday labors as "kingdom work." Or perhaps we can turn our common vocation into a holy one by somehow making it an avenue of personal evangelism or social transformation. Ironically, such anticlerical tendencies betray a deeper clericalism: namely, that every member of the church must be a minister. Like Peter, we find it difficult to *be served* by Christ (John 13:8–9) so that we can serve our neighbors in the world.

As we will see in this chapter, Calvin encountered something similar in monasticism, but especially in the Anabaptist movement, where every member was expected to follow a life similar to the monastic ideal. Today, evangelicals have created a subculture that is often a mirror of the world with an evangelistic and moralistic veneer. The danger is that we become like the world even while we are removed from it, busy in the beehive of "Christian" activities: we are of the world, but not in it, instead of in the world but not of it.

Vocations: Where Our Good Works Go

No less than Luther did Calvin affirm the priesthood of all believers, but for neither Reformer did this mean that all believers are ministers—that is, trained, tested, and ordained pastors and teachers of the visible church. Instead, Calvin believed that we come to church first of all to be served: to be fed richly by Christ, through his ministers; to be guided wisely by Christ, through his elders; and to be cared for in our temporal needs by Christ, through his deacons. Every Lord's Day is like a gathering of children in the living room on Christmas morning to receive and exchange gifts. From this ministry a host of spiritual gifts arise that circulate among all the members, who then love and serve neighbors in the world through ordinary vocations. Calvin offers rich insights on this distinction between the special offices (pastor, elder, deacon) and the general office (the priesthood of all believers).[1]

There is a large place for good works in the Reformers' piety, but it is now under the topic of vocation rather than justification. We bring our good works not to God for reimbursement, but to our neighbors for their good. As Luther expressed it, "We conclude, therefore, that a Christian lives not in himself, but in Christ and the neighbor. He lives in Christ through faith, and in his neighbor through love."[2] The church is where disciples are made, and the world is where discipleship goes.

Here again the rule of "distinction without separation" applies to the two kingdoms. We are heirs of the kingdom, "those sanctified in Christ Jesus" (1 Cor. 1:2), even when we are not directly advancing the kingdom of Christ. In other words, *we* are holy—set apart—even if the *callings* themselves are common. There is no such thing as Christian farming, holy medicine, or kingdom art, even though believers engaged in these callings alongside unbelievers are holy citizens of his kingdom. The service that a janitor, homemaker, doctor, or business person provides is part of God's providential care of his creatures. It requires no further justification.

The idea of working for God is therefore replaced with the conviction of God's working for us (in salvation) and through us (in our callings). When we care for a dying parent or dig a ditch or argue a case in court, God is the

---

[1] For example, see Calvin on Eph. 4:11, in *Calvin's Commentaries*, vol. 21, trans. William Pringle (Grand Rapids: Baker, 1996), 278; cf. Calvin, *Institutes of the Christian Religion*, ed. John T. McNeill, trans. Ford Lewis Battles (Philadelphia: Westminster, 1960), 4.1.3.

[2] Martin Luther, "The Freedom of a Christian," in *Luther's Works*, American Edition, 55 vols., ed. Jaroslav Pelikan and Helmut T. Lehman (Philadelphia: Fortress; St. Louis: Concordia, 1955–1986), 31:371.

primary actor and we are his instruments. When we pray, "Give us this day our daily bread," Luther says, God answers it "not directly as when he gave manna to the Israelites, but through the work of farmers and bakers." They are God's "masks."[3] He writes, "God who pours out his generosity on the just and the unjust, believer and unbeliever alike, hides himself in the ordinary social functions and stations of life, even the most humble. God himself is milking the cows through the vocation of the milkmaid."[4] Calvin shares this view: "From this will arise also a singular consolation, that no task will be so sordid and base, provided you obey your calling in it, that it will not shine and be reckoned very precious in God's sight."[5]

Look Outside Yourself: A Gift Ethic

Biblical piety, according to Calvin, directs our faith toward God and our love toward our neighbor. The Christian life is therefore extrospective: that is, looking outside ourselves. To be sure, there are times to examine ourselves. Yet this is primarily to discover our desperate need of Christ, rather than to find something meritorious within us that we can offer to God. Calvin exhorts us to flee the inner prison of our own sin and death and find our only asylum in Christ. If we look away from Christ, the search for inner peace, security, and purity will only lead to despair or self-righteousness. "If you contemplate yourself, that is sure damnation."[6] Ironically, it is only on this basis that you can finally turn away from self-obsession to embrace Christ in faith and your neighbor in love. The striving for an inner sanctity that will withstand God's judgment keeps you focused on yourself, ignoring both Christ and others. No one is helped by this sort of piety. It is a fool's errand that incurs God's wrath, avoids our neighbor, and, as it turns out, doesn't even help us.

Like that of other magisterial Reformers, Calvin's piety is marked by two emphases: (1) All good gifts come down to us from God; before God, we are only receivers (Acts 17:25–26; Rom. 11:35–36; James 1:17); (2) Not only does God love and serve us, but also through us he loves and serves our neighbors by means of our callings; before others, we are givers. So we

---

[3] Gene Edward Veith, "The Doctrine of Vocation: How God Hides Himself in Human Work," *Modern Reformation* 8, no. 3 (May/June 1999): 4. See also Veith, *The Spirituality of the Cross*, 2nd ed. (St. Louis: Concordia, 2010); Veith, *God at Work*, rev. ed. (Wheaton, IL: Crossway, 2011); Gustaf Wingren and Carl C. Rasmussen, *Luther on Vocation* (Eugene, OR: Wipf & Stock, 2004).
[4] Martin Luther, quoted by Veith, "The Doctrine of Vocation," 5.
[5] Calvin, *Institutes* 3.10.6.
[6] Ibid., 3.2.24.

bring only faith to God and good works to our neighbors. Our callings—as children, spouses, parents, volunteers, employers, and employees—are the channels through which these good works flow from God to others. And we're engaged simultaneously in many different vocations. So it's more of a gift ethic than a work ethic.[7]

In this way, first, *God is pleased.* He is pleased with us because he is pleased with Christ in whom we are hidden through faith. Now as our Father rather than our Judge, God treats us as children, forgiving by Christ's merits the sin clinging to our good works. Therefore, since we are in Christ, the Father is pleased not only with us but also with our works, whose imperfection would never satisfy him as a Judge. Following Augustine, Calvin observes that even the rewards that God has for us are the crowning of his own gifts.[8]

Second, *my neighbor is helped.* Instead of fretting over how we can bring gifts to God that will make him favorable toward us, inventing our own rules and habits that he never commanded, we are free to be instruments of his gift giving to others. God has given each of us different skills, knowledge, abilities, and interests, and his commandments are directed toward the actual needs of other people all around us.

Third, *I benefit as well.* Calvin frequently takes shots at Stoic philosophy, which he sees as underlying the monastic life. Stoics held that one must live in azure isolation, independent of others, simply doing one's duty. Nothing may be done out of self-interest. No, Calvin repeatedly counters, we were made for God and each other—in covenant. God doesn't need us, but we need him and we need each other. Therefore, my happiness does depend on my neighbor's good. When God is glorified and my neighbor is served, I too find great joy and satisfaction. Even in my service to others, I too am a recipient of God's good works in this economy of grace. It is not selfish but godly to find our own joy and happiness in God's glory and the good of others.

When our focus is on our own spiritual growth and rewards, we take ourselves out of the circulation of God's gift exchange. In effect, we reverse the flow of gifts, bringing good works to God instead of faith in the sufficiency of his work for us in Christ.

The Reformers believed that both Rome and the Anabaptists had re-

---

[7] For a helpful treatment of this as well as other aspects of vocation, see Veith, *God at Work.*
[8] Calvin, *Institutes* 3.18.1–10.

versed this flow of gift giving. Bringing their piety up the ladder to God, they focused more on themselves than on Christ and their neighbor. Of course, the monastic life is especially what Calvin has in mind: "Paul censures those lazy drones who lived by the sweat of others, while they contribute no service in common for aiding the human race. Of this sort are our monks and priests who are largely pampered by doing nothing, except that they chant in the temples for the sake of preventing weariness." Were they not hallowed with ignorant praise, they would be reckoned thieves.[9] The term *calling* or *vocation* was reserved for the clergy and monks. Yet in this scheme, nobody wins. Anabaptist leaders did not really challenge the monastic life, but expected the whole community to separate from the world in the pursuit of perfection.

Ever since Max Weber (1864–1920), it has been widely rumored that Calvinism is responsible for the Protestant work ethic that became the spirit of capitalism. Eager to prove their election by worldly success while frowning on conspicuous consumption, Calvinists created an embarrassment of riches. The result was a culture of hard work, savings, and giving to charitable causes. The so-called Protestant work ethic as we know it owes more to Ben Franklin than to John Calvin. It is really a *worth* ethic. Truly, you show that you are favored by Providence not by the station into which you are born, but by what you make of yourself. It is a rugged individualism that establishes your "market value" in society. We even speak today of a person's "net worth." Does this works-righteousness, defined in calculable terms, have anything to do with Calvin?

Weber perceived the effects of Reformation teaching, but his proposed cause is a speculation that can't be located in the primary sources. In fact, it's just the opposite. "If we are chosen in Christ," says Calvin, "we shall find no assurance of election in ourselves." To trust in Christ is to be assured of our election.[10] As Wilhelm Niesel reminds us, "The much discussed activism of Calvin is rooted in the fact that we belong to Christ and thus can go our way free from care and confess our membership in Christ; but it does not arise from any zealous desire to prove one's Christian faith by good works."[11]

Calvin reflects frequently on the fact that we don't deserve any good gift that we receive, that faithfulness is no guarantee of temporal prosper-

---

[9] Calvin on 2 Thess. 3:10, in *Calvin's Commentaries*, 21:355.
[10] Calvin, *Institutes* 3.24.5.
[11] Wilhelm Niesel, *The Theology of John Calvin*, trans. Harold Knight (Philadelphia: Westminster, 1956), 99.

ity, and that worldly success is more of a danger to faith than evidence of God's favor. He offers no encouragement to those who would draw a straight line from hard work to riches as a sign of God's blessing.[12] His emphasis is on generosity, which comes from thankfulness. "'For there is nothing in which we are more like God than in being bountiful.' . . . Apart from the rule of love for one's neighbor, Calvin gives no other rules."[13]

There is no virtue in austerity, according to Calvin. We can take ourselves out of the flow of God's gifts equally by luxurious self-indulgence and by asceticism. Biéler explains that for the Reformer sacrifice may have been spiritually valuable, but it had nothing to do with "the ancient Christian tradition of contrasting spirit and matter," much less with "a meritorious deed."[14] "Calvin dreaded avarice and hoarding. Hence he insisted on the fact that accumulated economic goods ought to be put again into circulation in view of mutual help."[15] He was also not obsessed with saving money like later, more secularized, generations.[16] Calvin writes that all good gifts come down to us from God and are meant for us to enjoy and to share with others. "In brief, just as Jesus Christ gave himself to us, so by charity we ought to impart to others the graces which he gave us. Riches are a means to help the needy. That is the way to proceed and to keep a happy medium."[17]

If our assurance does not come from *working* in the world, we also do not see *rest* as an end in itself. "The only reason that rest is prescribed to man is . . . in order that he may have access to the labor of God." Consequently, there is no place left for our work for God. There is only God's work for us and, through us and with us, for others. Because we rest in God, we can work for others. "Thus restored and reintegrated in the great work of God, work becomes again creative and liberating."[18] There is simply nowhere to locate a meritorious concept of work in Calvin's thinking: not in prosperity or in deprivation, not in working or in resting.

God does not even owe us a salary when we fulfill our duty. And yet he provides for us—not as an employer, but as our Father. However, those who

[12] Herman J. Selderhuis, *Calvin's Theology of the Psalms* (Grand Rapids: Baker Academic, 2007), 199. "Challenging a well-known hypothesis," Selderhuis writes, "Calvin's commentary on the Psalms disproves the idea that he was the father of capitalism."
[13] Ibid., 200, on Ps. 30:5.
[14] André Biéler, *The Social Humanism of John Calvin*, trans. Paul T. Fuhrmann (Richmond, VA: John Knox, 1960), 41.
[15] Ibid., 60–61.
[16] Ibid., 61.
[17] Calvin, quoted in ibid., 63.
[18] Ibid., 44–45.

abuse their employees or deprive them of just wages will answer to God for damming up this circulation of gifts.[19] It is "a strange cruelty" that violates God's law and the shared humanity of employer and employee.[20]

The Reformation coincided with the rise of nation states and mercantile capitalism. And the latter found ready actors in the former's ranks in part because of a new affirmation of secular callings. The Reformers encouraged an ethic of civic responsibility, freedom, and excellence in vocations that contributed to economic growth. However, there is no theological connection between Calvinism and capitalism—especially of the kind that Weber alleged. The monk offers his works to God for a reward, while today's secularist justifies work largely in terms of its material reward, self-worth, or individual rights. What is truly revolutionary in the Reformers' perspective is that even our most common and everyday labors are now brought back into the flow of God's gift giving. While it is surely an overstatement, Biéler argued that "Calvinism is the first Christian ethics which gave a religious character to work"—a "divine vocation" that is justified even apart from earning a living.[21] Here we are taken up in God's loving action toward his creation—not that we now become co-redeemers, but we do become instruments through whom he delivers his gifts of common and saving grace to others. In other words, we are not Santa, but his elves.

Pilgrims, Not Wanderers

Calvin frequently encourages us in our callings as an antidote to our natural tendency toward "wandering," intruding as busybodies into other people's affairs. We need God himself to call us to a *particular* station in the world.

> Lest through our stupidity and rashness everything be turned topsy-turvy, he has appointed duties for every man in his particular way of life. And that no one may thoughtlessly transgress his limits, he has named these various kinds of livings "callings." Therefore, each individual has his own kind of living assigned to him by the Lord as a sort of sentry post so that he may not heedlessly wander about throughout life.[22]

---

[19] Ibid., 48.
[20] Ibid., 49.
[21] Ibid., 59.
[22] Calvin, *Institutes* 3.10.6.

This is to be used not as a pretext for ignoring the needs of our neighbors, but to stir us to useful and excellent service, Calvin exhorts.[23] God has placed each of us at a certain post, and our neighbors need the service that our dedication to that calling provides, just as we need theirs. It is not just a job, but a calling, and it comes from God and not just from our employer.

Recall Calvin's reply when Beza rebuked the dying Reformer for taxing his energies by writing: "What, would you have the Lord find me idle when he comes?" Rather than take the monk for our example, we should look to David the pious ruler, Deborah the wise judge, Daniel the godly counselor in a pagan court, and Jesus in his father's carpentry shop. The church is the theater of God's grace, but the whole world is the theater of his glory. What would you do today if you knew that Jesus were to return this afternoon? Calvin replies that he would do exactly what he would do any other day, just as Paul encouraged the Thessalonians to continue in their callings with excellence in view of Christ's return (2 Thess. 3:1–13).

The carpenter building a house for a family is nobler than a monk who thinks that he is pleasing God and performing his pious works that God has not commanded. In fact, Calvin says that "the chastity the nuns pretend is nothing before God, in comparison with the calling he has appointed" to wives and mothers. Men have no place to look down on this vocation as if it were beneath them. "For a man is not born to idleness, nor is a woman." Let her say

> that [God] is well pleased with it. . . . So then let women learn to rejoice when they do their duty, and though the world despise it, let this comfort sweeten all respect they might have that way, and say, "God sees me here, and his Angels, who are sufficient witnesses of my doings, although the world do not allow of them."[24]

Since God has descended to us in swaddling clothes and in hanging on a cross, we should not consider any calling menial or unimportant. When Christ—the God of the universe—wrapped a towel around his waist to wash his disciples' feet, Calvin observes, he dignified the humblest callings. No one and no service is "beneath us" if it benefits others. A couple of genera-

---

[23] Calvin on 2 Thess. 3:13, in *Calvin's Commentaries*, 21:358.
[24] Calvin, sermon on 1 Tim. 2:13–15, in *A Sermon of Master John Caluine, vpon the first Epistle of Paul, to Timothie, published for the benefite and edifying of the Churche of God* (London: G. Bishop and T. Woodcoke, 1579).

tions later the poet-preacher George Herbert would express this piety well, addressing God in prayer:

> A servant with this clause
> Makes drudgery divine.
> Who sweeps a room as for thy laws,
> Makes that and th'action fine.
>
> This is the famous stone
> That turneth all to gold:
> For that which God doth touch and own
> Cannot for less be told.[25]

World Changing or World Engaging?

In his book *To Change the World*, sociologist James D. Hunter marshals convincing evidence to support his thesis that recent attempts by Christians to transform culture are short-sighted and often counterproductive. Instead, Hunter calls for "faithful presence": believers simply living out their callings not only as individuals but as parts of institutions.[26]

This model seems to me at least to fit well with Calvin's piety. I have been struck repeatedly by the extent to which Calvin ignored the impact of his ministry—much less his "legacy." Relentlessly committed to faithfulness in his calling, he knew that its effects were beyond his control.

> The restoration of the church is the work of God, and it no more depends on human hopes and opinions than does the resurrection of the dead or any other miracle of that description. . . . It is the will of our Master that his gospel be preached. Let us obey his command and follow wherever he calls. What the success will be is not ours to inquire.[27]

A reformer rather than a revolutionary, he displayed none of the impatience with the world's present condition exhibited by the radical Protestants of his day or ours. Precisely because he did not expect too much in "this sad world," he was able to take up his daily duties—even knowing that he would fall short of his calling. God did not expect him to change

---

[25] George Herbert, *Poets and Prophets: A Selection of Poems by G. Herbert* (Tring, UK: Lion, 1988), 38.

[26] James Davison Hunter, *To Change the World: The Irony, Tragedy, and Possibility of Christianity in the Late Modern World* (New York: Oxford University Press, 2010).

[27] Calvin, quoted in Scott H. Hendrix, *Recultivating the Vineyard: The Reformation Agendas of Christianization* (Louisville: Westminster John Knox, 2004), 94.

the world, but to fulfill his calling—loving and serving his neighbors with the gifts that God had given him. Like one of God's spies in the land, he knew that all would be made right at the last and that, in the meantime, Christ was building his kingdom and was even looking after Caesar's affairs behind his back.

This model of faithful presence also helps to explain Calvin's impact on so many others. As we've seen, Calvin was not "made for prime time." Unlike Luther, he was shy and private—"timid," perhaps even "cowardly," as Calvin himself divulged. One can imagine him collapsing in the anteroom after delivering his daring—anything but cowardly—speech before Emperor Charles V. When occasion called, which it seemed to do nearly every day, a powerful sense of his calling overcame his disposition to flee the bright lights of the public stage.

Nor was Calvin a phoenix rising from the ashes. He was indebted to the church fathers and the best of the Catholic heritage for his understanding of Scripture. Further, his ministry is inconceivable apart from the influences of the French Renaissance that gave him not only his remarkable exegetical skills, but also a profound knowledge of the world and coordinates for interpreting it. As Marilynne Robinson observes, "Calvin is never more French than in his insistence on the aesthetic character of perception. The beauty of what we see is burdened with truth."[28] She adds, "He was a classic Renaissance humanist by education, a great stylist in Latin, a sensitive interpreter of Greek and Hebrew, and one of the creators of French as a language of thought."[29] Just as Luther is regarded as the father of modern German, Calvin is remembered as the father of modern French. In fact, the Geneva Bible—produced by exiles during Calvin's ministry—shaped modern English. None of this was accomplished directly by Calvin alone; nor could he have done what he did without myriad predecessors, colleagues, and spiritual heirs, many of whose gifts were equal to and sometimes exceeded his own.

The ministers and professors attracted to Geneva in the heyday of Calvin's ministry (1550–1564) hailed "almost entirely from the urban classes of French-speaking Europe as well as France's nobility."[30] A scion of the Burgundy aristocracy, Theodore Beza, Calvin's associate and eventual suc-

[28] Marilynne Robinson, preface to *John Calvin, Steward of God's Covenant: Selected Writings*, ed. John F. Thornton and Susan B. Varenne (New York: Vintage, 2006), xxii.

[29] Ibid., xv.

[30] Scott M. Manetsch, *Calvin's Company of Pastors: Pastoral Care and the Emerging Reformed Church, 1536–1609* (New York: Oxford University Press, 2012), 47.

cessor, was a famous poet and Latinist in his own right. Others came from Italy, especially Venice. Some were former priests and even bishops and professors. Others were scientists, poets, craftsmen, musicians, doctors, and lawyers. For example, Geleazzo Caracciolo, Count of Vico in Naples, fled the court of his godfather Emperor Charles V in 1551, amid his wife's threats to turn him in to the Inquisition. The nephew of Pope Paul IV (who said he would burn his own grandmother if she embraced the Reformation), Caracciolo had given up everything and lived out his days helping with Geneva's Italian church and arriving refugees.[31]

Many students of the Geneva Academy went on to other Reformed universities like Heidelberg, Leiden, and Basel, as well as Oxford and Cambridge, the two English universities having been reformed by Vermigli and Bucer respectively. A number of English students, exiles during Mary's reign, returned to become leaders in church and state under Elizabeth. If the Renaissance was an unwitting carrier of the Reformation, the influence worked also in reverse. Wherever Reformed convictions gained a foothold, there was a revival of classical learning and interest in the arts and sciences—not only among the highly educated, but even among the daily laborer, who also had more access to basic education. Indeed, with "the new learning," as critics called it, spiritual and cultural rebirth usually went hand in hand. In short, Calvin's significance lies in the fact that he helped to shape a tradition that existed before and after him.

Calvin's faithful presence among the Company of Pastors and the consistory is evident not only in the restoration of teaching, but also in a vigorous system of shared pastoral care, spiritual oversight, and diaconal relief. The whole city was transformed, not because this was Calvin's aim, nor even because of Calvin's ministry alone. And it was transformed not only by ideas but also by historical factors beyond his control. After all, like any other minister in Europe, he was appointed by the state. Geneva's rulers adopted the confession, liturgy, and church order that he drafted. Even if it were not hubris, a pastor today could hardly expect to exert the same type of influence over our highly pluralistic nation-states.

In short, despite failures and setbacks, Calvin kept his focus on Christ in faith and neighbors in love rather than on his transformative influence. By keeping to his calling day in and day out, he had a far greater impact than he would have had if such an impact were his focus.

---

[31] William Monter, *Calvin's Geneva* (New York: John Wiley and Sons, 1967), 184–86.

Finding God in the Everyday

Revolutionaries are generally bored by the everyday world. They are themselves extraordinary, at least in their own estimation, and cannot settle
for an ordinary existence in an ordinary world. When looking for Calvin's
impact and influence, we are basically asking, How did he change the political, artistic, scientific, and educational landscape? Calvin himself would
have considered this indulging a theology of glory; it fails to appreciate the
much broader historical impact of his teaching on people from every walk
of life.

And yet, Calvin's cultural impact is undeniable. Ironically, this impact
is due not to cultural elitism, but to an emphasis on God's activity in the
ordinary, common, and everyday world. In his preaching style, Calvin mod-
eled his own rule of "simplicity and brevity," which spoke as much to the
farmer as to the professor. As we've seen, he discourages us from "soaring
above the clouds" to find God, but urges us to find him where he has found
us already: in nature, through general revelation, and in Christ, by the gospel. Monastic piety encouraged the mind to ascend away from this world
and its history in contemplative speculation, while Calvin's piety directed
us to the reality of God's presence in his Word and in his world. Focus on
the things to which the finger can point, instead of speculating, Calvin
constantly exhorts. The true, the good, and the beautiful are to be found
in the realm of the concrete, particular, and historical.

This emphasis resonated with scientists and artists as well as craftsmen, milkmaids, and homemakers. Calvin's interest in science and the arts
is not just academic; it is part of his piety. Although it may be overstating
Calvin's influence, Selderhuis observes, "The way that Calvin describes the
universe as a revelation of God's glory gives insight into why an impulse
towards the study of the natural sciences can ultimately be attributed to
Calvin."[32] His spiritual heirs were disproportionately represented among
leaders in the sciences and the arts. They were founders of the British
Academy and, though a persecuted minority, were among the founders of
France's Academy of Science and its Academy of Painting.

As art historians have often observed, far from inhibiting the arts, Calvin's piety encouraged their flourishing. Indeed, "sculpture and painting
are gifts of God." However, "only those things are to be sculpted or painted
which the eyes are capable of seeing." Under this class "are histories and

---

[32] Selderhuis, *Calvin's Theology of the Psalms*, 69.

events" as well as "images and forms of bodies." Both are acceptable, but the former alone "have some use in teaching or admonishing"; in any case, the purpose of art is to bring delight rather than to provide objects of veneration.[33]

The so-called Golden Age of art, literature, and science in Britain and the Netherlands coincided with the zenith of high Reformed orthodoxy. Attention to detail—the particular, the local, and daily life in the world of time—is the hallmark of the art and literature, as well as the science, that emerged from Calvin's heirs. Art historians often note that for the first time paintings were hung in blacksmith shops, taverns, and homes. Not only did the paintings and sculptures themselves revel in everyday life; they adorned everyday lives.

Drama also had to turn to everyday subjects. Here too, the church is not the great patroness and governess of the arts. The Word is to be preached, not staged. The liturgy was its own drama, with the Father as the playwright, the Son as the central character, and the Spirit as the casting director. It has its own script, props, and riveting plot. Yet space now opened for drama as in the other arts for natural, familiar, and everyday subjects. Not only did Calvin enjoy plays himself; Beza wrote the first French tragedy, and Arthur Golding, translator of Calvin's works into English, wrote the first English drama ever staged.

These artists did not bring their work into the sanctuary, but left the sanctuary each week to serve others in the world. The drama of sin and grace is woven through all of their work. Their convictions about God, truth, goodness, and beauty; providence and the apparent disorderliness of life; love and war; and "the hope of a better world" find less obvious and direct but nevertheless profound expression. Everyday life is suffused with elements and motifs of a deeply religious worldview.

We are familiar with the tendency of many contemporary attempts to use the arts as evangelistic or moralistic propaganda, with cheerfully upbeat and pleasant characters, plots, and subjects. However, Reformed theology provided a richer, fuller, and more realistic worldview that made room for the tragic as well as comic aspects of life. Along with *vanitas* (vanity), the *memento mori* ("remember you will die") theme became a notable genre in all of the arts, a striking example being Frans Hals's *Youth with a Skull*. The theological convictions and piety that we associate with Calvin

---

[33] Calvin, *Institutes* 1.11.12.

offer a richer palette than the sentimentalism that often pushes contemporary Christian artists to avoid the tragic aspect of life in a fallen world. Those who sang the Psalms while they worked in the field, lab, or studio had a fuller repertoire to draw from in their engagement with the world. And it made an enormous difference that their work did not have to serve an evangelizing or moralizing purpose, but was justified simply by the excellence with which it rendered loving service to others on God's behalf.

Scores of studies continue to roll off academic presses exploring the influence of Calvin's teaching on every department of life. He was convinced that Scripture, coming from God, gives us the "spectacles" through which we come more clearly to see the world as God's gift. However, for Calvin, the Bible is not an archive of subjects to be painted and sculpted for veneration in churches. He did not see Scripture as an encyclopedia of politics, law, medicine, economics, or science. He did not found a political party or advance a particular style of art or a distinct school of natural science, mathematics, or economics. This is not because he regarded these pursuits as insignificant, but because he understood them as venues of God's common grace. When we read in Psalm 136 that God made two great lights—sun and moon—to rule the day and the night, the Holy Spirit is accommodating his speech "to the simplest and most uneducated persons." "The Holy Spirit had no intention to teach astronomy."[34] The medieval unity of cult and culture produced distinctive architectural styles, the grand Gothic being the most obvious. However, Calvin bequeathed no general style to churches and, aside from the prominence of pulpit, table, and font, Reformed houses of worship display a remarkable diversity of styles.

The Diversity of Everyday Life

Wherever the particular, the concrete, and the local are emphasized, appreciation for diversity is bound to follow. Much like the modern era, the medieval worldview favored unity over diversity, sameness over difference. One civilization—Christendom—with its descending hierarchy, was the eternal and unchanging copy of its celestial archetype. All roads led to Rome. Even in China, a Roman Catholic parish looks like one that might be found anywhere in Italy. As Stephen Toulmin has argued, Renaissance humanism differed in this respect. It favored history over speculation; the

---

[34]Calvin on Ps. 136:7, in *Calvin's Commentaries*, vol. 6, trans. James Anderson (Grand Rapids: Baker, 1996), 184–85.

particular and concrete over abstract ideas; the local, timely, and practical over the universal, timeless, and theoretical.[35]

One of the distinctive characteristics of Calvin's thinking on nature and history is *diversity*, which derives from his emphasis on the particular. Like other classical humanists, Calvin shared the ancient philosophers' view of beauty as proper proportion and the ordering of all the parts into a whole. However, his aesthetic sensibilities express a more dynamic outlook. For him, the beauty of God's order is not its sameness, but the difference that each particular person, place, and thing contributes to the whole.

Reflecting his humanist background, Calvin's interest in diversity and difference as essential to God's order can be discerned across his whole theology. We have seen how, in discussing the Trinity, he is as struck by "the splendor of the Three" as by the unity of the essence. While we affirm the unity of the divine essence, Calvin says that "it is not fitting to suppress the distinction" between the divine persons and their distinct way of acting in every external work of the Godhead.[36] It is clear enough from his argument in the *Institutes* that he thinks Western theology has in fact tended sometimes to blur the differences in emphasizing the unity. And, with the aid of the Eastern fathers, he seeks greater balance.

This triune God also created a world of diversity to reflect his beauty and to bring us pleasure: "To what purpose are there produced so many kinds of fruit, and in so great abundance, and why are there so many pleasant and delightful countries, if it is not for the use and comfort of people?"[37] Notice how he himself connects diversity in nature with diversity in cultures. Furthermore, he revels in the diversity of the human constitution, affirming the body as well as the soul. He discerns this diversity in providence as well: "Nothing is more natural than for spring to follow winter; summer, spring; and fall, summer—each in turn," he writes. "Yet in this series one sees such great and uneven diversity that it readily appears each year, month, and day is governed by a new, a special, providence of God."[38]

What is the purpose of so much diversity in nature and providence? It does not seem merely to serve mathematical order, much less practical

---

[35] Stephen Toulmin, *Cosmopolis: The Hidden Agenda of Modernity* (Chicago: University of Chicago Press, 1992), 30–35.
[36] Calvin, *Institutes* 1.13.18.
[37] Calvin on Ps. 24:1, in *Calvin's Commentaries*, vol. 4, trans. James Anderson (Grand Rapids: Baker, 1996), 402.
[38] Calvin, *Institutes* 1.16.2.

utility. It would seem that God created so much difference in the world simply for his pleasure—and ours. Calvin adds later:

> In grasses, trees, and fruits, apart from their utility, there is beauty of appearance and pleasantness of odor. For if this were not true, the prophet would not have reckoned them among the benefits of God, "that wine gladdens the heart of man, that oil makes his face shine." . . . Has the Lord clothed the flowers with great beauty that greets our eyes, the sweetness of smell that is wafted upon our nostrils, and yet will it be unlawful for our eyes to be affected by that beauty, or our sense of smell by the sweetness of that odor?

Continuing, he strikes out again at Stoic philosophy, which he sees behind the monastic insistence on the necessities of life apart from pleasure:

> What? Did he not so distinguish colors as to make some more lovely than others? What? Did he not endow gold and silver, ivory and marble, with a loveliness that renders them more precious than other metals or stones? Did he not, in short, render many things attractive to us, apart from their necessary use? Away, then, with that inhuman philosophy which, while conceding only a necessary use of creatures, not only malignantly deprives us of the lawful fruit of God's beneficence but cannot be practiced unless it robs man of all his senses and degrades him to a block.[39]

If God created such diversity—more colors, shapes, cultures, callings, styles, and flavors than we need—then we would be ungrateful not to delight in it. "However many blessings we expect from God, his infinite liberality will always exceed all our wishes and our thoughts." Indeed, "it is no small honor that God for our sake has so magnificently adorned the world, in order that we may not only be spectators of this *beauteous theatre*, but also enjoy the *multiplied abundance* and *variety of good things* which are presented to us in it."[40]

We have seen the same reference to diversity in his rejection of the insistence that all nations submit to the Mosaic law.

> How malicious and hateful toward public welfare would a man be who is *offended by such diversity*, which is perfectly adapted to maintain the

---

[39] Ibid., 3.10.2–3.
[40] Calvin, quoted in Howard L. Rice, *Reformed Spirituality: An Introduction for Believers* (Louisville: Westminster John Knox, 1991), 59, emphasis added.

observance of God's law! For the statement of some, that the law of God given through Moses is dishonored when it is abrogated and new laws preferred to it, is utterly vain.[41]

Calvin even expresses delight in the diversity of Scripture. The Bible's one central plot unfolds through a variety of twists and turns through different ages, with a remarkable diversity among its human authors and supporting cast. The whole range of emotion, personalities, and characters that we encounter in everyday life is reflected from Genesis to Revelation.[42] In each passage we must discern the wider context in the book and in the wider canon of Scripture. The preacher no less than the artist, scientist, or farmer must give due attention to the trees, not just the forest. Calvin is taken with the Psalms in part because there we discover "an anatomy of all feelings of the soul."[43] "The varied and resplendent riches which are contained in this treasury it is no easy matter to express in words," he says.[44]

Calvin brings the same appreciation for diversity even to his discussion of life in the church. Universal ideas, principles, and laws may be applied without discrimination in every situation at every time and place. God's Word delivers a clear gospel, with the elements of worship, government, and commands for daily life spelled out insofar as God is pleased to reveal them. However, circumstances will be diverse. The outward form of ceremonies may differ across times and places.[45] As I have pointed out, this diversity in circumstances is reflected in the fact that there is no "Calvinist style" analogous to Byzantine or Gothic styles of the Eastern or Latin churches. Biblical elements (visually prominent in the pulpit, font, and table) are the focus of unity, while the circumstances concerning architecture, liturgical order, musical style, and church order may differ from culture to culture.

Where God speaks, we must obey; where he has not spoken, we are free to exercise godly wisdom, looking to the particular context. Even biblical commands have to be applied in concrete, particular, and diverse situations that may differ from case to case. One has to exercise circumspection: "looking around" at the specific circumstances.[46]

---

[41] Calvin, *Institutes* 4.20.8, 14, emphasis added.

[42] Calvin on Heb. 1:1–2, in *Calvin's Commentaries*, vol. 22, trans. John Owen (Grand Rapids: Baker, 1996), 31–32.

[43] Calvin, quoted in Selderhuis, *Calvin's Theology of the Psalms*, 23.

[44] Calvin, preface to *Commentary on the Psalms*, in *Calvin's Commentaries*, 4:xxxvi.

[45] Andrew Pettegree, "The Spread of Calvin's Thought," in *The Cambridge Companion to John Calvin*, ed. Donald K. McKim (Cambridge: Cambridge University Press, 2004), 207–8.

[46] Toulmin, *Cosmopolis*, 32: "Modern moral philosophy was concerned not with minute 'case studies' or particular moral discriminations, but with the comprehensive general principles of ethical theory. In

Calvin's emphasis on the diversity of situations in the particulars of everyday life offers wisdom that we need today. While Calvin had much to say from the biblical text against oppressing the poor, he never proposed a policy—such as the proper wage or an interest-rate limit on loans. If the pastor fulfills his vocation with his superior knowledge of Scripture, then the parishioners can fulfill theirs. They have more circumstantial data and experience to bring to bear beyond general rules. The Reformed confessions give significant attention to "the light of nature" on such matters. Though not "the light of grace," it is essential for making decisions, especially where Scripture does not provide its own obvious applications.

In short, unity did not mean uniformity. In the church as in culture, as in creation itself, diversity is not a falling away from the unity of being; it is intrinsic to that unity that the triune God creates and blesses. God's beautiful order in creation and redemption is not set over against difference, but against sin, which turns diversity into violent opposition and resentment. Calvin worked against the xenophobia of native Genevans, encouraging them to welcome the stranger. Eventually, not only French families but also Spaniards, Italians, and Eastern Europeans became citizens and even senators there. In myriad ways, Calvin welcomed difference as essential to the unity of God's good creation.

The piety that Calvin encouraged certainly colors the way in which Christians engage culture, but Calvin would not have understood what was meant by appeals to create a "Calvinist culture." Given his warnings against demanding uniformity in rites, even the church—indeed, especially the church—must not be allowed to become a mirror of a monolithic ethnic, generational, socioeconomic, or cultural demographic.

"Places, Everyone!"

Calvin could say with Luther, "The Word did it all." Philip Benedict summarizes:

> Every aspect of the city had been transformed. According to the leading historian of Genevan government, the city fathers of this once tumultuous and faction-ridden town "had evolved from carefree demagogues into

---

a phrase, general principles were in, particular cases were out." The Puritans especially wrote detailed "cases of conscience," in which they related specific counseling situations and the application of Scripture and godly wisdom in contexts where there wasn't a one-size-fits-all application. Toulmin points out the extent to which Calvin and his spiritual heirs focused on particular cases in pastoral ministry, in contrast with the abstract principles of modern ethics.

the grave and painfully honest stereotype of Calvin's ideal magistrate."
. . . The thousands of new immigrants who had taken their place had introduced the fine textile and clock-making industries that would in time
make the city's fortunes. The sizable number of printers and booksellers
among them had enabled the output of the city's presses to increase from
three titles in 1537 to forty-eight in 1561. Laurent de Normanie, the well-
heeled former mayor of Calvin's home town of Noyon, had put into place
a vast clandestine distribution network by which the output of these
presses reached across France, Savoy, Lorraine, Alsace, and Poland.[47]

In short, in Calvin's piety, cultural engagement is certainly part of
Christian discipleship, but it takes place in our worldly callings rather than
in the church. Instead of seeking to bring the culture into the church, diverse strangers of God are made one family in Christ and are then sent out
into the culture to pursue their callings. "Let us not be ashamed to take
pious delight in the works of God open and manifest in this most beautiful
theater," Calvin encourages.[48]

The sort of evangelical piety that Calvin encourages is riveted to the
economy of grace, fastening our attention to the one whose descent, ascent,
and return keep us looking up in faith, forward in hope, and out to our
neighbor in love. In the meantime, believers know roughly how the story
ends. They look upon this world as the theater of God's glory, fallen into
disrepair and disorder, but still preserved by God's hand and to be restored
even beyond its original integrity one day. And so they participate in the
common joys and trials of their neighbors in this time between Christ's
two advents and gather together regularly to savor the scent of a banquet
that never ends.

---

[47] Phillip Benedict, *Christ's Churches Purely Reformed: A Social History of Calvinism* (New Haven, CT: Yale University Press, 2002), 108.
[48] Calvin, *Institutes* 1.14.20.

CHAPTER 14

LIVING TODAY FROM THE FUTURE: THE HOPE OF GLORY

The piety in which many of us were raised encourages a heavenly minded-ness that sometimes tends to denigrate our common lives and callings here and now. Reacting against this flight away from the here and now, others preach a more this-worldly salvation. This message comes in two seemingly different packages: a prosperity gospel, focusing on either personal peace and happiness, or a social gospel, focusing on redemptive political policies and action. But whether it promises "your best life now" or "our best world now," the assumptions are similar. We're tired of waiting for "pie in the sky bye and bye," and if God is going to be relevant, we have to see results now. Both versions make God a means to an end and make us rather than Christ alone the agent of redemption. Either one plays better in our culture than the call of Jesus Christ to die to ourselves and be raised with Christ. It is being baptized into Christ as the firstfruits of the age to come that gives us faith, hope, and love to endure the present evil age with neither resentment nor triumphalism.

In his treatment of the "helps" to Christian living in the *Institutes*, Calvin exhorts readers to "meditation upon the future life."[1] It's interesting

---

[1] Calvin, *Institutes of the Christian Religion*, ed. John T. McNeill, trans. Ford Lewis Battles (Philadelphia: Westminster, 1960), 3.25.1.

that he calls it "the future life," not "the other world." It is not an escape from the realm of earthly embodiment. "Plato recognized man's highest good as union with God," but that was by the soul's release from the body and this physical world at death. Plato "could not even dimly sense [the] nature" of this union apart from Christ. Far from raising their minds away from the body to incorporeal universals, says Calvin, "they alone receive the fruit of Christ's benefits who raise their minds *to the resurrection.*"[2]

Unlike the me-centered and us-centered gospels of our day, this emphasis on the future makes the point that we are still awaiting the full effects of God's rescue operation. We can't make our lives or our world heaven on earth by our agendas, programs, and activity. It is a gift, and only Christ can consummate his kingdom, which he will do when he returns in glory. Yet this is no reversion to the "I'll fly away," "Late Great Planet Earth" approach either. As the phrase suggests, "meditation on the *future* life" focuses on the complete renewal of this world, including our bodies, at the end of the age.

"Even though among the ancient philosophers," says Calvin, "Plato enjoys the distinction of having recognized that 'man's highest good . . . is union with God,' none of the philosophers understood that the achievement of this good depends on the 'sacred bond' of union with Christ."[3] Yet the good news is also not a gospel of self-salvation through personal or social transformation. Rather, says Calvin, with such meditation we look to Christ, who is the firstfruits of the resurrection: as he is, so we shall be also.[4] He has not assumed our flesh only to divest himself of it at the ascension. Rather, he ascended to enthrone our flesh at the right hand of the Father. Sending his Spirit as a down-payment to indwell us, he will bring his elect—and the wider creation—into that glorious condition beyond the reach of sin and death.

The Resurrection of the Dead and Life Everlasting

Calvin is simply synthesizing the best Christian wisdom. Meditation on the future life is less like waiting at the airport for a flight than like a child's quivering with excitement on Christmas Eve. While we rejoice in the promise of being in God's presence upon death, the ultimate confidence of Christians is "the resurrection of the body and the life everlasting." Under

---

[2] Ibid., 3.25.2, emphasis added.
[3] Cornelis P. Venema, "Calvin's Doctrine of the Last Things," in *A Theological Guide to Calvin's Institutes: Essays and Analysis*, ed. David W. Hall and Peter A. Lillback (Phillipsburg, NJ: P&R, 2008), 446.
[4] Calvin, *Institutes* 3.25.2.

the reign of sin and death, our history does not have any living seeds that could grow into full flower for a new world. This present age cannot be transformed by us into the age to come. And yet, assuming our humanity, God the Son has delivered our destinies from this dead end. Our history is now united with his, inseparably, for all eternity. Christ already wears the glorious immortality that we too will "put on" in the resurrection.[5] The whole cosmos will be renewed. And, paradoxically, focusing on that future changes our lives in the present.

On Romans 8:19–25, Calvin comments, "I understand the passage to have this meaning: that there is no element and no part of the world which, being touched, as it were, with a sense of its present misery, does not intensely hope for a resurrection."[6] How tragic it is that the whole creation, through our fault alone, should be subject to a curse![7] Yet the whole creation also longs for its redemption in the train of the last Adam, together with his coheirs. "For God will restore to a perfect state the world, now fallen, together with mankind." We should not give our speculation free rein here. "Let us then be content with this simple doctrine—that such will be the constitution and the complete order of things that nothing will be deformed or fading."[8]

Yet creation groans with us, awaiting its redemption. It is not yet complete and we cannot bring it about, so we must wait for it patiently.

> [God] does not call his people to victory before he exercises them in the warfare of patience. But since it has pleased God to lay up our salvation, as it were, in his closed bosom, it is expedient for us to toil on earth, to be oppressed, to mourn, to be afflicted, yea, to lie down as half-dead and to be like the dead; for they who seek a visible salvation reject it, as they renounce hope which has been appointed by God as its guardian.[9]

For now, we live by a promise—what we hear, no matter how it is contradicted by what we see.

Therefore, the focus of this daily meditation is our life at the intersection of the "already" and the "not yet." On the one hand, we are assured of our election, justification, and adoption. We have been definitively

---

[5] Calvin on Rom. 8:25–26, in *Calvin's Commentaries*, vol. 19, trans. John Owen (Grand Rapids: Baker, 1996), 310–16.
[6] Ibid., 303.
[7] Ibid., 305.
[8] Ibid.
[9] Ibid., 310.

regenerated by the Spirit and are being conformed to Christ's image. In the Psalms Calvin finds supreme comfort in the knowledge of God as our Father in Christ. Yet he also finds solace in the knowledge that our Father is also our Judge. After all, he is the Judge who has justified us. "Just as in Luther's thought, Calvin's notion of the righteousness of God does not mean the righteousness God demands of us but the righteousness he gives us."[10] It especially underscores God's covenantal faithfulness and encourages us to endure the false accusations and insults of other people.[11]

Yet we are a long way off from our destination. Precisely because of what we already possess—including the indwelling Spirit—we long for the more that awaits us up ahead. Precisely because we have already been touched by the powers of the age to come, we long for its consummation. Precisely because our inner self is regenerated, we long for the resurrection of the body. Precisely because we are justified, we long to be glorified. In the meantime, we put up with the anxieties of a fallen world and struggle against indwelling sin as part of a curse that no longer defines us or controls our destiny. So we live in patience, not as a matter of stoic resolve, abandoning ourselves to fate, nor in blind optimism as if the future were always in principle better than the present. Rather, our patience is reasonable because of the promise that has already been proved in the gifts that we have already received and have begun to enjoy in Christ.

Frequently Calvin echoes Paul's confidence: "If God is for us, who can be against us? . . . Who shall bring any charge against God's elect?" (Rom. 8:31–33). Calvin rejects Rome's view that even while the transgression might be forgiven, its punishment remains. No, nothing God sends our way comes from justice, but it arises from mercy; the goal is not to punish us, but to help us.[12] "In God's anger, Calvin says, he does not stop being a father. Moreover, properly speaking, God is never angry with his elect. . . . When it seems otherwise, he 'wears a human mask.'"[13] David's confession in Psalm 51 "should not be taken as proof that a person's repentance makes God gracious towards the sinner."[14] For believers the verdict of the future judgment has already been rendered; it's just that our actual condition and experience have not yet caught up with that verdict. With such a secure future in place, we can bear our cross in the present.

---

[10] Herman J. Selderhuis, *Calvin's Theology of the Psalms* (Grand Rapids: Baker Academic, 2007), 157.
[11] Ibid., 157–58.
[12] Ibid., 164.
[13] Ibid., 165, on Ps. 74:1, 9.
[14] Ibid., 168, on Ps. 51:5.

The Way of the Cross

Calvin began preaching on the Psalms every Sunday afternoon from 1549 to 1554. The commentary appeared in 1557. In just one decade (1550–1560), Geneva had nearly doubled its population, largely from foreign exiles. The Reformer saw himself in David, and the church of sojourners and martyrs in the remnant of Israel. In fact, this commentary is the nearest we come to an autobiography. "I must confess that by nature I have not much courage and that I am timid, faint-hearted and weak," he tells us in the preface.[15] Calvin saw other parallels with David. "David vehemently resisted these people, Calvin writes, not because of his name but for the sake of the well-being of the church."[16] Selderhuis notes, "Calvin's descriptions of the moral aberrations of David often give us information about the way Calvin has struggled with his own shortcomings."[17] Surely with sound exegetical warrant, but no doubt a lively sense of relevance to his own life, a motif of "asylum" and "exile" is shot through the commentary.[18]

> The Psalms, however, reveal to us the true God—a God who is so great as to be able to "forgive sins free of charge." "In this book," writes Calvin, "the most important thing we can wish to have is presented to us, namely, not only that we might be on intimate terms with God but also that we might openly confess to him the weaknesses which, casting shame on us, we kept hidden from others."[19]

While Calvin was drawn to David's experience, he saw him chiefly as prefiguring Christ.[20] "David is a mouth of Christ and of all those who belong to Christ."[21] Like John the Baptist, David points away from himself to the true King—the Lion who is also a Lamb. Calvin discerned in the Psalms two kinds of anxiety: "mortal fear," which drives to despair, and "dying struggle," which can be oddly reassuring when we flee to Christ. David often expresses the latter.[22] With the fall in Paradise, humanity "lapsed into '*superbia*.'" This is pride and vanity. "Only God's merciful intervention led to the restoration of order. This order is restored in Christ and takes the form

---

[15] Calvin, quoted in ibid., 27–28, from Calvin, preface to his *Commentary on the Psalms*.
[16] Calvin, quoted in ibid., 32.
[17] Ibid., 34.
[18] Ibid., 34–35.
[19] Ibid., 39.
[20] Calvin, *Institutes* 2.10.15–18; 2.12.2.
[21] Selderhuis, *Calvin's Theology of the Psalms*, 36, quoting Calvin on Ps. 69:4.
[22] Ibid., 41.

of an ordered Christian and ecclesiastical life." Yet until Christ returns, Calvin writes, "this world remains in confusion."[23] We find asylum only in God's mercy in Christ, yet this refuge brings us "exile, oppression, and disgrace" as we share in Christ.[24] "It is characteristic of the theology of the cross that reality is manifested in its opposite just as the victory of Christ over death shrouded itself in the crucifixion. . . . For example, God can deprive us of all his gifts in order thereby to give us back our trust in him."[25]

This is why we must close our eyes and listen only to God's promises, which are *not* hidden and give us an open and free access to the Father of all mercies.[26]

In medieval piety, self-denial was the fast track to the saving blessing of the beatific vision. This is why monks took a vow of poverty and celibacy. Calvin also recognizes that self-denial lies at the heart of the Christian life. Yet he begins this section by counseling us to take our cues not from moral philosophy but from the gospel, which "shows that God the Father, as he has reconciled us to himself in his Christ, has in him stamped for us the likeness to which he would have us conform." The philosophers "wish particularly to exhort us to virtue, announce merely that we should live in accordance with nature," Calvin notes. "But Scripture draws its exhortation from the true fountain." This true fountain is Christ with all of his benefits, the only proper ground and motive for following Christ in taking up our cross.[27] Thus, self-denial is not the means to salvation, but the pattern that our salvation takes in this pilgrimage. Indeed, self-denial is "the sum of the Christian life."[28]

Once again, there is distinction without separation between Christ and the Christian, his cross and our cross. The difference is not just quantitative (greater and lesser), but qualitative. His cross alone redeems us. Nevertheless, united to him through faith alone, we are caught up in his baptism into death and resurrection unto life. In relation to God, this means that we renounce our own claims to righteousness, security, and ownership over our own lives. In relation to our neighbors it means that we give up our "insolent pride and self-love" that "looks down upon [them] as inferior." We all tend to "admire ourselves" while belittling others. "If there are any faults

---

[23] Ibid.
[24] Ibid., 42.
[25] Ibid., 188, on Ps. 30:8.
[26] Ibid., 193, on Pss. 102:16; 119:123.
[27] Calvin, *Institutes* 3.6.3.
[28] Ibid., 3.7.1.

in others, not content with noting them with severe and sharp reproach, we hatefully exaggerate them."[29] Especially in our culture—even the culture of American Christianity—the call to die to ourselves is crucial, as it is often absent from our piety. "You will never attain true gentleness," Calvin instructs, "except by one path: a heart imbued with lowliness and with reverence for others."[30] When we find all of our security in God's free reconciliation in Christ, apart from our merits, we can love our neighbors in view of God's mercies rather than because of their merits. Scripture teaches us "that we are not to consider what men merit of themselves, but to look upon the image of God in all people, to which we owe all honor and love."[31]

Where prosperity gospels assume that possessing all spiritual blessings in Christ entails temporal abundance, Calvin teaches, "For whomever the Lord has adopted and deemed worthy of his fellowship ought to prepare themselves for a hard, toilsome, and unquiet life, crammed with very many and various kinds of evil."[32] Our Father sends us trials not to punish us for our sins but to humble us and drive us to himself.

> But even the most holy persons, however much they recognize that they stand not through their own strength but through God's grace, are too sure of their own fortitude and constancy unless by the testing of the cross he brings them into deeper knowledge of himself. . . . In peaceful times, then, they preened themselves on their great constancy and patience, only to learn when humbled by adversity that all this was hypocrisy.[33]

He adds, "Now we see how many things, interwoven, spring from the cross. For, overturning that good opinion which we falsely entertain concerning our own strength, and unmasking our hypocrisy, which affords us delight, the cross strikes at our perilous confidence in the flesh."[34] It is not only in the manner of our salvation, but also in the way that it is worked out in our daily lives that we remain fastened to a theology of the cross rather than a theology of glory.

We are so drawn to a theology of glory that we can even turn cross bearing into a good work that we offer to God and for which we praise our

---

[29] Ibid., 3.7.4–5.
[30] Ibid., 3.7.4.
[31] Ibid., 3.7.6.
[32] Ibid., 3.8.1.
[33] Ibid., 3.8.2.
[34] Ibid., 3.8.3.

virtue. The monks go looking for a cross, thinking that they are pleasing God by their stoic resolve. We encounter this sometimes in our own circles today, as believers often feel obliged to smile in public even if they collapse at home in private despair. Calvin counters, "Such a cheerfulness is not required of us as to remove all feeling of bitterness and pain."

> It is not as the Stoics of old foolishly described "the great-souled man": one who, having cast off all human qualities, was affected equally by adversity and prosperity, by sad times and happy ones—nay, who like a stone was not affected at all. . . . Now, among the Christians there are also new Stoics, who count it depraved not only to groan and weep but also to be sad and care-ridden. These paradoxes proceed, for the most part, from idle men who, exercising themselves more in speculation than in action, can do nothing but invent such paradoxes for us. Yet we have nothing to do with this iron philosophy which our Lord and Master has condemned not only by his word, but also by his example. For he groaned and wept both over his own and others' misfortunes. . . . And that no one might turn it into a vice, he openly proclaimed, "Blessed are those who mourn."[35]

Especially given how some of Calvin's heirs have confused a Northern European "stiff upper lip" stoicism with biblical piety, it is striking how frequently he rebuts this "cold" philosophy that would "turn us to stone."[36] Suffering is not to be denied or downplayed, but arouses us to flee to the asylum of the Father, in the Son, by the Spirit.

It is quite unimaginable that this theology of the cross will top the best-seller lists in our "be good–feel good" culture, but those who labor under perpetual sorrows, as Calvin did, will find solidarity in his stark realism:

> Then only do we rightly advance by the discipline of the cross when we learn that this life, judged in itself, is troubled, turbulent, unhappy in

---

[35] Ibid., 3.8.8.

[36] Calvin, "To Monsieur de Richebourg" (Ratisbon, April 1541), in *Selected Works of John Calvin: Tracts and Letters*, ed. Henry Beveridge and Jules Bonnet, 7 vols. (Grand Rapids: Baker, 1983), 4:253. At the beginning of the letter, Calvin expresses his own grief: "When I first received the intelligence of the death of Claude and of your son Louis, I was so utterly overpowered that for many days I was fit for nothing but to grieve" (246). The Reformer saw it as great consolation that the Lord had taken Louis, not fate or destiny (248). "Now certainly because the Lord himself, who is the Father of us all, had willed that Louis should be put among the children as a son of his adoption, he bestowed this benefit upon you, out of the multitude of his mercies, that you might reap the excellent fruit of your careful education before his death; whence also you might know your interest in the blessing that belongs to you, 'I will be thy God and the God of thy seed'" (249–50). "Neither do I insist upon your laying aside all grief. Nor, in the school of Christ, do we learn any such philosophy as requires us to put off that common humanity with which God has endowed us, that, being men, we should be turned to stones" (253). Calvin also asked Melanchthon and Bucer to send letters of condolence (253).

countless ways, and in no respect clearly happy; that all those things which are judged to be its goods are uncertain, fleeting, vain, and vitiated by many intermingled evils. From this, at the same time, we conclude that in this life we are to seek and hope for nothing but struggle; when we think of our crown, we are to raise our eyes to heaven. For this we must believe: that the mind is never seriously aroused to desire and ponder the life to come unless it is previously imbued with contempt for the present life.[37]

Yet precisely because "this life, *judged in itself*," is filled with misery, the obvious evidences of God's grace to us in the gospel fill us with hope. For our life is not merely judged in itself.

Only when the burden of this life presses us to lodge our entire confidence in Christ and the blessings of the age to come do we not only find the strength to endure this life, but also recognize bright beams of God's kindness even in our temporal circumstances. "Since, therefore, this life serves us in understanding God's goodness, should we despise it as if it had no grain of good in itself?" Only when we are made certain that our only hope is in the kindness, love, and mercy of God—and not at all in the circumstances of our lives now—can we begin to wonder at so many blessings instead of complain at the slightest adversity. "When we are certain that the earthly life we live is a gift of God's kindness, as we are beholden to him for it we ought to remember it and be thankful."[38]

In spite of some of his bleak comments, Calvin makes it clear that the misery of this present life is not natural. He longs to be liberated not from creation, but from sin. "Of course," he says, the present life "is never to be hated except in so far as it holds us subject to sin; although not even hatred of that condition may ever properly be turned against life itself."[39]

Meditation on our frailty—even death—is not an end in itself. It is meant to lead us to hope in the resurrection. Ironically, it is the denial of death and the resurrection of the body that leads pagans to suppress the tragic aspect of life, even while "the brute animals and even inanimate creatures—even trees and stones—conscious of the emptiness of their present condition, long for the final day of resurrection" and know that "this earthly decay" does not have the last word.[40] "To conclude in a

---

[37] Calvin, *Institutes* 3.9.1.
[38] Ibid., 3.9.3.
[39] Ibid., 3.9.4.
[40] Ibid., 3.9.5.

word: if believers' eyes are turned to the power of the resurrection, in their hearts the cross of Christ will at last triumph over the devil, flesh, sin, and wicked men."[41]

As it turns out, then, Calvin's "meditation on the future life" is not a flight from this world, but a deeper identification with it. It is a realism and hope grounded in the gospel that opens us up to his grace and our callings in the world. We are not monks, depriving ourselves of everything but the basic necessities. "And we also cannot avoid those things which seem to serve delight more than necessity. Therefore we must hold to a measure so as to use them with a clear conscience, whether for necessity or delight."[42] Paradoxically, those who have let go of this life, no longer slaves to its promises of health, wealth, and happiness, are free to enjoy its gifts as pleasures directing our gratitude to a generous Father. He gives them "not only to provide for necessity but also for delight and good cheer."[43]

Glorification of the Saints

Calvin's treatment of the last things follows from his discussion of the benefits we receive in union with Christ the Mediator. As Cornelis Venema observes, "Considering the location of chapter 25 in the *Institutes*, it might well be titled 'The Believer's Glorification in Union with Christ.'"[44] The chapter focuses on the resurrection of the dead, which is the climax of God's saving work. Here, the believer is raised, body and soul, in everlasting glory—immortal and as much like God in moral excellence as is possible for a creature. It is meditating on this that Calvin has in mind—and believes that Paul has in mind—when he calls us to fix our minds on heaven, where we are seated with Christ.[45] We have already seen the importance of glorification in Calvin's treatment of the order of salvation.

Where the goal of the monk's meditation was the beatific vision of God in his glorious majesty, Calvin calls us to meditate on the most particular and concrete, revealed in that which is small, foolish, and even disgusting in the eyes of the world. To see God is to find him wrapped in swaddling clothes and hanging on the cross. True contemplation dwells daily on the gifts of our union with Christ, culminating in glorification. This glory is

---

[41] Ibid., 3.9.6.
[42] Ibid., 3.10.1.
[43] Ibid., 3.10.2.
[44] Venema, "Calvin's Doctrine of the Last Things," 445.
[45] Calvin, *Institutes* 3.25.1.

not something that we attain by cooperating with God's deifying grace, but is a gift of our union with Christ. As Jesus Christ now is, so we will be; as goes the Head, so go the members. In fact, Calvin can even say that "Christ considers himself in some measure imperfect" until his whole body shares with him in everlasting glory.[46] That is how real the bond is between Christ and his church.

On a number of topics, Calvin draws deeply from church fathers, in the East especially.[47] He does so again here, in treating glorification. He writes, "Let us mark that the end of the gospel is to render us eventually conformable to God, and, if we may so speak, to deify us." Nevertheless, he adds:

> But the word nature [in 2 Pet. 1:4] is not here *essence* but *quality*. The Manicheans [Gnostics] formerly dreamt that we are a part of God, and that after having run the race of life we shall at length return to our original. There are also at this day fanatics who imagine that we thus pass over into the nature of God, so that he swallows up our nature. . . . But such a delirium never entered the minds of the holy Apostles; they only intended to say that when divested of all the vices of the flesh, we shall be partakers of divine and blessed immortality and glory, so as to be as it were one with God *as far as our capacities will allow.*[48]

Resurrection and glorification are two sides of the same coin, then, in the view of Calvin and the tradition that he helped to shape. William Ames could say that glorification "is actually nothing but the carrying out of the sentence of justification. . . . In glorification the life that results from the pronouncement and award given to us: We have it in actual possession."[49] In his commentary on the Westminster Confession, Thomas Watson rhapsodizes concerning the soul's reunion with its flesh, concluding, "The dust of a believer is part of Christ's mystic body."[50]

All of this follows from the emphasis on union with Christ, the full benefits of which we do not enjoy until we are raised bodily in incorruptible glory. Our condition will be far greater than that of Adam and Eve before the fall. The consummation is not "Paradise Restored," but something

---

[46] Calvin on Eph. 1:23, in *Calvin's Commentaries*, vol. 21, trans. William Pringle (Grand Rapids: Baker, 1996), 218.

[47] I point this out at length in *People and Place: A Covenantal Ecclesiology* (Louisville: Westminster John Knox, 2008), 124–52.

[48] Calvin on 2 Pet. 1:4, in *Calvin's Commentaries*, 22:371, emphasis added.

[49] William Ames, *The Marrow of Theology*, trans. John D. Eusden (Boston: Pilgrim, 1968; repr., Durham, NC: Labyrinth, 1983), 172.

[50] Thomas Watson, *A Body of Divinity* (Edinburgh: Banner of Truth Trust, 1986), 309.

that "no eye has seen nor ear heard" (1 Cor. 2:9). It is the reward that Adam forfeited on behalf of himself and his posterity, but has been won for us by the last Adam, our elder Brother. All will be raised, either to immortal shame or to glory. Yet, it is the latter upon which Calvin focuses attention. Although he clearly affirms everlasting punishment, there is much more on this cosmic restoration than on hell. "He also dismisses as too harsh the common interpretation he has encountered that, in Christ's victory over his enemies, so much blood will flow that it will form a stream from which Christ will drink."[51]

Venema notes concerning Calvin's view, "Since Christ came 'properly not for the destruction of the world but for its salvation,' this is the chief emphasis to be found in the Word of God."[52] In fact, Calvin interprets "judgment" as "reformation" in John 12:31—in other words, "the world must be restored to due order." Calvin explains, "For the Hebrew word *mispat* which is translated as judgment means a well-ordered constitution," and Calvin surmises that this was Jesus's meaning reported in the Gospel. "Now we know that outside Christ there is nothing but confusion in the world. And although Christ had already begun to set up the kingdom of God, it was His death that was the true beginning of a properly-ordered state and the complete restoration of the world."[53] The Redeemer is the Creator, and eschatology (future things) recalibrates our settings for life here and now.

"In Calvin's thought there is thus no preoccupation with personal salvation to the exclusion of any concern with the restoration of all of reality. Rather, he writes that God will put an end to the great confusion and will restore the original order."[54] Just as this "future life" will be an everlasting union of soul and body, it will unite the diverse peoples, languages, and cultures in one global family. In Greek thinking (especially Platonism), the fountain of all being is one, and diversity is a falling away from this origin of unity; "salvation" is returning to this unity where no differences exist. Yet, as we've seen, Calvin is delighted in the diversity that God has created in nature and history, and this diversity continues in glory.

There is also a Trinitarian vision in this meditation on the future life: a unity of humanity with God in Christ. "Christ rose again that he might

---

[51] Selderhuis, *Calvin's Theology of the Psalms*, 176, on Ps. 110:7.
[52] Venema, "Calvin's Doctrine of the Last Things," 451, citing *Institutes* 3.25.9.
[53] Venema, "Calvin's Doctrine of the Last Things," 451.
[54] Selderhuis, *Calvin's Theology of the Psalms*, 173, on Ps. 94:15.

have us as companions in the life to come," says Calvin. "He was raised by the Father, inasmuch as he was Head of the church, from which the Father in no way allows him to be severed. He was raised by the power of the Holy Spirit, the Quickener of us in common with him."[55] In short, Calvin teaches that the justification that believers enjoy now will be fully revealed and its effects fully and publicly realized in our resurrection-glorification. It is in this sense that Calvin is willing even to call this event a deification (*theōsis*) of the saints.[56]

In this glorification the effects of our union with Christ will be fully complete. Calvin sees in Hebrews 4:10 "a definition of that perpetual Sabbath in which there is the highest felicity, when there will be a likeness between men and God, to whom they will be united." The ancient pagan ideal of union with the oneness of the divine All is actually selfish, part of that essence of sin itself, which Augustine defined as being "curved in on ourselves."

> For whatever the philosophers may have ever said of the chief good, it was nothing but cold and vain, for they confined man to himself, while *it is necessary for us to go out of ourselves to find happiness*. The chief good of man is nothing else but union with God; this is attained when we are formed according to him as our exemplar.[57]

One final time we see that the gospel calls us out of our individualistic preoccupation with ourselves, to look up in faith to God and out to our neighbors in love. It is a social and socializing vision that Calvin has in mind when he meditates on the future life.

From all of this we see how Calvin's version of "meditation on the future life" fuels our life and vocations in the world rather than drawing us away from our temporal responsibilities. It is not the flight of the soul from the weary world, but the longing of the whole person for that everlasting joy that only the returning Savior can bring to the earth. "Since Christ is the one who carries out the judgment, believers themselves should not take up the sword, but they should instead patiently bear their cross."[58] We can bear our cross in this pilgrimage knowing what lies up ahead.

---

[55] Calvin, *Institutes* 3.25.3.
[56] Calvin on 2 Pet. 1:4, in *Calvin's Commentaries*, 22:371. For more on this point, see Michael Horton, *Covenant and Salvation: Union with Christ* (Louisville: Westminster John Knox, 2007), chap. 12.
[57] Calvin on Heb. 4:10, in *Calvin's Commentaries*, 22:98, emphasis added.
[58] Selderhuis, *Calvin's Theology of the Psalms*, 177, on Ps. 21:9.

Our Only Comfort in Life and in Death

For insights into how this piety shaped his own life, Calvin's death is as illustrative as his life. Once a rising star in a constellation of the French Renaissance, he was, as he put it, "subdued" by the God of grace. And now, at the age of fifty-five, he succumbed to a long list of ailments. He died, as he lived, by meditating on the future life.

Calvin had experienced the pangs of loss frequently, including the death of his only son, Jacques, shortly after the boy's premature birth. Just as he felt increasingly alone, God took his wife, Idelette. Her death, he confided to Pierre Viret, "has been exceedingly painful to me." He cherished the support of friends. "But you know well enough how tender, or rather soft, my mind is. . . . And truly mine is no common source of grief. I have been bereaved of the best companion of my life." She who "has been the willing sharer of my indigence," he said, would even have shared willingly in his martyrdom.[59] After years of saying goodbye to close friends and colleagues—some to martyrdom, others to the plague, and others (including the one that grieved him most) who returned to Rome—Calvin was now in the position of allowing others to send him off to his rest.

In November 1563 he wrote to Melanchthon that he was trying to follow the doctors' prescription, "except that in my burning thirst I allow myself to drink a little more copiously." The problem, he complained, is that the doctors "wanted to kill me outright" with cheap wine until he prevailed upon them to prescribe a fine Burgundy.[60]

Calvin's last will and testament (dated April 25, 1564) provides some insight into his personal spirituality. He took the occasion to offer his final "sermon" to the city's leaders. In it he begins by giving thanks to God for his mercy in delivering him from idolatry "into the light of his Gospel."

> I have no other defense or refuge for salvation than his gratuitous adoption on which alone my salvation depends. With my whole soul I embrace the mercy which he has exercised towards me through Jesus Christ, atoning for my sins with the merits of his death and passion, that in this way he might satisfy for all my crimes and faults, and blot them from his remembrance.

---

[59] Calvin, "To Viret" (April 7, 1549), in *Select Works of John Calvin: Tracts and Letters*, ed. Henry Beveridge and Jules Bonnet, 7 vols. (Grand Rapids: Baker, 1983), 5:216–19.
[60] Calvin, "To Melanchthon" (Geneva, November 19, 1558), *Select Works of John Calvin*, 6:483.

I testify also and declare that I suppliantly beg of Him that he may be pleased so to wash and purify me in the blood which my Sovereign Redeemer has shed for the sins of the human race, that under his shadow I may be able to stand at the judgment seat. I likewise declare that, according to the measure of grace and goodness which the Lord hath employed toward me, I have endeavored, both in my sermons and also in my writings and commentaries, to preach His Word purely and chastely, and faithfully to interpret His sacred Scriptures.[61]

He also testifies that in all of the controversies of his life, he has "acted candidly and sincerely in defending the truth," adding:

But, woe is me! My ardor and zeal (if indeed worthy of the name) have been so careless and languid, that I confess I have failed innumerable times to execute my office properly, and had not He, of His boundless goodness, assisted me, all that zeal had been fleeting and vain. Nay, I even acknowledge that if the same goodness had not assisted me, those mental endowments which the Lord bestowed upon me would, at His judgment seat, prove me more guilty of sin and sloth. For all these reasons, I testify and declare that I trust to no other security for my salvation than this, and this only, viz., that as God is the Father of mercy, he will show himself such a Father to me, who acknowledge myself to be a miserable sinner.[62]

After this expression of ultimate gratitude, Calvin disposed his meager estate to the Boys' School, "poor strangers," and to children of close friends. The rest he left to his nephews and nieces.[63] All told, it was a modest sum indeed. Calvin said, "If some will not be persuaded while I am alive, my death, at all events, will show that I have not been a money-making man."[64]

Calvin called for the four syndics and all of the senators to address them one last time in the senate chamber. They preferred to come to him, given his condition. Thanking them "for having conferred so many honors on one who plainly deserved nothing of the kind, and for having so often borne patiently with my very numerous infirmities," he confessed that he had "performed so little in public and in private, compared with what I ought to have done." The senators had "borne patiently with my vehemence, which was sometimes carried to excess; my sins, in this respect,

---

[61] Theodore Beza, "Life of Calvin," in *Selected Works of John Calvin*, 1:lxxxvi–lxxxvii.
[62] Ibid.
[63] Ibid., lxxxvii–lxxxviii.
[64] Ibid., c.

I trust, have been pardoned by God also." "But in regard to the doctrine which I have delivered in your hearing," he added, "I declare that the Word of God entrusted to me I have taught, not rashly or uncertainly, but purely and sincerely; as well knowing that His wrath was otherwise impending on my head, as I am certain that my labors in teaching were not displeasing to Him." From his own sense of mixed feeling, both of gratitude to God and of regret for not having served more diligently, Calvin exhorted his comrades:

> Therefore, whether in prosperity or adversity, have this, I pray you, always present before your eyes, that it is He alone who establishes kings and states, and on that account wishes men to worship Him. . . . For He alone is the supreme God, the King of kings, and Lord of lords, who will give honor to those by whom He is honored, but will cast down the despisers. Worship Him, therefore, according to His precepts; and study this more and more, for we are always very far from doing what it is our duty to do. . . . In the decision of civil causes let there be no place for partiality or hatred; let no one pervert justice by oblique artifices; let no one, by his recommendations, prevent the laws from having full effect; let no one depart from what is just and good.[65]

On May 11, Farel—eighty, and feeble himself—intended to visit Calvin one last time. In a letter in Latin, Calvin replied, "Farewell, my best and most right-hearted brother; and since God is pleased that you should survive me in this world, live mindful of our friendship of which, as it was useful to the Church of God, the fruit still awaits us in heaven."[66] On the twenty-fourth, Calvin was carried one last time to the senate chamber. With a faltering voice, he read some notes on New Testament passages he was still writing, asking the leaders for their opinion. After introducing the new rector of the academy, he departed "amidst sobs and tears."

> On the 2d day of April, which was Easter day, although much exhausted, he was carried into the church in a chair, and was present during the whole service. He received the Lord's Supper from my hand, and sang the hymn along with the others, though with tremulous voice, yet with a look on which joy was not obscurely indicated on his dying countenance.[67]

---

[65] Ibid., xc–xcii.
[66] Ibid., xciv.
[67] Ibid., lxxxv.

According to Beza, "The interval to his death he spent in almost constant prayer."[68]

> I have also heard him say, "Thou, O Lord, bruisest me; but it is enough for me that it is thy hand." . . . In this way, resigned in himself, and consoling his friends, he lived till the 19th of May, on which day we ministers were wont to have our private censures, and to dine together as a mark of our friendship; Pentecost and the dispensation of the Lord's Supper being to follow two days after.[69]

Calvin died on May 27, 1564, after issuing final encouragement, apologies, and exhortations to the weeping rulers of Geneva. Having so frequently blocked his reforms of the church in former days, the republic's leaders allowed him his dying request: to be buried at "the common cemetery" without pomp, in an unmarked grave. "There is nothing that man's nature seeks more eagerly than to be flattered," he once wrote.[70]

The announcement of his death caused weeping throughout the city and "as the curiosity became excessive," even the English ambassador was denied permission to view his body.[71] Calvin died as he lived: confident in God's mercies in Jesus Christ despite his shortcomings, and in the profound awareness of that truth which he had professed when Geneva recalled him to his post many years previously: "But when I remember that I am not my own, I offer up my heart, presented as a sacrifice to the Lord."[72]

---

[68] Ibid., xciv–xcv.
[69] Ibid., xcv.
[70] Calvin, Institutes 1.1.2.
[71] Beza, "Life of Calvin": "That night and the following day there was a general lamentation throughout the city—the whole State regretting its wisest citizen—the Church deploring the departure of its faithful pastor—the academy grieving at being deprived of so great a teacher, and all lamenting the loss of one who was, under God, a common parent and comforter. Many citizens were eager to see the body, and could scarcely be torn away from it. Some foreigners also, who had come from a distance to see and hear him, among them the illustrious ambassador of the Queen of England to the court of France, were anxious to have a look at his corpse. At first admission was given; but as the curiosity became excessive, and might have given occasion to calumny, it was thought advisable, on the following day, which was the Lord's Day, to wrap the body in linen, in the usual manner, and inclose it in its coffin" (xcvi–xcvii). "He was buried in the common cemetery of Plein Palais, with no extraordinary pomp, and, as he had commanded, without any grave-stone" (xcvii).
[72] Calvin, "To Farel" (Strasbourg, August 1541), in Selected Works of John Calvin, 4:281.

GENERAL INDEX

SCRIPTURE INDEX

GAINING WISDOM FROM THE PAST FOR LIFE IN THE PRESENT

Other volumes in the Theologians on the Christian Life series

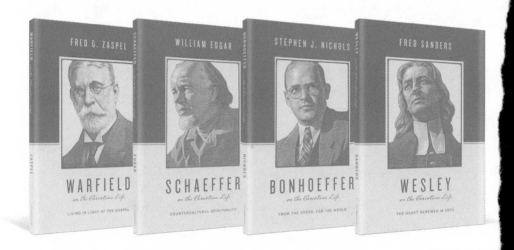